Microsoft® FoxPro® 2.5
Programming

Microsoft® FoxPro® 2.5 Programming

Les Pinter

Windcrest®/McGraw-Hill

New York San Francisco Washington, D.C. Auckland Bogotá
Caracas Lisbon London Madrid Mexico City Milan
Montreal New Delhi San Juan Singapore
Sydney Tokyo Toronto

FIRST EDITION
FIRST PRINTING

© 1993 by **Les Pinter**.
Published by Windcrest Books, an imprint of TAB Books.
TAB Books is a division of McGraw-Hill, Inc.
The name "Windcrest" is a registered trademark of TAB Books.

The title of the first edition of this book is FoxPro Programming (No. 3525). The title of
the second edition is FoxPro Programming—2nd Edition (No. 4057).

Library of Congress Cataloging-in-Publication Data
Pinter, Les.
   Microsoft FoxPro 2.5 programming / by Les Pinter. — 3rd ed.
     p. cm.
   Rev. ed. of: FoxPro programming. 2nd ed. c1992.
   Includes index.
   ISBN 0-8306-4398-2
   1. Data base management. 2. FoxPro (Computer file) I. Pinter,
Les. FoxPro programming. II. Title.
QA76.9.D3P525 1993
005.75'65—dc20   93-3278
                                                  CIP

Editorial team: Jennifer Holt DiGiovanna, Acquisitions Editor
                 Kellie Hagan, Book Editor
Production team: Katherine G. Brown, Director
                 Tina M. Sourbier, Typesetting
                 Rose McFarland, Layout
                 Nancy Mickley, Proofreading
Index: Jodi L.Tyler
Design team: Jaclyn J. Boone, Designer
             Brian Allison, Associate Designer
Cover Design and Illustration: Sandra Blair, Harrisburg, Pa.

                                                   WP1

Acknowledgments

The techniques developed here precede me. My menu-driven examples are based on examples generated from Luis Castro's ViewGen, FoxView, and Stage models. My event-driven models are derived from both the sample applications included with FoxPro and written by Dr. Dave Fulton, Walt Kennamer, and other MicroSoft/Fox staff, and also from the excellent work of Alan Griver and Tom Rettig. In all cases, their work develops these concepts at a more advanced level than was appropriate for this book, and I encourage you to look further into these excellent resources.

If you don't feel like typing in the code I present in the book, order the source-code disk from the coupon at the end of the book. You might also want to request a sample copy of the *Pinter FoxPro Letter*, the monthly publication from which this and all my books are extracted. A newsletter is a very timely vehicle for communicating new programming concepts. In a dynamic environment like FoxPro, new ideas can take hold even faster than I can get them to my esteemed publisher. If you're interested, I even have a Russian edition, published monthly in Moscow!

Contents

Foreword

One of the nicest things about working for Fox Software and now Microsoft has been watching the FoxPro community grow and prosper. Les Pinter is one of the real "old-timers" and has written about our products for years. It's a pleasure to see him continue his success with this new project.

I've always felt that the best way to learn a programming language is to study working code and modify it to fit your needs. Les puts a great deal of emphasis on programming code, as you can tell from a casual thumbing of the book. I think this is a wise approach.

Les's book takes an interesting and different approach to explaining how to design FoxPro programs. He draws a distinction between menu-driven and event-driven programming, and goes into substantial detail on the advantages and disadvantages of each technique. Indeed, this distinction is one of the major themes of the book and most of the large examples are built around it. I think these examples will be very valuable to someone just getting started with FoxPro programming, and they differentiate his book from most others, which typically recommend either menu-driven or event-driven programming exclusively.

Congratulations to Les for completing this new book. It's apparent that he has invested a lot of time in it, and it has paid off in a book that should be helpful to all FoxPro users.

Walter Kennamer
Software Design Engineer
Microsoft Corporation

Introduction

In 1979, I was asked to take over the management of Small Business Applications, a two-man startup that had developed one of the first word-processing programs for microcomputers, Magic Wand. Bill Radding and Mike Griffin, two brilliant guys from Houston, had spent over a year working on the project, and were finally ready to market it.

Jerry Pournelle wrote a review in *Byte* magazine saying that Magic Wand was "better than WordStar," and we hit the jackpot. Within eight months, we'd sold over a million dollars' worth of software and hired eight more employees.

One day, I got a message from Bill Gates, the 23-year-old chairman of Microsoft. He wanted to buy our source code. Two days later, the deal was done (and three months later, so was our business). He came to Houston, gave us a check and a noncompetition agreement, and went back to Seattle. At a party in Seattle last year, Bill told me that my nondisclosure agreement had lapsed, which is why you're reading this now.

I tried to go back to mainframe programming, but the success of that one little program was impossible to forget. I drifted over into Lotus 1-2-3, wrote the first Lotus add-on (Real Estate Guide), and eventually started doing databases with dBASE II. The rest has been like riding a rocket.

A short history of FoxPro

FoxPro is heir to the line begun by Wayne Ratliff when he was working for Jet Propulsion Laboratories in the early '70s. A unique feature of the language was the concept of storing the file description in the file itself, as a header. Thus, when a program opened a file, it read in the file's description (names, types, and sizes of fields, as well as the number of records in the file). Because of this one innovation, programs didn't have to contain a description of each file used. The addition of procedures, such as those for indexing, sorting, and browsing the contents of the files, further simplified programming.

The result was a language that nonprogrammers could understand and use almost immediately. For the first time, professionals from other disciplines were building their own database applications. This openness didn't always lead to code that followed textbook techniques, but at least the door was opened. You didn't have to be a programmer to write programs!

The dBASE language, as Ashton-Tate developed it, was widely viewed as a good idea badly executed. The proliferation of clones, each of which was superior to the original product, validated that view. Finally, a much better program emerged— FoxBASE. I discovered it while doing a contract for LucasFilm, the home of the Star Wars trilogy. My DBASE III programs ran seven times faster under FoxBASE, and I was an instant convert.

FoxBASE became FoxPro, and the war was on. Initially it was a lawyers' war, but eventually the courts determined that xBASE was not copyrightable, returning the competition to the technical sphere. By that time, Microsoft had bought Fox Software, and technical competition is a field in which Microsoft excels. The result was FoxPro 2.5, the first generation of xBASE products from Microsoft. So I again find my path crossed with that of Bill Gates. This time, I'm sure it will be all for the good.

How does FoxPro stack up to the competition?

FoxPro still has a few competitors; Clipper (bought from Nantucket by Computer Associates) and dBASE IV (purchased by Borland) are the two largest, but a half-dozen others continue to share the market. Clipper has taken an object-oriented approach that appeals to trained programmers, and produces .EXE files that, although once considered too large, now seem minuscule compared to the 1Mg+ giants generated by FoxPro. Read a Clipper code listing, however, and you'll think you're reading Armenian. I've been programming in xBASE since 1984, and I literally can't read a Clipper program. So I suspect that Clipper is going somewhere else, and the path they've chosen will deter beginning to intermediate programmers.

What about dBASE IV? Borland was the company that marketed Turbo Pascal, the first development environment in which the programmer could edit, compile, and test without exiting to DOS. Borland has led the market many times in developing high-quality, inexpensive software for programmers.

If Borland follows the formula that made them successful in the past, they'll follow a two-pronged plan of attack: dBASE IV will continue to be technically enhanced, and the price will be about half that of FoxPro. If they don't, they'll likely disappear from the xBASE market. You can't compete with Microsoft wearing nothing but marketing hype.

I personally hope that Borland does follow their formula. Competition with Ashton-Tate is what pushed the Fox team into the lead. Without competition, we'll get pretty much what all monopolies sell—less product for more money. Witness government. Besides, in a fair fight, Dave Fulton and his group can clean Borland's clock any time. And Microsoft does more to find out what its customers want and give it to them than any other software company.

Event-driven vs. menu-driven software

The main topic of discussion in FoxPro is whether to use traditional menu-driven techniques, or the event-driven approach that predominates in the Windows environment. The decision to write one type of software rather than the other is not changed by the arrival of FoxPro 2.5. It might surprise you to learn that event-driven techniques aren't exclusive to Windows; in fact, there are only a very, very few differences between FoxPro for DOS and FoxPro for Windows, and the technique for writing event-driven software is *exactly* the same for both.

What then do you base that decision on? In this book, you'll see the same application developed using both techniques. I leave it to you to determine what your users need, and what you'll need to do to give them what they want. Small event-driven applications are pretty easy to write, but large-scale commercial software is very hard, and large-scale event-driven commercial software is much, much harder. The number of things that can ruin your day goes up exponentially when your users determine the order in which things happen.

How to use this book

I've always contended that knowing all of the words in the English language won't guarantee that you can write like Shakespeare. Words have meaning only in the context of sentences and paragraphs. Similarly, FoxPro's commands and functions make sense only when assembled into user-defined functions, procedures, and applications.

My books target FoxPro programmers who are looking for tools, techniques, and prototypes. If you're a beginner in the FoxPro world, you might need to nail down FoxPro's commands and functions. My goal here is to skip the introductory stuff and jump straight into putting commands and functions together into building blocks and prototypes. So the material might appear a little advanced to novices. I can recommend books by Tom Rettig, John Hawkins, Miriam Liskin, and others for the basics. These guys are also very competent in the most advanced phases of FoxPro programming, but they've taken the time to write introductory texts that do things that this book doesn't do.

You can use this book as a reference work, but you'll miss the point unless you dig into the code and understand what's there. I wouldn't dive in and memorize all of the code, though. Start by identifying what you're interested in. Then take it apart and find out how it works.

Learning theorists point out that remembering isolated facts is much more difficult than recalling pieces of a larger structure. In the Middle Ages, learning was always done within a physical "memory gym"—often the floor plan of an imaginary thousand-room cathedral. By attaching facts to a physical, albeit imaginary, structure, medieval scholars were able to recall vast numbers of facts. So you might want to learn FoxPro commands and syntax within the framework of working programs. Start by running the programs. If you see something that interests you, take it apart and find out how it works. Then you can learn commands and functions within a meaningful context.

A different approach

Every month I read articles about advanced topics in object-oriented programming and event-driven techniques. These are topics that place their authors on the cutting edge—or what my friend Alan Schwartz refers to as the "bleeding edge" of FoxPro development. I've gotten many, many calls from subscribers informing me that they don't even understand the topics, and asking about their relevance.

I was fortunate enough to be at the bottom of my class in the graduate program in Economics at Rice University. By virtue of that honor, I feel I have a special insight into the difficulties of average programmers. Through daily contacts with subscribers to my monthly newsletter, I get a pretty good feel for what many programmers are looking for. The need that I intend to try to fill is for good, solid, relevant examples of complete applications.

Therefore, the chapters on event-driven techniques start with a simple case and then bring up a new wrinkle, show why something's missing, and add the required code. Hopefully, you'll end up with an appreciation for every single DEACTIVATE, VALID, and WHEN clause.

Compare the event-driven model in chapter 4 with the menu-driven model in chapter 5. The differences are partly cosmetic, and partly structural. The important difference is how much work is involved. I strongly believe that the additional effort and cost of event-driven software might not be justified in many cases. You be the judge.

1
Programming paradigms

All computer languages have certain features: assignment, conditional branching, iteration, I/O, and the like. But FoxPro has a few special characteristics that determine how programs are written in its own language, as opposed to C or COBOL. The xbase lineage has become one of the most popular languages in the world precisely because of the way it does things. I've talked with many, many of my subscribers who always wanted to write programs, but couldn't get past introductory BASIC or COBOL. Then they discovered FoxBASE, and they were unstoppable.

You can write FoxPro programs as if you were writing in C, and some programmers take particular delight in doing so. But I believe that the entire charm of xbase derives from its simplicity. I sincerely hope that the folks who want to turn FoxPro into C lose the war. If it ain't broke, don't fix it.

File structures

There are several types of files used in FoxPro applications: program code, data files (tables), indexes, and all of the components of an application.

Program files

FoxPro programs are generally written as ASCII text files with the extension .PRG. Programs generally begin with assignments, opening files, and generally getting ready to do whatever their mission in life is. Functions called by the program can be included at the bottom of the program listing, like this:

```
* Main program
* program code
```

1

```
FUNCTION first
* program code
FUNCTION second
* program code
```

When you call a function, FoxPro looks for it within the body of the current program file, toward the end of the code. In FoxPro, there are many places where, instead of writing the code yourself in linear fashion, you insert it into pigeonholes called *code snippets*. The Screen Builder and Menu Builder described later in this chapter let you insert such code snippets, which they then insert into the generated code at the appropriate locations.

Perhaps the most important of these code snippets is the CLEANUP snippet. Anything you insert there will be placed at the end of the generated code. So, if you insert all the functions that a data entry program will need into the CLEANUP snippet, they'll end up at the end of the program listing—exactly where FoxPro looks for functions.

As time goes by, you might end up with a large number of functions that are useful in other applications. Inserting them into CLEANUP snippets for each screen is certainly possible, but there might be a better way. If you bundle a bunch of functions and procedures into a file and call it MYPROCS, you can use the statement:

```
SET PROCEDURE TO MYPROCS
```

to inform your application that this library exists. If you call a function in your program that isn't included in the functions at the end of the currently executing program, FoxPro will look in the table of function names created with your SET PROCEDURE TO MYPROCS, and execute the function. If you really must, you can tell FoxPro to:

```
DO functionname IN filename
```

FoxPro will read *filename* on the fly, locate *functionname*, and execute it. You generally don't want to do this because it's slow, but it's the usual way to refer to functions included in menus. For example, DO MENUHIT IN MYMENU.MPR will find the program that processes menu selections, regardless of which program is running at the time or which procedure file is open.

Data files

FoxPro, like all xBASE dialects, reads database files that end with the extension .DBF. If a file has at least one index, it's usually contained in an associated structural index file with the same name as the .DBF file, but with the extension .CDX. If the file contains at least one memo field, there will be an associated memo file with the same name as the .DBF file, but with the extension .FPT.

Headers

Data files begin with a header of 32 bytes, followed by one 32-byte field descriptor for each field in the file, and ending with one more byte. If the header is damaged, you won't be able to read your file, although all the data is still there. If you accidentally zap your file, FoxPro will reset the record count to zero, but leave the data intact. If FoxPro can't find your structural .CDX file and there's a 1 in byte 29, your program will return an error.

All these things and more have happened to me, and will probably happen to you. Not to worry; thanks to the personal tutoring of my good friend Paul Heiser, the original guru of file repair, I'll be providing you with some file-repair utilities in a later chapter.

Fields and records

FoxPro files have *fields*, which can be one of five types:

- Character
- Numeric or floating point
- Logical
- Date
- Memo, picture, or general

The last three types are stored in an .FPT file, so their size in your DBF is limited to 10 bytes. I *never* use logical fields in data files, so as far as I'm concerned, there are four types of fields. FoxPro's CREATE TABLE statement lists these as eight different field types and, although I'm sure there are important internal distinctions, until they've insinuated themselves into my life, ignorance is bliss.

The delete byte

A record's size consists of the size of all its fields, plus one byte for the "delete flag." FoxPro doesn't actually delete records until they're packed. Instead, it inserts an asterisk into the delete flag field. The DELETED( ) function will report .True. for these records, and SET DELETED ON will make them seem to disappear.

One of the important controversies in application programming is how to deal with the deletion of records. Prior to the appearance of compound indexes (described in the following section), deleting and packing was such a headache that a technique called *record recycling* was often used to avoid the issue entirely. Compound indexes and Rushmore technology give rise to a solution that will be described later in this book.

Indexes

FoxPro lets you move through your file in physical sequential order—record number 1, number 2, and so forth. But you can add any number of index tags and view your data any way you want.

In FoxPro version 1, each index occupied its own file. That caused a lot of problems with applications that had to be reindexed from time to time, because records would be added or deleted with one of the indexes detached. Never mind that with good programming practices you could avoid the problem. Remember Murphy's Law.

In versions 2.0 and 2.5, you can't forget to attach an index, because they all live in a single .CDX file. These .CDX files can hold more indexes than you'd want or need. To add an index, use the expression:

```
INDEX ON expression TAG name
```

Using the command SET ORDER TO TAG name, you can switch from one index tag to another as needed. If you attach an index, the index will tell FoxPro which is the next record. If you have a file with names in it like this:

```
Record # Name
1        BAKER
2        ALLEN
3        CHARLES
```

and if you had an alphabetical index on the Name field, the command:

```
SET ORDER TO TAG NAME
```

would present the file to you like this:

```
Record # Name
2        ALLEN
1        BAKER
3        CHARLES
```

You can't match different types of expressions—logical, numeric, and character—in an index expression. That is, you can't index on NAME + DATE + AMOUNT, where NAME is a character expression, DATE a date expression, and AMOUNT a numeric expression. Instead, I always convert each field in an index tag expression to its character equivalent. In the preceding example, I'd use something like:

```
UPPER(NAME) + DTOC(DATE,1) + STR(Amount,10,2)
```

In many applications, the greatest benefit that FoxPro brings is its ability to efficiently extract subsets of data. Whenever possible, FoxPro extracts data using information stored in the index tags. Because the indexes can actually live completely in memory, the speed can be unbelievable. The trick to using "Rushmore optimizable expressions" is to refer to the database in the same way it's expressed in the index tags.

Recycling deleted records

Remember when I mentioned the delete flag? That was the point of this discussion. Deleting and packing records, and adding records back into a file, can be really, really slow on a network. So ingenious techniques for record recycling have been developed—which has led to a trick that's becoming more popular. For each modifiable file, add:

```
INDEX ON DELETED() TAG DELETED
```

If DELETED() is one of your index tags, managing the recycling of deleted records is fast and easy. When I talk more about networked applications, you'll see how important this is.

FoxPro's internal files

I wondered for years whether the concept of including a header in a file was going to disappear. Other languages didn't use it. Either it was a terrific idea that went right over COBOL programmers' heads, or it was a lousy idea and we xBASE dopes were the only ones who hadn't figured that out. Well, guess what? It was such a good idea that Fox decided to use the same format for all of its internal files as well. Just about everything in FoxPro is stored in a file whose structure is exactly like that of DBFs—screens, projects, menus, reports, and labels, even FoxPro's color schemes and the size and location of your last BROWSE! So I guess that answers my question.

You can do anything with these files that you'd do with data files: read and report, do global search-and-replace operations, or just browse. In fact, for one particular programming trick (doing Lotus-like spreadsheets in FoxPro), the fastest way to enter the validation code that lets you move in any direction around the screen is to insert it manually while browsing the screen file.

I/O for data entry

There are three ways that FoxPro gets data from the keyboard: @...GET and READ, BROWSE, and INKEY( ). (Menus and menu popups are a fourth input method, but they're rarely used in data entry.)

@...GET and READ

The basic input mechanism in FoxPro consists of any number of statements of the form:

```
@ row, col GET memvar | field
  [FUNCTION expC1]
  [PICTURE expC2]
  [FONT expC3 [, expN1]]
  [STYLE expC4]
  [DEFAULT expr1]
  [ENABLE | DISABLE]
  MESSAGE expC5]
  [[OPEN] WINDOW window name]
  [RANGE [expr2] [, expr3]]
```

```
[SIZE expN2, expN3]
[VALID expL1 | expN4
[ERROR expC6]]
[WHEN expL2]
[COLOR SCHEME expN5 | COLOR color pair list]
```

GETs are "stacked" as you issue them, and can be activated only by the
READ command. READ processes the GETs in the order in which they
were issued. If the GETs were issued in more than one window, the appropriate window is made foremost when its first GET is processed.

The presence of any of the 14 available subcommands can cause *huge*
differences in the way each variable is processed. In particular, if a VALID
clause or function is present, that clause or function is executed the instant the cursor attempts to leave the related variable's GET region. *This
one feature represents for many applications the biggest difference between
FoxPro and other languages.*

FoxPro distinguishes between GET for data and GET for vitiating CON-
TROLS. Parameters passed to the PICTURE or FUNCTION clause can
cause FoxPro to display a very different kind of GET. In particular, controls with names like Checkbox, List, and Radio Button allow you to spice
up the interface.

In Windows, you can display .BMP (bit map) files to add graphics to
your screens. While I don't have the patience to create these things one
byte at a time, I love to use bit maps created by artsy types to spice up my
applications.

BROWSE

This command has the following syntax:

```
BROWSE
  [FIELDS field list]
  [FONT expC1 [, expN1]]
  [STYLE expC2]
  [FOR expL1]
  [FORMAT]
  [FREEZE field]
  [KEY expr1 [, expr2]]
  [LAST]
  [LEDIT]
  [REDIT]
  [LOCK expN2]
  [LPARTITION]
  [NOAPPEND]
  [NOCLEAR]
  [NODELETE]
  [NOEDIT | NOMODIFY]
  [NOLGRID] [NORGRID]
  [NOLINK]
```

```
[NOMENU]
[NOOPTIMIZE]
[NOREFRESH]
[NORMAL]
[NOWAIT]
[PARTITION expN3]
[PREFERENCE expC3]
[REST]
[SAVE]
[TIMEOUT expN4]
[TITLE expC4]
[VALID [:F] expL2 [ERROR expC5]]
[WHEN expL3]
[WIDTH expN5]
[[WINDOW window name1]
[IN [WINDOW] window name2 | IN SCREEN]]
[COLOR SCHEME expN6 | COLOR color pair list]
```

BROWSE presents a table of fields from the currently selected work area. You can add calculated fields, consisting of anything else you might want to look at, and also VALID field clauses in order to add any functionality you feel is lacking.

BROWSE is a language in itself, with 34 subcommands to modify its mode of operation. More than any other, this command vastly enhances the ability of power users to work with their data in ways that make sense to them. Using the mouse or pull-down menus, users can rearrange columns, resize the Browse window, or split the display into coordinated table and form views. In Windows, this capability is especially spectacular.

Paradoxically, I've spent more time doing work-arounds for aspects of BROWSE that bothered me—principally speed—than any other single feature of FoxPro. More power means more complexity, and presumably, more horsepower requirements. I'll deal with both BROWSE and work-arounds for BROWSE-like applications.

INKEY( )

Before FoxPro added its many controls and enhancements to READ, programmers used keystroke trapping to provide complete control for their applications. I know a programmer in Mexico who develops his applications without using GET or READ at all. The resulting code, while a bit laborious, is *unbelievably* fast.

I guess what I'm getting at is that there's more than one way to skin a cat. If FoxPro's built-in features don't do what you want, try writing your own. It's still FoxPro, and the flexibility of the language is amazing. There's an API for writing functions in C, but you'd be surprised what you can do with nothing more than INKEY( ).

Low-level file I/O (LLIO)

In case your needs for exotic I/O go beyond the screen, FoxPro supports commands for reading and writing byte streams to disk that will add whatever you need. Commands include the following:

```
FCLOSE()
FCREATE()
FEOF()
FERROR()
FFLUSH()
FGETS()
FOPEN()
FPUTS()
FREAD()
FSEEK()
FSIZE()
FWRITE()
```

The sections of this book on data conversion and file repair will give you some notion of the power of LLIO.

Windows

A window is a rectangular area of the screen that you can write to without destroying the underlying screen. Only one window is active at a time, although many can be displayed simultaneously. Windows can be defined so as to be moved, resized, and minimized; this last feature allows the window to shrink to the size of its title, then be "docked" elsewhere on the screen until needed.

If your programs are coded so as to support it, activating a window (usually by clicking on it with the mouse) will activate the code associated with the window. This feature permits a program to be event-driven; menu, window-selection, or hot-key events can trigger the same action. In particular, applications like those that ship as demonstration software in the FoxPro box are of this type, which is sometimes referred to as "modeless."

Windows are an essential part of design in both FoxPro for DOS and FoxPro for Windows. If you have too many fields to fit on the screen, you can design a multiwindow screen set and thus break the 25×80 barrier. Also, you can use windows to group related fields together. And if nothing else compels their use, FoxPro's Screen Builder makes screen design a snap, and generates @ SAY...GET statements with coordinates that are relative to the upper left-hand corner of the window. Once you use windows for your applications, I'm sure you'll stick with them.

Popups

A *popup* is a vertical list of selections displayed in a window that appears and disappears without destroying the screen display under it. The syntax follows:

```
DEFINE POPUP popup name
  [FROM row1, column1]
  [TO row2, column2]
  [IN [WINDOW] window name | IN SCREEN]
  [FOOTER expC1]
  [KEY key label]
  [MARGIN]
  [MARK expC2]
  [MESSAGE expC3]
  [MOVER]
  [MULTISELECT]
  [PROMPT FIELD expr | PROMPT FILES [LIKE skel]
   | PROMPT STRUCTURE]
  [RELATIVE]
  [SCROLL]
  [SHADOW]
  [TITLE expC4]
  [COLOR SCHEME expN | COLOR color pair list]
```

Popups are used as menu pull-downs, as pick lists for data-entry field validation, and as scrollable information displays. For the first of these, Menu Builder will write the code for you, probably much more easily than you could write it yourself. For listing all the values of a particular field in a file, there's a special syntax:

```
DEFINE POPUP FROM coordinates PROMPT FIELD fieldname
```

If SET CONFIRM is turned off, you can make a selection from the popup either by pressing the first letter of one of its members, by pressing a hot key if one is defined, or by highlighting a choice and pressing the Enter key. Popups can be scrolled if more elements are present than can fit in the rectangular display area.

If you specify SET CONFIRM OFF, pressing a key that matches the first letter of one of your popup bars will immediately terminate the popup and return. If SET CONFIRM is turned on, pressing Enter is required to terminate the popup. In either event, the FoxPro function PROMPT( ) returns the selected value of the popup. If ESCAPE is pressed, PROMPT( ) will return a null string. When you specify RELEASE POPUP popupname, PROMPT( ) will lose its memory, so use something like:

```
Selected = Prompt()
RELEASE POPUP X
```

There are many additional modifiers you can use to enhance this command. You can use it to return multiple selections, or provide you with a popup containing only the filenames that match a wildcard specification. You might be able to design major parts of your application around this one command. There's even a third-party product from Joe Gotthelf, called JKEY, that turns BROWSE into a popup with incremental searching, i.e., it builds a search string as you type and automatically positions itself on the first matching record in the BROWSE. A copy of JKEY is on the source-code disk available from the coupon at the back of the book. If you like it, please send Joe twenty bucks.

Executing programs and functions

There are three ways to execute a program or function:

```
DO programname
=PROGRAMNAME()
@ coord GET...VALID PROGRAMNAME()
```

The first format is used to run programs from the Command window, and can be used anywhere else as well. As noted previously, you can use:

```
DO programname IN filename
```

which is a syntax usually used to call functions that live in the MENU CLEANUP code. DO *programname* was the syntax that characterized DBASE II/III and all of its heirs up to FoxPro. I think I avoid it because it reminds me of the bad old days.

The second format is what I generally use inside programs because I like the way it looks. To me, a sequence like:

```
=Initialize()
=Process()
=Cleanup()
```

just *looks* the way code should look. Use the third format wherever FoxPro expects a user-defined function—generally a VALID or WHEN clause, e.g.:

```
@ 10,2 GET m.NAME VALID MakeProper(m.NAME)
...
FUNCTION MakeProper
m.Name = PROPER ( m.Name )
```

Function or procedure?

FoxPro lets you declare every subroutine as either a function or a procedure. The theory is that functions return a value explicitly, as in:

```
IF MowGrass()
   WAIT WINDOW [ I can't play golf today ] NOWAIT
ENDIF
FUNCTION MowGrass
RETURN IIF ( CDOW(DATE() = [Saturday], .T. , .F. )
```

while procedures don't. Well, actually, they do. So do whatever's consistent with your personal value system. I'm going to call them functions.

Control structures

I once calculated the number of lines of assembly-language code that an 80486 could process in one second. If there was no looping or branching, at an average of 8 cycles per instruction, it came out to 6 million instructions per second. This means that, if you printed a program that an assembly language took 1 second to run and printed it on fan-fold paper, it would produce a stack over 20 feet high!

Of course, few programs run from top to bottom with no branching or looping. FoxPro has several mechanisms for managing flow of control.

Looping

Looping in FoxPro is accomplished either in conjunction with movement through a file (SCAN) or as a simple mechanism for incrementing a counter (FOR...ENDFOR). The DO WHILE...ENDDO command used to serve both of these purposes, but has been relegated to a third use (described in a following section).

Note that all these looping structures can be scoped using the FOR modifier SCAN FOR Name = [A]. Also, the EXIT command will instantly pass control to the first statement beyond the end of the loop.

SCAN...ENDSCAN

SCAN...ENDSCAN allows you to read through a file. If there's a FOR clause, it will read only the records that match the FOR scope. If there's a WHILE clause, processing will stop as soon as a record is found that doesn't match the scope. Before Rushmore, if you had an index that guaranteed that all of the records you wanted to process—e.g., invoices for a particular customer—would all be found together, it was usually worthwhile to SEEK the first record that matched, then use SCAN WHILE to ensure that your program would look only at the matching records. With Rushmore, FOR is usually as efficient, and the initial SEEK isn't necessary.

Note that SCAN does its own SKIP, so you don't need to use the SKIP command. Note also that SKIP will go nuts if you SELECT another file area and then forget to SELECT back to the one you started with. You'll get some very unexpected results.

FOR...ENDFOR

The FOR loop automatically increments its declared counter as it loops, so it's especially handy for array processing. For example:

```
DIMENSION X(1)
COPY TO ARRAY X FIELDS NAME
FOR I = 1 TO ALEN ( X )
  ? I,  PROPER ( X(I) )
ENDFOR
```

DO WHILE...ENDDO

There used to be only DO WHILE NOT EOF( ), and you had to manage your own movement through the file. Now that there's SCAN, I pretty much reserve DO WHILE for INKEY( ) loops and the like.

```
DO WHILE .T.
  KeyPressed = INKEY(0)
  DO CASE
    CASE KeyPressed = UpArrow
      ...
  ENDCASE
ENDDO
```

REPORT/LABEL FORM

You might not think of it as a control structure, but REPORT FORM and
LABEL FORM work just like SCAN. In fact, I suspect they were the inspi-
ration for SCAN. They both can use a FOR *scope* parameter to limit the
records included, and can use Rushmore if the scope is optimizable.

Branching

Branching is used to conditionally execute code. In BASIC, COBOL, and
some other languages, this is often used in conjunction with a GO TO. In
FoxPro, you use functions that go do their thing, then continue down
through the code. I personally wouldn't use a GO TO unless there was also
a COME FROM.

IF...ENDIF

Use IF...ENDIF when a section of code applies only sometimes. For example:

```
IF LineCount > 55
  =PageHeader()
ENDIF
```

Often, an IF is used within a loop to handle some records differently:

```
SCAN FOR Balance > 0 AND ( DATE() - LastPayment ) > 29
  IF ( DATE() - LastPayment ) < 60
    =PaymentDue()
  ELSE
    =PaymentLate()
  ENDIF
ENDSCAN
```

CASE...ENDCASE

If there are several possibilities, IF...ELSE...ENDIF can get tedious and
complex. Also, if only one of a series of IFs is expected to apply, you'll
waste a lot of processor cycles because all of the IFs will be evaluated.

For such cases, CASE...ENDCASE is better. After a case that evaluates
to .True. is processed, FoxPro will drop out of the CASE...ENDCASE structure. This is especially useful when evaluating a single variable:

```
DO CASE
  CASE LASTKEY() = 27
    DO EscapeRoutine
  CASE LASTKEY() = 13
    DO PickOne
  ...
ENDCASE
```

A hybrid case

If you have particularly complex conditions to evaluate, you can use a hybrid that I occasionally make use of. It looks like this:

```
DO WHILE .T.
  IF condition
   =Process()
   EXIT        <== Leave NOW
  ENDIF
ENDDO
```

The power tools

Most of the looping and control structures I've described in this chapter aren't new to FoxPro, but the power tools are a real treat for programmers coming from other environments. They consist of programmer productivity tools and neat objects to include in your own applications.

The three programmer tools that will be your home from now on are the Project Manager, Screen Builder, and Menu Builder. These three elements manage much of the drudgery of application development.

Project Manager

When you start a programming project, start by giving it a name; then enter FoxPro and type:

```
MODIFY PROJECT MYAPP
```

or whatever. You'll get a screen that looks like the illustration in Fig. 1-1. The control on the right invites you to Add. What you're supposed to add is a screen, menu, program file, or any of the other things that go into an application. I generally start with a menu and then design file structures and design screens and reports.

The command MODIFY PROJECT creates a pair of files with the extensions .PJX and .PJT. The .PJT file is where the MEMO fields in the .PJX file are—analogous to the relationship between .DBF and .FPT files. Project Manager uses memo fields in project records to store what used to live in .FXP files—compiled code. But you can also store absolutely everything in your application into the project file. For example, reports—which live in .FRX/.FRT files—are stored in the project file, as are .PLB (library) files, which are used to add commands to FoxPro. In fact, if you have tables that

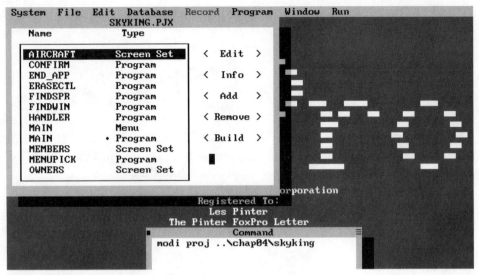

Figure 1-1 The Project Manager screen.

don't change often—State abbreviations, for example—you can store them in the project file.

You can also insert references to pieces of the project file that can be modified by users, like data files. If so, there's a way to mark them as modifiable; you can use the Greek letter phi (φ) to tell the Project Manager that the file is referenced solely for documentation purposes.

SET MAIN and application structures

One of the new aspects of the Project Manager is that you have to tell it where the program begins, using the SET MAIN bar from the Project pulldown menu. When you use SET MAIN, a dot appears beside the program or screen that's the starting point for your application.

Not long ago, there was only one way to design software. You could use a DO WHILE .T., display a menu, and then process choices until an option was chosen that called it quits, e.g:

```
MenuChoice = []
DO WHILE .T.
  =ShowMenu()
  DO CASE
   CASE MenuChoice = [R]
     =ShowReportMenu()
   ...
   CASE MenuChoice = [X]
     EXIT
  ENDCASE
ENDDO
```

You can still do that, but there's another way that's not intuitively obvious. FoxPro allows you to put the program into a wait state, then use *events* to trigger subroutine execution. You still have a MAIN program, but the menu gets loaded first; you can pull it down at any time in the same way you activate FoxPro's menu, using either the Alt or F10 key, or one of the menu bar's hot keys. I'll give you examples of both types of programs later on.

Screen Builder

For many FoxPro programmers, the screen builder is the most exciting aspect of the language. If your application consists mainly of low-level file I/O, you might be less impressed. But in my experience, the look and feel of the interface is where I spend 80% of my time, and that's where Screen Builder makes a world of difference.

The command MODIFY SCREEN *name* brings up a blank screen. In most cases, you would select the WINDOW button and define the screen as a window. This would cause FoxPro to generate code that defined a window and write everything in your screen design to the window. In traditional applications, this is desirable; in event-driven ones, it's essential. So plan on using the window option every time.

Pressing Alt–C will display the SCREEN BUILDER Screen Layout dialog screen (see Fig. 1-2). This is where you'll define other characteristics of the screen, and optionally write up to seven code snippets that Screen Builder will insert into seven different places in the generated code.

Screen Builder writes programs. These programs are exactly like programs that you would write yourself; there's not some strange new nonlinear flow of control that you haven't caught on to yet. In the screen in Fig. 1-2,

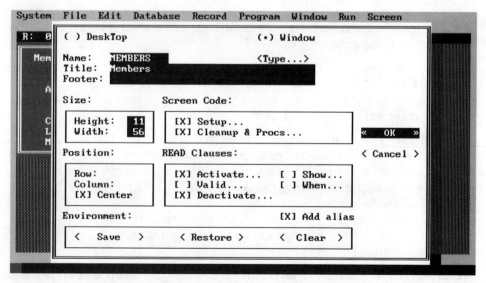

Figure 1-2 Screen Builder screen layout dialog.

you click on SETUP and the SETUP CODE window opens up. Whatever you type there is inserted verbatim into the setup portion of the generated program. The setup portion, as you would expect, is the very beginning. The CLEANUP portion is placed—you guessed it—at the end of the generated code, right after the READ.

The READ clauses

There are a few new items for non-FoxPro types. READ has five new clauses, each of which generally refers to a user-defined function. These five clauses are:

- VALID
- SHOW
- WHEN
- ACTIVATE
- DEACTIVATE

The generated code for all of these five clauses goes at the end of the CLEANUP code, as does the code from all VALID and WHEN snippets for GET variables. Their mission in life is to be executed when certain things happen.

READ VALID The VALID clause is executed if your program tries to exit the READ for a screen, which it will do if you:

- Press Escape
- Press Ctrl–W
- Exit the last field on the screen (if you didn't use READ CYCLE)
- Click on another window
- Click on a control defined as *terminating*

If the VALID clause returns a .T., your READ will end. If it returns .F., the READ will remain active.

READ SHOW The READ SHOW clause is executed every time the command SHOW GETS is issued. This can be used to display information that's related to the record on the screen, but not part of a GET field (e.g., a record number).

READ WHEN The WHEN clause is executed when the READ is first activated. READ WHEN clauses are used for two purposes: to do things you want done just when READ is executed, and to suppress the READ entirely. If you're using memvars, the command SCATTER MEMVAR at this point will load all the field data into memvars with the same names. If the READ WHEN clause returns a .F., the READ isn't executed at all. (Note that there's a new directive to suppress the READ command entirely, which will be explained later.)

READ ACTIVATE and DEACTIVATE Your application might display several screens at the same time. If you want to force some processing—saving on-screen information to a file, for example—the DEACTIVATE clause will process that request before deactivating the current window. Also, if you don't want your user to leave a screen unless certain fields have been filled in, the DEACTIVATE clause is where you do it.

Screen objects

There are four types of "objects" you can put on the screen:

- Text
- Boxes
- SAY/GET fields or memvars
- Controls

I'm ordinarily not fond of using a new word to describe something that already has a name—it makes me think that someone is trying to put something over on me—but I guess *object* is better than *thing*. Text can be placed anywhere. Boxes, which can also be displayed as lines, are useful for grouping related elements. Variables can be either memvars or fields. I almost never use fields. The amount of extra work required to use memvars is minimal, and philosophically I feel better about writing data to fields when I know that I want to save them.

Controls

Finally, FoxPro provides a half-dozen controls—more in the Windows product—that can be used to communicate with the READ statement. These controls also animate the screen in ways you'd have to program yourself if FoxPro hadn't already done it for you. Controls include:

- Push buttons
- Popups
- Lists
- Check boxes
- Radio buttons
- Invisible buttons

Controls are special cases of memvars. First, they can display and process choices in ways that used to take a *lot* of programming. Push buttons that permit easy selection of one of several choices are commonly used as on-screen menus. Radio buttons are mutually exclusive controls that typically don't terminate the read, but serve to remind users that one of a group of choices is the default, unless they override the default by choosing something else. Popups are useful for lists of choices that need to be displayed only at the moment they're chosen, while lists are displayed on the screen at all times, typically as an important part of the screen design.

Invisible buttons are used to turn areas of the screen into menu choices. (For an excellent design example, see FoxFire! from MicroMega Systems.)

You can designate controls as *terminating*, usually by including a T in the FUNCTION or PICTURE clause. When a terminating control is selected, FoxPro reacts as if Ctrl–W had been pressed, and any READ DEACTIVATE and READ VALID clauses are activated.

VALID clauses

Each control, as well as each GET object on the screen, can have both a WHEN and a VALID clause. WHEN clauses are relatively rare, but VALID clauses are the heart of FoxPro design.

As you exit a GET field, FoxPro always executes the field's VALID clause. You can use VALID clauses to check for valid values entered by the user. A typical VALID clause for a short character field might look like this:

```
@ 5,30 GET m.Warehouse
FUNCTION WHCodes
   Valid WHCodes()
IF NOT m.Warehouse $ [ABC]
   DEFINE POPUP CODES FROM 5,15 TITLE [ Warehouse codes ]
   DEFINE BAR 1 OF CODES PROMPT [A - Atlanta]
   DEFINE BAR 2 OF CODES PROMPT [B - Boston ]
   DEFINE BAR 3 OF CODES PROMPT [C - Columbus]
   ON SELECTION POPUP CODES DEACTIVATE POPUP CODES
   ACTIVATE POPUP CODES
   m.Warehouse=IIF(EMPTY(PROMPT()),[ ],LEFT(PROMPT(),1)
   RELEASE POPUP CODES
ENDIF
```

The changed value of m.Warehouse is automatically redisplayed. Of all of the features of FoxPro, I think the VALID clause has the greatest effect on our ability to write powerful and intelligent applications. I'll demonstrate dozens of types of VALID clauses in this book, but there are probably more ways to use this feature than any one book could ever show.

Snippets

Once you've entered a few dozen VALID clauses, if you click on the Display All Snippets option of the Control window, you'll see dozens of rectangular windows tiled one on top of the other. Each one will contain one of the VALID or WHEN clauses, or one of the five READ clauses, or any SETUP and CLEANUP code that you might have entered. Each of these pieces of code will get written to the bottom of the generated code for your screen (except SETUP, which is written to the TOP of the generated code).

FoxPro generally provides unique names for procedure snippets. The names look like this:

```
FUNCTION qc70u9cr7
```

If you want to use your own function names, you can do so by including the generator directive:

```
#NAME snippetname
```

as the first line in a snippet. FoxPro makes no attempt to ensure the uniqueness of function names you supply thusly, so don't get carried away. Besides, once you've learned to have faith in the generated screen program code, you'll probably never look at it. If you publish a monthly newsletter about FoxPro, however, you'll probably use it a lot . . . If you save your screen, go back to the Command window, and type:

```
USE MyScreen.SCX
BROWSE
```

You'll be looking at what appears to be a .DBF. That's where all those snippets are stored. In particular, tab over to the VALID column and press Ctrl–PgDn, and you'll be looking at your code. If the snippet is empty, the word *memo* will be all lowercase; if it contains some code, the first *M* will be capitalized.

On rare occasions, I've decided to add a single validation clause to a large number of fields on a screen. FoxPro permits valid clauses of the form:

```
VALID FirstExpr() AND SecondExpr()
```

If you design a screen that's supposed to act like a spreadsheet, you might use the first VALID function to recalculate row and column totals, and the second to determine which cell to move to, based on the last keystroke. But, on a 20×7 spreadsheet, we're talking about a *lot* of typing! I find it easier to browse the VALID clause field for the screen file and manually add the missing code, or even use FoxPro's REPLACE ALL command. The point is that this is just like a DBF, and you can use FoxPro's interactive commands to manipulate it.

SETUP and CLEANUP

You can use SETUP to ensure that needed files are open. I like to use the expression:

```
IF USED ( [CLIENTS] )
   SELECT CLIENTS
   ELSE
   SELECT A
   USE &dbfs..CLIENTS
ENDIF
SET ORDER TO CLIENTNAME
```

I used to use this kind of routine to reuse a file area for a group of mutually exclusive tables, but because FoxPro 2.5 permits a huge number of open file areas, area management is generally no longer an issue. So you can replace SELECT A with SELECT 0.

CLEANUP is where you put all the functions and procedures that are used by the current screen. The generated code will look just like any other FoxPro program, with all of the functions at the bottom (CLEANUP goes before the READ clauses and any GET...VALID clauses). The only time you might have to put some functions that are used exclusively by a single screen into a file by themselves is during debugging; once they work, they can be moved to CLEANUP.

If a function is used by several screens, just include it in the project file. You *could* put a function common to several screens into just one screen, then use `DO function IN XXX SPR` to run it from other screens, but the performance penalty is just too great. If you have functions called by several applications, put them all into a procedure library—a program file like any other, and use:

```
SET PROCEDURE TO myproclib
```

Each application will have to read it only once to table the location of its component functions, and the speed will be very acceptable.

Directives

You can use compiler directives to tell FoxPro how to deal with certain compile-time and generation-time features. There are a number of new ones in FoxPro 2.5:

```
#DEFINE/UNDEF
#IFDEF...ELIF...ENDIF
#INSERT
#ITSEXPRESSION char
#NAME snippet name
#NOREAD
#READCLAUSES clauses
#REDEFINE
#SECTION 1 | 2
#WCLAUSES clause1, clause2, ...
```

All of these commands can be (and usually are) expressed as the first four letters, e.g., `#READ COLOR ,W+/R`.

#DEFINE and #UNDEF are used to define and undefine constants in your code, to be evaluated at compile time. You can use this to simplify your code for different amounts of memory. For example, you might produce one version of your program for users running on 286 machines with 1 meg of memory, and another for people who have more hardware and memory resources.

The #IFDEF...ELIF...ENDIF directives are used in conditional compilation. The following is FoxPro's example code from the HELP file:

```
#IF 'WINDOWS' $ UPPER(VERSION())
   ? 'This is FoxPro for Windows'
#ELIF 'MAC' $ UPPER(VERSION())
```

```
    ? 'This is FoxPro for Mac'
#ELIF 'UNIX' $ UPPER(VERSION())
    ? 'This is FoxPro for UNIX'
#ELSE
    ? 'This is FoxPro for DOS'
#ENDIF
```

Conditional compilation means that the compiler will include only the code that passes the #IF test in the compiled .FXP or .APP. This trivial example might belie the value of the directive, but in multiplatform software, version-specific code can run to thousands of lines. In such cases, the resulting size reduction can be important.

The #INSERT menu and screen-generator directive inserts the contents of the file into generated menu or screen code. You can use #INSERT to place #DEFINE...#UNDEF statements from a file into the beginning of a generated menu or screen program. The included file cannot include other screen-generator directives. #INSERT is the only directive available for menus.

#ITSEXPRESSION allows you to specify a character that indicates that picture clauses, window titles, and window footers are character expressions instead of literal strings.

#NAME lets you use your own name for snippets produced by clauses such as SHOW, WHEN, and VALID. Only blank lines or comments can precede the #NAME directive.

Sometimes you'll want to display a screen without activating a READ. Include the #NOREAD screen-generator directive in a screen setup snippet to prevent the generation of the READ command.

#READCLAUSES allows you to specify clauses to be placed at end of a READ command that aren't available through the Screen Builder. Typical clauses to include are TIMEOUT, SAVE, OBJECT, NOMOUSE, and COLOR. One that I use often is:

```
#READ COLOR ,W+/R
```

which makes the GET field that the cursor is in appear in bold white on red. Users really appreciate this one.

#REDEFINE allows you to suppress the generation of commands that check for the existence of a window and automatically redefine the window. This has the same effect as:

```
IF WEXIST ("WindowName")
    RELEASE WINDOW WindowName
ENDIF
DEFINE WINDOW WindowName...
```

#SECTION 1 and #SECTION 2 let you split the setup code for a screen into two sections. Section 1 is generated at the beginning of the .SPR program. If you use it, #SECTION1 must precede the first executable line of code. Section 2 is generated after the DEFINE WINDOW commands and before the screen-layout commands. A common use of SECTION directives is to split the setup code to include a PARAMETER statement or ON ERROR in the screen program.

The #WCLAUSES screen-generator directive lets you specify additional DEFINE WINDOW clauses. It goes in the SETUP snippet of your screen window.

#WNAME lets you substitute a generated window name for a string wherever it occurs in the screen code. This allows you to create generic code. For example, if you include:

```
#WNAME JoeBob
```

in a screen's SETUP code, and the following code in the ACTIVATE clause for the window:

```
IF WONTOP('JoeBob')
    statements
ELSE
    statements
ENDIF
```

a unique name for the current window will be substituted for JoeBob.

Two approaches to screen design

The big decision facing you is whether to use FoxPro's event-driven capabilities, or rely on more traditional techniques. The choice is not obvious, regardless of what you might have been told. If you're asked to write an event-driven application, the choice has been made for you—presumably by people aware of the additional cost and complexity who are willing to bear it. If not, you owe it to your users to make the usual "how much software for how much money" decisions that have always been a part of software design. If you decide to develop a Rolls-Royce for every customer, you're doing what the American Medical Association has done to this country. The honest and decent thing to do in both cases is to let the customer choose.

I use modeless designs more heavily in applications where most of the application consists of picking and choosing. For example, the ABSTRACT program included on the disk for this book does a keyword search of all of the articles ever published in my newsletter, then displays a short abstract of the selected article. There's no data entry or editing. This is a perfect application for the modeless approach. For heavy data entry, I would *never* use a modeless model. I still haven't decided whether it will ever be desirable to use a modeless interface for the invoice screen, the model that dominates my commercial applications.

Menu Builder

FoxPro contains a built-in menu bar, displayed at the top of the screen, called _MSYSMENU (see Fig. 1-3). You can redefine _MSYSMENU by re-

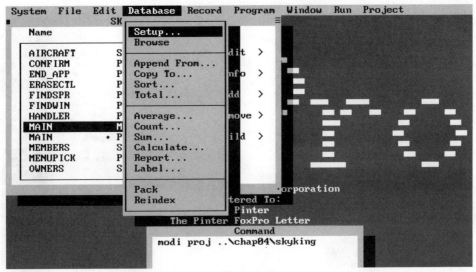

Figure 1-3 FoxPro's menu bar.

placing it entirely with your own menu, adding more pads with associated pull-downs, or changing the existing pull-downs. Your application's menu will act exactly the same way FoxPro's does, because it's the same one. Thus pressing Alt or F10 will activate the menu bar, and (if you set up hot keys) pressing Alt plus the hot key letter for one of the pad's choices will pull down the selected menu pad. FoxPro makes menus incredibly easy to write. The command:

```
MODIFY MENU menu program name
```

will open up the Menu Builder screen, as shown in Fig. 1-4. You can use this facility to begin to design your application. It includes a preview facility, which allows you to see what the finished menu will look like without exiting Menu Builder. Typically, you insert "stubs" to indicate that a particular part of the application isn't finished yet. I use the FoxPro command:

```
WAIT WINDOW [ ** not yet implemented ** ] TIMEOUT 1
```

Special menu entries

In addition to choices like DO *programname*, you can select from one of the hundred or so reserved menu words that represent entries from FoxPro's own menu. To get a list of them, type:

```
? SYS(2013)
```

For example, _MST_CALCU will activate the calculator window, while _MST_DIARY will invoke the Calendar/Diary. ACTIVATE WINDOW CALENDAR

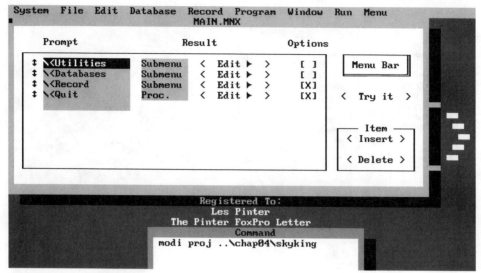

Figure 1-4 The Menu Builder screen.

will display the calendar, but it won't necessarily interact with the rest of the program in a useful way, as you'll see in chapter 5.

Some programmers seem to delight in providing users with dozens of options. In particular, I've seen a number of FoxPro applications that seem to include just about everything in FoxPro's own menu except the program development tools. One wonders if the users asked for them, or even know what to do with them. Before you add a menu item to display the time, see if your customer already has a watch. If he does, suppress the urge.

Going anywhere from anywhere

One of the benefits of being able to pull down a menu at any time is the ability to do something else briefly and then return to your screen without saving and exiting. This is something that almost all of my clients have asked for at one time or another. A typical case is medical-office software, which constitutes probably a third of my total consulting work. No matter where you are, being able to take a payment or schedule an office visit is a constant requirement.

Well, one way to do that is to write your software so that anyone can pull down the menu and do anything else at any time. Another way is to add the functions Schedule Appointment and Record Payment as hot keys on each of your principal screens. This is a practical and very inexpensive solution, one which works in every case I've seen.

However, there are indeed cases where having access to every menu option from within any other menu option is actually required. If so, use the techniques described in chapter 4. If some features should be suppressed from time to time, you can conditionally disable them using the

SKIP FOR *memvar* parameter, where a .False. value of *memvar* will indicate that the menu item is unavailable by "dimming" it.

Color

Another very exciting tool in FoxPro is the use of color. Color sets are collections of a dozen color schemes, which are in turn groups of ten color pairs that affect various screen elements. For example, color scheme 1 affects your windows (and other TO SCREEN output):

```
User Windows (Scheme 1)
   Color Pair 1  SAY field
   Color Pair 2  GET field
   Color Pair 3  Border
   Color Pair 4  Title, active
   Color Pair 5  Title, idle, & message
   Color Pair 6  Selected item
   Color Pair 7  Clock, Hot keys
   Color Pair 8  Shadow
   Color Pair 9  Enabled Ctrl
   Color Pair 10 Disabled Ctrl
```

Screen elements whose color is similarly managed include:

Element	Colors
User Wind	Scheme 1
User Menus	Scheme 2
Menu Bar	Scheme 3
Menu Popups	Scheme 4
Dialogs	Scheme 5
Dialog Popups	Scheme 6
Alert	Scheme 7
Windows	Scheme 8
Window Popups	Scheme 9
Browse	Scheme 10
Report	Scheme 11
Alert Popups	Scheme 12

The difference between a window popup and a dialog popup might seem obscure, and in fact the etymology of many computer terms is a mystery to me, but the distinctions are documented and useful. The variety is amazing. (For the limiting case of color sets, you might want to take a look at Wayne Harless' *The Harless Color Sets*, a smashing exercise in overkill that's a delight to see.)

Granted, if your design involves having several user windows on the screen at one time, each with a different color scheme, this isn't going to help you much; when you change a color scheme, it changes for all objects that use it, and it changes immediately. I usually manage my own user window objects' colors, and let FoxPro handle everything else.

Error trapping

FoxPro programs should always have an error trap—a program that does what you want it to do if the program encounters an error. For some years I've believed that 100% bug-free software is an unattainable goal, especially with highly complex software; languages like FoxPro may never be absolutely free of undesirable bugs. Somewhere, somehow, some Gonzo patch to DOS in conjunction with some obscure sequence of FoxPro commands is going to leave a dirty cup and saucer in the AX register, and even FoxPro is going to blow up. Just keep in mind that if your software blows up, they'll call *you*, not Microsoft. To trap errors, use:

```
ON ERROR DO ERRTRAP WITH parameters
```

Then, any error will send control to your ERRTRAP routine. Whatever you do there, you can return control to the command that caused the error with the RETRY command, or to the next command after the one that caused the error with a simple RETURN. There are a number of automatic error-handling capabilities (e.g., SET REPROCESS), but they're more appropriate for the user interface than for your programs. I like to be in control.

Parameters that can be passed to your error routine include the name of the program that was running when the error happened, the text of the error message, what line number it was on, and even the source code that caused the error. To pass all of the above, use:

```
ON ERROR DO ERRTRAP WITH ;
PROGRAM(), MESSAGE(), LINENO(), MESSAGE(1)
```

It's important to include PROGRAM( ) and LINENO( ) in your ON ERROR routine, because FoxPro knows their correct values only at the point the error occurred. If you display PROG( ) and LINE( ) at the top of your error routine, you'll get `ERRTRAP.FXP` and `LINE 1`, respectively.

Be sure to save the current value of any settings that might interfere with error reporting (e.g., SET PRINT, SET DEVICE, SET TALK), then set them back to their original settings if RETRY or "next statement" are selected.

Good error trapping, while not perfect, sure beats *error no. 12* messages that scare the pants off your users and don't help solve the problem. I sometimes prefer to log all of the technical information to a file that you can dial in and download without ever worrying your users with details. Just give them a screen with the error message and a note to call you, and then reopen all databases and `RETURN TO MASTER`.

Multiuser programming

As of version 2.5, every copy of FoxPro can be used to write and run multiuser applications. That means that you can write your software so that several users at once can write to the same file. The means for accomplishing this is through the use of file and record locking, implemented both explicitly through the FLOCK( ) and RLOCK( ) commands, and implicitly by means of commands that lock the current record, do their thing, and unlock it.

The literature on multiuser FoxPro programming ranges from the ridiculous to the sublime. I spent much of my MBA program in Operations Research working on "corner solutions"—the one in a million shots that thrill hardcore math freaks. Some papers on multiuser programming seem to think that everyone's trying to write an airline reservation system. Or, more likely, they're so obsessed with appearing academically pure and rigorous that they overlook the little matter of cost effectiveness.

I'm going to deal with multiuser programming in a bit more depth than I ever have before, because I think it's something we all have to do on virtually every job. But don't make a big deal of it. Try the inexpensive approach first. Usually, multiuser programming carries a very small incremental cost over single-user programming. And there are a few tricks that really speed things up.

Summary

This chapter presents the characteristics of FoxPro that seem to me to determine the flavor and texture of applications written in this language. In the next chapter, we'll look at the steps involved in writing an application.

2
Writing an application

FoxPro is pretty flexible about how you organize your application; you can scatter bits and pieces all over the hard disk. But a set of recommended practices has surfaced, much of it recommended by Microsoft/Fox, and its adoption is pretty compelling.

The raw materials

The executable portion of a FoxPro application consists of program files, screen and menu programs (programs that were generated from screens and menus respectively), reports, library code (from .PLB files generated using C), and other .APP files built within other projects. All of these elements end up as lines in the project file, which then tells FoxPro how to build an .APP or .EXE file.

In the Project Manager, there's a lot more going on than meets the eye. If you select EDIT while the Customer Screen is highlighted, or simply press Enter, you're moved to the Customer Screen. These actions "point to" the location of the screen files and source code—they're not actually stored in the .PJX/.PJT files. However, when you build the application, the Project Manager does several things:

- It generates the source code for the screen, giving it the extension .SPR.
- It compiles the generated code and saves the compiled version in a memo field in the project file.
- If saving the screen's generated source code wasn't requested, it deletes it. So if you don't ever want to see the generated .SPR code, you never will.

Menus are given similar treatment. .PRG files are compiled to .FXP format, but the .FXP code is also stored directly into memo fields in the project file. So a lot of the "directory bloat" possible in systems involving hundreds of programs can be eliminated.

This feature has a major impact on application execution speed—not because of FoxPro, but because of DOS. If DOS has fewer than 128 directory entries, it tables them. Directory searches are instantaneous. However, if DOS has more than 128 entries in a directory, it rereads the directory every time you look for something—for example, a function that your program needs. And, if you create 150 files in a directory and then erase them, DOS *still* thinks they're there (until you defragment your hard drive), at least for the purpose of determining whether to scan its internal file table or reload from disk. So avoiding cluttering up your directories is one of the many fringe benefits of using the Project Manager.

Once the .APP or .EXE is built, the pieces are no longer needed to run the application. FoxPro copies all the parts it needs and binds them into the generated application. Not only don't you need the source code, you don't need the .FXPs, reports, or labels. In fact, if you have .DBFs that are tables you read but don't write to, you can also include them in the .APP by marking them with the Greek letter phi (ϕ).

What goes where

I build my applications in a subdirectory directly off the root directory. Under that structure, I add directories for data, screens, source code, reports, and work files. A sample would look like this:

```
C:\MYAPP (.APP file goes here)
   \DBFS (.DBF/CDX files go here)
   \SOURCE (.PRG files go here)
   \MENUS (.MNX/MNT files go here)
   \REPORTS (.FRX/FRT files go here)
   \SCREENS (.SCX/SCT files go here)
```

If you type the command:

```
SET PATH TO SOURCE
```

FoxPro will find your program files without any other help. With this command:

```
MODIFY COMMAND PLANNER
```

FoxPro will look first in the current directory and then in subdirectory SOURCE for a program named PLANNER.PRG. I don't use SET PATH. While I'm writing a program, it lives in the MYAPP directory. I copy it from SOURCE using:

```
! COPY source\progname.PRG
```

then delete the current reference to *source\progname.prg* in the project file list, and add the copy I just moved to the MYAPP directory. Once it's debugged, I copy it to SOURCE and erase it from the MYAPP directory, using the commands:

```
! COPY progname.PRG source
! DEL progname.PRG
```

Then I rebuild the project, which asks me to locate the copy of the copy that's now back down in the SOURCE directory. That way, the current production source is always in the SOURCE directory, and I don't replace it until a new version of a .PRG is put into production.

The .PJX/.PJT project files also live in the MYAPP directory. The project file remembers the location of your source-code files. If you USE MYAPP.PJX, then browse the file and you'll see that each program filename is referred to with a fully qualified path name unless it's located in the current directory. Note that, when you finalize a program and copy it to the SOURCE directory, you have to update the project file to point to the new location by deleting the original reference to the .PRG and then using Add to include the copy that's now in the SOURCE directory.

A sample application

To demonstrate how all of this goes together, you're going to build a sample application. I'll use the example of a flying club, because I fly small planes and have spent an inordinately large amount of my money on them. (Actually, "flying club" is a euphemism for "airplane rental company." There's no club involved, but the name makes you feel a bit better about spending that much money on something that isn't deductible.)

Flying clubs lease airplanes from people who've realized that they can't make the monthly payments on their new toy, and rent them to student pilots. Students' licenses must be current as of the date they take up a rental plane. If they haven't been up within the last 60 days, they have to go up with an instructor before they can rent another airplane. Every quarter, owners get a report of their planes' activity.

The principal files, then, are AIRCRAFT, OWNERS, MEMBERS, CHARGES, and PAYMENTS. You won't use all of these files for several chapters, but I'm trying to be organized, so here they are. The file structures have been designed as shown in Listing 2-1.

Each .DBF file has an index of the same name and the extension .CDX. Although you can have any number of index tags in a structural .CDX file, don't overdo it. The performance and size penalties are pretty steep compared to the actual benefit.

I use an AIRCRAFT ID because all airplanes have a six-character identification number. OWNERS is a small file and typically has so few records that it doesn't need to be indexed.

Listing 2-1 The generated code for AIRCRAFT.SPR.

Structure for database: AIRCRAFT.DBF

Field	Field Name	Type	Width	Dec	Index
1	AIRCRAFTID	Character	6		Asc
2	MAKE	Character	8		
3	MODEL	Character	6		
4	YEAR	Character	4		
5	COLORS	Character	10		
6	PARKING	Character	4		
7	ENGINES	Character	1		
8	SEATS	Character	3		
9	LASTANNUAL	Date	8		
10	TOTALTIME	Numeric	6	1	
11	SMOH	Numeric	6	1	
12	SMOHRIGHT	Numeric	6	1	
13	HOURLYRATE	Numeric	3		
14	OWNER	Character	40		
** Total **			112		

Index tag: AIRCRAFTID   Key: AIRCRAFTID

Structure for database: OWNERS.DBF

Field	Field Name	Type	Width	Dec	Index
1	NAME	Character	40		Asc
2	ADDRESS1	Character	40		
3	ADDRESS2	Character	40		
4	CITY	Character	17		
5	STATE	Character	3		
6	ZIP	Character	10		
7	COUNTRY	Character	3		
8	HOMEPHONE	Character	12		
9	WORKPHONE	Character	12		
10	CELLPHONE	Character	12		
** Total **			190		

Index tag: NAME   Key: UPPER(NAME)

Structure for database: MEMBERS.DBF

Field	Field Name	Type	Width	Dec	Index
1	MEMBERID	Character	10		Asc
2	NAME	Character	40		Asc
3	ADDRESS1	Character	40		
4	ADDRESS2	Character	40		
5	CITY	Character	14		
6	STATE	Character	3		
7	ZIP	Character	10		

```
    8   COUNTRY      Character      3
    9   LICENSE      Character     15
   10   MEDICALDAT   Date           8
   11   BALANCEDUE   Numeric        7        2
** Total **                      191
```

```
Index tag:    MEMBERID    Key: MEMBERID
Index tag:    NAME        Key: UPPER(NAME)
```

```
Structure for database: CHARGES.DBF
Field   Field Name   Type       Width   Dec   Index
    1   MEMBERID     Character     10           Asc
    2   DATE         Date           8
    3   TYPE         Character      1
    4   AIRCRAFTID   Character      6           Asc
    5   DESCRIP      Character     20
    6   HOURS        Numeric        4     1
    7   AMOUNT       Numeric        7     2
** Total **                       57
```

```
Index tag:    AIRCRAFTID   Key: AIRCRAFTID
Index tag:    MEMBERID     Key: MEMBERID + DTOC ( DATE , 1 )
```

```
Structure for database: PAYMENTS.DBF
Field   Field Name   Type       Width   Dec   Index
    1   MEMBERID     Character     10           Asc
    2   DATE         Date           8
    3   DESCRIP      Character     20
    4   AMOUNT       Numeric        7     2
** Total **                       46
```

```
Index tag:    MEMBERID    Key: MEMBERID + DTOC ( DATE , 1 )
```

The use of the expression DTOC (DATE , 1) in the two transaction file index expressions buys you two things. First, it displays transactions in date order. Second, if you specify SET TAG TO MEMBERID DESCENDING, then the command:

```
SEEK m.MemberID
```

will find the most recent transaction for that member. If that transaction's date is more than two months old, the member gets scheduled for some "dual" time.

Designing screens

Any application starts with its file structures and screens. I've done the file design already, so we'll do the screens next. You're going to start with a simple task, and then build the rest of the application around it. For the first screen, develop the one that manages the stable of aircraft. To begin, use the following commands:

```
USE AIRCRAFT
MODIFY SCREEN SCREENS\AIRCRAFT
```

and the screen shown in Fig. 2-1 will appear. I find that the easiest way to start is to use the QuickScreen feature, and then move things around. Pull down the Screen Menu by pressing Alt–C (which will get you the System Menu), and then press Q or highlight the last item on the pull-down menu and press Enter (see Fig. 2-2).

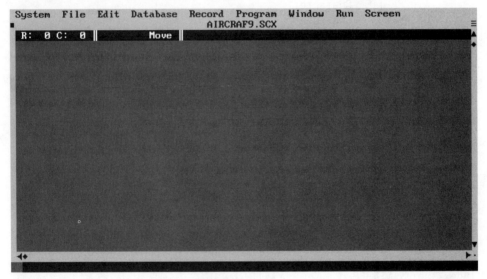

Figure 2-1   Starting to design a screen.

The QuickScreen option presents the dialog shown in Fig. 2-3. Notice the options beside the check boxes. Any time you see a dialog like this, you can bet that what you select will affect the result. In this case, accept the defaults and see what the consequences are. So press Enter a few more times, and you'll get the screen in Fig. 2-4. The fields from the file have become GET objects on the screen, and their names are the associated text SAY fields.

Here's where most newcomers to FoxPro get converted to using a mouse. By far the easiest way to manipulate objects in the Screen Builder is with a mouse. It's possible to do so without one, but, believe me, it's just not worth the effort. You don't have to make your users use a mouse—and

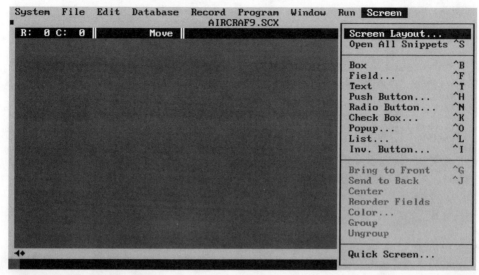

Figure 2-2 The Screen menu.

Figure 2-3 The QuickScreen option.

unless you're programming in Windows you probably won't—but you won't want to use the Screen Builder without using a mouse yourself.

This type of screen is called a *form* (as opposed to a *table*, which uses one line of the screen for part of each record in the file). I've moved things around a bit and changed the prompts to reflect what I think the screen should look like. There's just one other thing to do, and that's to make sure that this all gets done in a window instead of on the screen. Use Alt–C

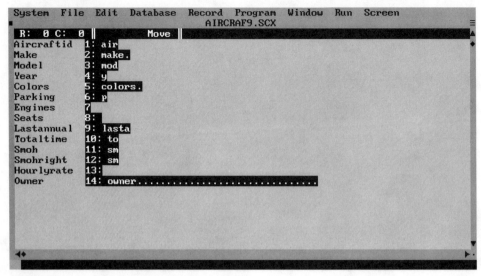

Figure 2-4 A QuickScreen-generated screen.

again to pull down the Screen Menu, then select the first option, Layout. You'll get the screen seen in Fig. 2-5.

Using the Layout window, select Window and then enter the name AIR-CRAFT. In fact, you could call it anything, or let FoxPro generate a name for it. But window naming turns out to be kind of a big deal later on, so get used to naming them yourself. Now, let's generate some source code and see what it looks like. Use Alt–P to pull down the Program Menu, and then select Generate (see Fig. 2-6).

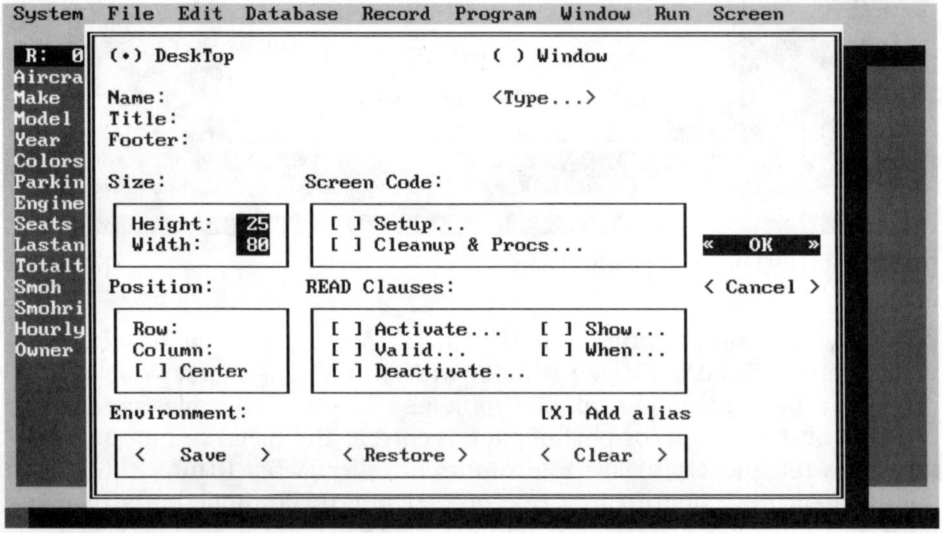

Figure 2-5 The Layout dialog.

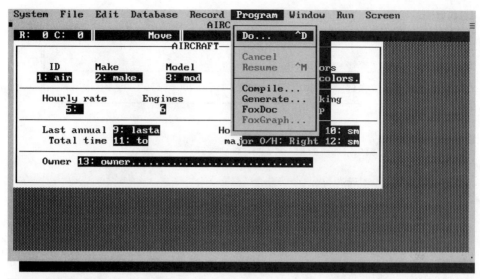

Figure 2-6 The Program/Generate menu.

The screen you'll see next is shown in Fig. 2-7. Because some of these defaults (whether or not to generate code to open the AIRCRAFT file each time this screen program is run and whether or not to release the AIRCRAFT window after the READ command is executed) are going to be the same every single time you generate this code, you might wonder whether you're going to have to go up and click the appropriate boxes every single time. Relax—you aren't. The Project Manager file remembers what options you picked. Finally, you'll get the program shown in Listing 2-2.

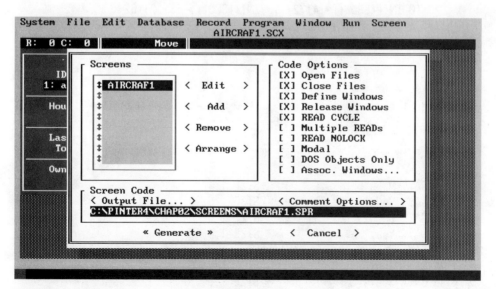

Figure 2-7 The Screen Program Generation Options dialog.

Listing 2-2 The fixed generated screen code.

```
*
*      ┌─────────────────────────────────────────────────────┐
*      │                   AIRCRAFT.SPR                        │
*      ├─────────────────────────────────────────────────────┤
*      │  This program was automatically generated by GENSCRN  │
*      └─────────────────────────────────────────────────────┘
*

#REGION 0
REGIONAL m.currarea, m.talkstat, m.compstat

IF SET("TALK") = "ON"
   SET TALK OFF
   m.talkstat = "ON"
ELSE
   m.talkstat = "OFF"
ENDIF
m.compstat = SET("COMPATIBLE")
SET COMPATIBLE FOXPLUS

IF NOT WEXIST("aircraft") ;
   OR UPPER(WTITLE("AIRCRAFT")) == "AIRCRAFT.PJX" ;
   OR UPPER(WTITLE("AIRCRAFT")) == "AIRCRAFT.SCX" ;
   OR UPPER(WTITLE("AIRCRAFT")) == "AIRCRAFT.MNX" ;
   OR UPPER(WTITLE("AIRCRAFT")) == "AIRCRAFT.PRG" ;
   OR UPPER(WTITLE("AIRCRAFT")) == "AIRCRAFT.QPR"
   DEFINE WINDOW aircraft ;
      FROM INT((SROW()-14)/2)   ,INT((SCOL()-63)/2)      ;
        TO INT((SROW()-14)/2)+13,INT((SCOL()-63)/2)+62 ;
      TITLE "AIRCRAFT"   NOFLOAT NOCLOSE SHADOW ;
      NOMINIMIZE    COLOR SCHEME 1
ENDIF

#REGION 1
IF WVISIBLE("aircraft")
   ACTIVATE WINDOW aircraft SAME
ELSE
   ACTIVATE WINDOW aircraft NOSHOW
ENDIF
@  1,21 SAY "Make"                SIZE 1,4, 0
@  1,36 SAY "Model"               SIZE 1,5, 0
@  1,50 SAY "Colors"              SIZE 1,6, 0
@  1,43 SAY "Year"                SIZE 1,4, 0
@  4,48 SAY "Parking"             SIZE 1,7, 0
@  4,21 SAY "Engines"             SIZE 1,7, 0
@  4,36 SAY "Seats"               SIZE 1,5, 0
@ 10, 4 SAY "Owner"               SIZE 1,5, 0
```

2-2 Continued.

```
@  1, 9 SAY "ID"               SIZE 1,2, 0
@  7, 4 SAY "Last annual"      SIZE 1,11, 0
@  8, 5 SAY "Total time"       SIZE 1,10, 0
@  4, 4 SAY "Hourly rate"      SIZE 1,11, 0
@  7,47 SAY "Left"             SIZE 1,4, 0
@  7,34 SAY "Hours since"      SIZE 1,11, 0
@  8,35 SAY "major O/H:"       SIZE 1,10, 0
@  8,46 SAY "Right"            SIZE 1,5, 0
@  3, 0 TO 3,60
@  6, 0 TO 6,60
@  9, 0 TO 9,60
@  5,37 GET aircraft.seats        SIZE 1,3     DEFAULT " "
@  5,48 GET aircraft.parking      SIZE 1,4     DEFAULT " "
@  7,16 GET aircraft.lastannual   SIZE 1,8     DEFAULT {  /  /  }
@  2,36 GET aircraft.model        SIZE 1,6     DEFAULT " "
@  2,44 GET aircraft.year         SIZE 1,4     DEFAULT " "
@  2,48 GET aircraft.colors       SIZE 1,10    DEFAULT " "
@  2, 7 GET aircraft.aircraftid   SIZE 1,6     DEFAULT " "
@  2,21 GET aircraft.make         SIZE 1,8     DEFAULT " "
@  5, 8 GET aircraft.hourlyrate   SIZE 1,3     DEFAULT 0
@  5,24 GET aircraft.engines      SIZE 1,1     DEFAULT " "
@  7,52 GET aircraft.smoh         SIZE 1,6     DEFAULT 0
@ 10,10 GET aircraft.owner        SIZE 1,40    DEFAULT " "
@  8,16 GET aircraft.totaltime    SIZE 1,6     DEFAULT 0
@  8,52 GET aircraft.smohright    SIZE 1,6     DEFAULT 0


IF NOT WVISIBLE("aircraft")
   ACTIVATE WINDOW aircraft
ENDIF


READ CYCLE


#REGION 0
IF m.talkstat = "ON"
   SET TALK ON
ENDIF
IF m.compstat = "ON"
   SET COMPATIBLE ON
ENDIF
```

FoxPro's generated code

Several things about the generated code stand out. First, there's some "save and restore settings" code that might be crucial to your environment. Second, it defines SIZE and DEFAULT for every GET field Third, it generates a READ command—READ CYCLE in this case, which is what had been checked. Fourth, the GETs are reading from .DBF fields, which is something I *never* do. Finally, the order of the GET fields is scrambled.

As far as the save-and-restore environment stuff and the SIZE and DE-FAULT clauses, they're harmless and you can't get rid of them. But the last two items are more serious. Applications that use database fields in edit/add screens are seriously flawed. For one thing, you have to lock the record to edit it. For another, you have to specify APPEND BLANK before you can add a new record, which means that you have to delete the record if the user decides not to save it halfway through the ADD. And the order of the GETs is pretty much a matter of common sense; this one is seriously messed up.

Fields or memvars?

Remember back in Fig. 2-5, where the code asked whether you wanted memory variables? The answer is almost always yes. This is sort of a trick question. The alternative is to use the fields in your database records for direct data entry.

This particular prompt reminds me of one of the oddities of flying in America. If you fly small planes, you'll be turned away from a tower-controlled field if the visibility is only between one to three miles. If you say the magic words "request special VFR," however—which means "I know what I'm doing"—the tower will *instantly* clear you for final approach. They just want to know that you're sure you can handle the landing and are prepared for the consequences if you can't. Sounds silly, but it's true.

FoxPro generates screens with field variables by default because, in spite of all of their drawbacks, they don't require any special programming. But editing field variables directly has more serious consequences. If you ask for memvars, you're taking responsibility for doing what has to be done to make your application work.

Rearranging GETs

Getting the GETs in the right order is another matter. As you edit screen objects, their order gets shuffled around. By the time you select GENERATE, there's no telling what order they'll be in. But there's an easy way to fix them. If you press Alt–E (for Edit), then choose Select All—or alternatively, press Ctrl–A (the global hot key for the Select All menu option)—all the objects on the screen will change color, indicating that they've been "grabbed." If you then press Alt–C to pull down the Screen Menu and then pick Reorder, you'll get the normal left-to-right, top-to-bottom scan order.

If the screen has a lot of boxing and grouping, the normal scan order might not apply. If that's the case with your screen, you'll have a slightly more tedious job ahead of you. Here's what you do: Hold down the Shift key and click on the GET fields on the screen in the order in which you want them scanned. Be careful not to move the mouse while you're doing this. When you're done, use Alt–C to pull down the screen menu, and then select Bring to Front. That's all there is to it!

Now, generate the screen again and take a look at the code in Listing 2-3 (spurious code omitted). To run the program, type:

```
DO AIRCRAFT.SPR
```

(Remember to use ESCAPE or Ctrl–W to exit the screen's READ CYCLE loop.) Nice screen. It looks good, and it acts like a screen should. But, it doesn't *do* anything! The data you type in doesn't get saved. Well, you didn't tell it to save the data.

Listing 2-3 The Valid snippet for m.What2Do.

```
*
*                ┌──────────────────────────────────────────────────┐
*                │                  AIRCRAFT.SPR                     │
*                ├──────────────────────────────────────────────────┤
*                │  This program was automatically generated by GENSCRN │
*                └──────────────────────────────────────────────────┘

IF NOT WEXIST("aircraft") ;
   OR UPPER(WTITLE("AIRCRAFT")) == "AIRCRAFT.PJX" ;
   OR UPPER(WTITLE("AIRCRAFT")) == "AIRCRAFT.SCX" ;
   OR UPPER(WTITLE("AIRCRAFT")) == "AIRCRAFT.MNX" ;
   OR UPPER(WTITLE("AIRCRAFT")) == "AIRCRAFT.PRG" ;
   OR UPPER(WTITLE("AIRCRAFT")) == "AIRCRAFT.QPR"
   DEFINE WINDOW aircraft ;
      FROM INT((SROW()-14)/2)    ,INT((SCOL()-63)/2)     ;
         TO INT((SROW()-14)/2)+13,INT((SCOL()-63)/2)+62 ;
      TITLE "AIRCRAFT"    NOFLOAT NOCLOSE SHADOW ;
      NOMINIMIZE    COLOR SCHEME 1
ENDIF

#REGION 1
IF WVISIBLE("aircraft")
   ACTIVATE WINDOW aircraft SAME
ELSE
   ACTIVATE WINDOW aircraft NOSHOW
ENDIF

@  1, 0 SAY "ID"        SIZE 1,2, 0
@  1,13 SAY "Make"      SIZE 1,4, 0
@  1,25 SAY "Model"     SIZE 1,5, 0
@  1,38 SAY "Year"      SIZE 1,4, 0
@  1,50 SAY "Colors"    SIZE 1,6, 0
```

```
@  4, 4 SAY "Hourly rate"   SIZE 1,11,0
@  4,21 SAY "Engines"       SIZE 1,7, 0
@  4,36 SAY "Seats"         SIZE 1,5, 0
@  4,48 SAY "Parking"       SIZE 1,7, 0
@  7, 4 SAY "Last annual"   SIZE 1,11,0
@  8, 5 SAY "Total time"    SIZE 1,10,0
@  7,34 SAY "Hours since"   SIZE 1,11,0
@  8,35 SAY "major O/H:"    SIZE 1,10,0
@  7,47 SAY "Left"          SIZE 1,4, 0
@  8,46 SAY "Right"         SIZE 1,5, 0
@ 10, 4 SAY "Owner"         SIZE 1,5, 0
@  3, 0 TO 3,60
@  6, 0 TO 6,60
@  9, 0 TO 9,60

@  2, 3 GET m.aircraftid    SIZE 1,6    DEFA " " WHEN _qc80jd925()
@  2,13 GET m.make          SIZE 1,8    DEFA " " FUNC "!" VALID _qc80jd9ju()
@  2,25 GET m.model         SIZE 1,6    DEFA " "
@  2,38 GET m.year          SIZE 1,4    DEFA " " PICTURE "####"
@  2,48 GET m.colors        SIZE 1,10   DEFA " "
@  5, 8 GET m.hourlyrate    SIZE 1,3       DEFAULT 0
@  5,24 GET m.engines       SIZE 1,1       DEFAULT " "
@  5,37 GET m.seats         SIZE 1,3       DEFAULT " "
@  5,48 GET m.parking       SIZE 1,4       DEFAULT " "
@  7,16 GET m.lastannual    SIZE 1,8       DEFAULT {  /  /  }
@  7,52 GET m.smoh          SIZE 1,6       DEFAULT 0
@  8,16 GET m.totaltime     SIZE 1,6       DEFAULT 0
@  8,52 GET m.smohright     SIZE 1,6       DEFAULT 0
@ 10,10 GET m.owner         SIZE 1,40      DEFAULT " "

IF NOT WVISIBLE("aircraft")
   ACTIVATE WINDOW aircraft
ENDIF

READ CYCLE
```

Adding controls to a screen

To make screens actually do things, Microsoft/Fox recommends the use of
controls. The usual control for this type of screen is called a *push button*.
Push buttons are displayed as a series of prompts enclosed in angle brack-
ets. To add a push button, either select Push Button from the Screen
Menu, or hot-key to it directly with Ctrl–H. The Push Button dialog is
shown in Fig. 2-8.

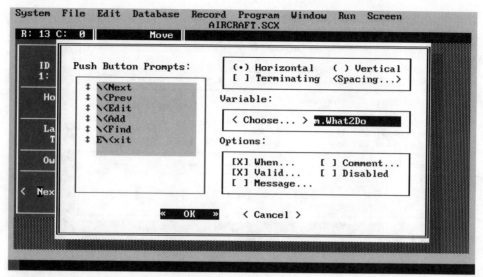

Figure 2-8 The push-button dialog screen.

A push button requires a memvar name and a series of prompts. Within each prompt, the string \< can be used to designate a hot-key letter. Prompts can be displayed either horizontally or vertically.

The terminating check box refers to a unique property of controls. As you know, you can end a READ by pressing either Ctrl–W or one of its surrogates (PgDn, Ctrl–Enter), pressing Escape or Ctrl–Q, or exiting the last GET in the read if READ CYCLE wasn't used. If a control has been designated as *terminating*, selecting it either by clicking on it or by pressing Enter will also attempt to terminate the READ. I say "attempt to terminate the READ" because if a READ VALID clause is present it must return a .True. before the READ will actually terminate.

This is the key to designing a wide variety of interesting and useful screens in FoxPro. READ CYCLE moves you from field to field without exiting when you get to the "last" field on the screen. Controls can be used to run the entire process, with a READ VALID clause to determine whether the program stays in the READ or continues on to the next statement.

The use of controls adds a new look to screen design. You'll find that you can write your software as a series of dialogs that guide users through the choices to be made at each step of their work with relatively little effort.

In particular, the options to move the user from record to record (Next/Previous), add or delete a record, search for a particular record, and exit the screen are required by most "form" screens of this type. In the screen in Fig. 2-9, I've added a control with these options. In Fig. 2-10, I've checked the Valid box to indicate that I want to enter some code as a valid clause for variable What2Do.

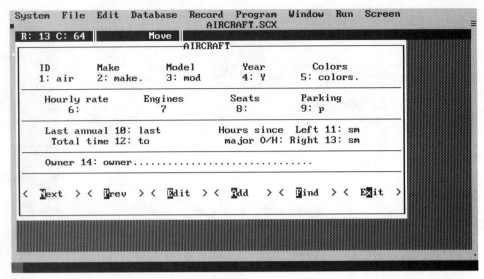

Figure 2-9 The Aircraft screen with a control added.

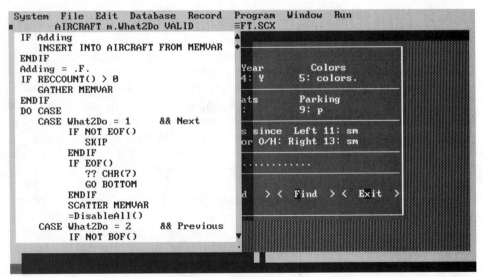

Figure 2-10 Adding a valid clause for the m.What2Do control.

If the code were just a few lines, I'd type it into the text region that the snippet dialog uses for initial display. But because it's a little longer, I click on Edit and then Ok to make the dialog disappear, and it leaves me in the editor in the valid snippet for m.What2Do. Listing 2-3 shows what I typed.

Listing 2-4 Making a file available.

```
FUNCTION _qc60x4szj                && m.What2Do VALID
#REGION 1
IF Adding
   INSERT INTO AIRCRAFT FROM MEMVAR
ENDIF
Adding = .F.
GATHER MEMVAR                       && Write memvars to file
DO CASE
   CASE What2Do = 1                 && Next
      SKIP
      IF EOF()
         ?? CHR(7)
         GO BOTTOM
      ENDIF
      SCATTER MEMVAR
      SHOW GETS
   CASE What2Do = 2                 && Previous
      SKIP -1
      IF BOF()
         ?? CHR(7)
         GO TOP
      ENDIF
      SCATTER MEMVAR
      SHOW GETS
   CASE What2Do = 3                 && Add
      Adding = .T.
      SCATTER MEMVAR BLANK
      SHOW GETS
      _CurObj = 1
   CASE What2Do = 4                 && Search
      DEFINE WINDOW VIEWER FROM 2,7 TO 21,73 SHADOW
      BROWSE WINDOW VIEWER NOMODIFY ;
      FIELDS AIRCRAFTID, Make, Model, Year
      RELEASE WINDOW VIEWER
      SCATTER MEMVAR
      SHOW GETS
   CASE What2Do = 5                 && Quit
      CLEAR READ
ENDCASE
```

The m.What2Do control becomes the last GET on the screen, and looks like this:

```
@ 13,0 GET m.What2Do ;
  PICTURE "@*HN \<Next;\<Prev;\<Edit;\<Add;\<Find;\<Exit" ;
  SIZE 1,10,1 DEFAULT 1 VALID _qc60x4szj()
```

More on memvar GETS

Why does the m.What2Do VALID snippet start by saving the memvars to a record in the database? Because you're using memvars, you're responsible for saving data after making any changes. So any time you move away from the current record, you do a GATHER MEMVAR to store the changes. If Add has been selected, you'll have to add a record before you can save data to it, so use a logical memvar m.Adding to determine whether Add was clicked just before the current edit. This logic ignores the problem of users pressing Escape, but you can't assume that m.What2Do was the current object when they pressed Escape, so this isn't the place to handle it anyway. This is the valid clause for this variable only.

Notice that every time you move to a new record using Next or Previous, you're also responsible for doing a SCATTER MEMVAR *and* a SHOW GETS. If you hadn't used memvars, this wouldn't be necessary, but then you would have had other problems. The SHOW GET is needed because the mere fact that the memvars have been assigned new values with SCATTER MEMVAR doesn't mean that the new values will be redisplayed automatically. In fact, the only automatic redisplay of a changed value occurs upon return from a memvar's VALID clause.

Another modification necessitated by this code fragment is that you have to declare m.Adding in the setup code. If not, it won't have an assigned value the first time the code is executed. So use MODIFY SCREEN AIRCRAFT, pull down the Screen Menu, select Layout, and click on Setup Code. This time, the selected option will simply change color to indicate that it's been selected; the same thing would have happened to CLeanup if you had checked it. You don't get to type into the editor windows for these two options until you select Ok (or press Ctrl–W). Once you're in the Setup Edit Window, type the line:

```
Adding = .F.
```

I also added my own code into SETUP to ensure that the AIRCRAFT file was open:

```
IF NOT USED ( 'AIRCRAFT' )
   SELECT 0
   USE DBFS\AIRCRAFT
ENDIF
SET ORDER TO 1
SCATTER MEMVAR
```

The last line is required to give all the memvars displayable values the first time the screen is shown. At the same time, uncheck the boxes for Open Files and Close Files on the Setup screen. You can do your own file management.

Now generate the code and try the controls. Add a few records so you'll have something to work with, then use the Next, Previous, and Find options. (I used BROWSE because it's easy to code and I only had one index order to worry about.) The colors are a bit ugly, but that's easy to fix. Now you have everything you need. This is a basic model for event-driven screens.

Turning EDIT off

Perhaps the most difficult aspect of this model, when compared to traditional menu-driven models, is that you enter the screen in the first GET field. This is called a *modeless* approach, but in fact it stays in what used to be called the "edit mode." I much prefer to force users to take an action when they want to change something on the screen, but it can be disconcerting to new users who are afraid to touch anything. If they press Z to see what happens, they'll inadvertently enter a Z into the first input field—not exactly intuitive.

There's a small design change you can use to fix this problem. If you define all of the fields on the screen as disabled by entering Screen Builder and clicking on the Disabled check box for each field, then the users can't get into them. Then you can add an additional option, Edit, to the m.What2Do control, and add code to the Edit and Add options to do a SHOW GET *memvar* ENABLE for each GET on the screen.

This is one time when having the generated code is useful. I went into the generated .SPR code with the editor, grabbed the GETs and pasted them into a temporary program file, reworked them a bit, and came up with the following two functions for the CLEANUP code (see Listing 2-4). This is one of the few cases where looking at the generated code is useful.

The modifications required by m.What2Do are shown in Listing 2-5. I also added three IFs to deal with the first time you run the program, when the file is empty. You can't GATHER MEMVAR if you're at EOF( ), which you will be if there are no records in the file. Similarly, you can't SKIP at EOF( ) or SKIP -1 at BOF( ). This code is important only the first time you run the program, but it doesn't help user confidence if it blows up the first time, either. Remember this trick; in the next chapter, we'll look at an improvement that sidesteps the problem entirely.

This necessitates a small change to the GET for m.What2Do, the control. Add a WHEN clause to the GET for m.What2Do:

```
@ 13,0 GET m.What2Do ;
    PICTURE "@*HN \<Next;\<Prev;\<Edit;\<Add;\<Find;\<Exit" ;
    SIZE 1,10,1 DEFAULT 1 WHEN DisableAll() VALID
    _qc60x4szj()
```

Listing 2-5   Two new functions to support an explicit EDIT.

```
FUNCTION EnableAll
SHOW GET m.aircraftid    ENABLE
SHOW GET m.make          ENABLE
SHOW GET m.model         ENABLE
SHOW GET m.year          ENABLE
SHOW GET m.colors        ENABLE
SHOW GET m.hourlyrate    ENABLE
SHOW GET m.engines       ENABLE
SHOW GET m.seats         ENABLE
SHOW GET m.parking       ENABLE
SHOW GET m.lastannual    ENABLE
SHOW GET m.smoh          ENABLE
SHOW GET m.totaltime     ENABLE
SHOW GET m.smohright     ENABLE
SHOW GET m.owner         ENABLE


FUNCTION DisableAll
SHOW GET m.aircraftid    DISABLE
SHOW GET m.make          DISABLE
SHOW GET m.model         DISABLE
SHOW GET m.colors        DISABLE
SHOW GET m.year          DISABLE
SHOW GET m.hourlyrate    DISABLE
SHOW GET m.engines       DISABLE
SHOW GET m.seats         DISABLE
SHOW GET m.parking       DISABLE
SHOW GET m.lastannual    DISABLE
SHOW GET m.smoh          DISABLE
SHOW GET m.totaltime     DISABLE
SHOW GET m.smohright     DISABLE
SHOW GET m.owner         DISABLE
```

Listing 2-6   Changes to the m.What2Do VALID clause.

```
FUNCTION _qc60x4szj              && m.What2Do VALID
#REGION 1
IF Adding
   INSERT INTO AIRCRAFT FROM MEMVAR
ENDIF
Adding = .F.
IF RECCOUNT() > 0
   GATHER MEMVAR
```

```
ENDIF
DO CASE
    CASE What2Do = 1              && Next
        IF NOT EOF()
            SKIP
        ENDIF
        IF EOF()
            ?? CHR(7)
            GO BOTTOM
        ENDIF
        SCATTER MEMVAR
        =DisableAll()
    CASE What2Do = 2              && Previous
        IF NOT BOF()
            SKIP -1
        ENDIF
        IF BOF()
            ?? CHR(7)
            GO TOP
        ENDIF
        SCATTER MEMVAR
        =DisableAll()
    CASE What2Do = 3              && Edit
        =EnableAll()
        _CurObj = 1
    CASE What2Do = 4              && Add
        Adding = .T.
        SCATTER MEMVAR BLANK
        =EnableAll()
        _CurObj = 1
    CASE What2Do = 5              && Search
        DEFINE WINDOW VIEWER FROM 2,7 TO 21,73 SHADOW
        BROWSE WINDOW VIEWER NOMODIFY ;
        FIELDS AIRCRAFTID, Make, Model, Year
        RELEASE WINDOW VIEWER
        SCATTER MEMVAR
        =DisableAll()
    CASE What2Do = 6              && Quit
        CLEAR READ
ENDCASE
```

Remember that a GET...WHEN clause is used to either allow or prevent the activation of a GET, or run a procedure just before the cursor enters the field. In this case, it's the latter; the WHEN clause is used to DISABLE all of the other input fields. The only time you'll be entering this field from another field is when you're coming out of an EDIT.

Why does the m.What2Do VALID snippet start by saving the memvars to a record in the database? Because you're using memvars, you're responsible for saving data after making any changes. So any time you move away from the current record, you should do a GATHER MEMVAR to store the changes. If Add has been selected, you'll have to add a record before you can save the data to it, so use the logical memvar m.Adding to determine whether Add was clicked just before the current edit.

This logic ignores the problem of users pressing Escape, but you can't assume that m.What2Do was the current object when they pressed Escape, so this isn't the place to handle it anyway. This is the valid clause for this variable only.

Data entry validation

There are a few cosmetic details to deal with. Most of the input fields should be uppercase, so you should go back and add the appropriate number of exclamation points to the PICTURE clauses of the relevant character fields. The only aircraft you have are CESSNA, PIPER, BEECH, and MOONEY, so the Make field should validate for those values. If the Aircraft ID is empty, it should probably begin with a capital N (for North America). These are best dealt with using WHEN and VALID clauses, entered on a field-by-field basis.

The WHEN clause is perfect for entering the N prefix. Just enter this in the WHEN snippet for m.AircraftID:

```
IF EMPTY ( m.AircraftID )
    KEYBOARD "N"
ENDIF
```

Notice that the WHEN (as well as the VALID) dialog asks whether you want to enter a procedure or an expression. The difference is that an *expression* has to be a single line of code, and is generated as part of the GET expression. So, if you enter the name of a UDF as an expression, don't prefix it with DO or the equals sign; if you do, the generated code will look like this:

```
@ 5,5 GET x VALID DO WHATEVER()
```

which isn't correct. If you pick *procedure*, FoxPro will generate one of its funky little function names, like fzr20brxz( ).

For the Aircraft Make field, first check whether what was entered was one of the valid values. If it wasn't, the user gets a popup from which he has to pick a value. See the following:

```
FUNCTION _qc7Osz2fa        &&  m.make VALID
#REGION 1
IF TRIM(m.Make) $ [CESSNA/MOONEY/PIPER/BEECH/]
   RETURN
ENDIF
DEFINE POPUP MAKES FROM $,$+10 SHADOW
DEFINE BAR 1 OF MAKES PROMPT [CESSNA  ]
DEFINE BAR 2 OF MAKES PROMPT [PIPER   ]
DEFINE BAR 3 OF MAKES PROMPT [MOONEY  ]
DEFINE BAR 4 OF MAKES PROMPT [BEECH   ]
ON SELECTION POPUP MAKES DEACTIVATE POPUP MAKES
ACTIVATE POPUP MAKES
m.Make = PROMPT()
RELEASE POPUP MAKES
RETURN IIF ( EMPTY ( m.Make ) , .F. , .T. )  && Can't leave empty
```

Building a project

This screen is beginning to look pretty good. It's clear that FoxPro has a variety of features that make application programming a lot easier. But the application consists of three screens (Aircraft, Members, and Owners), plus the Charges and Payments screens. What is the implication of adding more screens? And how do you use a menu to tie them together? Let's start a project file and add the rest of the application. Type:

```
MODIFY PROJECT SKYKING
```

and press Enter. Then click on Add, go down to the File Type box at the lower left of the screen and pick Screens, and then add your Aircraft

Figure 2-11 The SkyKing Startup screen.

screen. Now you've put the Aircraft screen into a project. But when you start up the application, you don't necessarily want to be looking at Aircraft. You need a starting place, and perhaps a nice logo. I like the one in Fig. 2-11. The program that produces it is shown in Listing 2-7.

Listing 2-7 The SKYKING startup program.
```
* Program-ID.....: Main.PRG
* Purpose........: Controls SKY KING application

SET TALK    OFF
SET CONFIRM OFF
SET SAFETY  OFF

CLOSE DATABASES
USE DBFS\AIRCRAFT IN 1 ORDER 1

DEFINE   WINDOW FULLSCREEN FROM 1,0 TO 24, 79
ACTIVATE WINDOW FULLSCREEN
@ WROWS()/2, 0 SAY PADC( ' Sky King Flying Club' , WCOLS() )
@ WROWS()-1, 0 SAY PADC( ' Press F10 for Menu  ' , WCOLS() )

Done = .F.             && Required so that menu can end the APP
DO MAIN.MPR            && Load the system menu

READ VALID HANDLER()   && Don't stop until HANDLER() returns .T.

CLOSE DATABASES
CLEAR

RETURN                 && QUIT in production



FUNCTION HANDLER

IF Done                && Set to .T. if QUIT is chosen from the menu
   RETURN .T.
   ELSE
   RETURN .F.
ENDIF
```

This simple structure runs the application until the user pulls down the menu and selects Quit. That's when you assign the memvar Done and the value .T., and force execution of the READ VALID command using CLEAR READ ALL (see Listing 2-8).

Listing 2-8 The menu for SKYKING.APP.

```
*
*       ┌╓───────────────────────────────────────────────╖┐
*       │║ 01/04/93              MAIN.MPR          14:07:04 ║│
*       │║                                                 ║│
*       │║ This program was automatically generated by GENMENU. ║│
*       └╙───────────────────────────────────────────────╜┘

SET SYSMENU TO
SET SYSMENU AUTOMATIC

DEFINE PAD _qc70u9cmo OF _MSYSMENU PROMPT "\<Utilities" COLOR SCHEME 3
DEFINE PAD _qc70u9coc OF _MSYSMENU PROMPT "\<Databases" COLOR SCHEME 3
DEFINE PAD _qc70u9cow OF _MSYSMENU PROMPT "\<Quit" COLOR SCHEME 3
ON PAD _qc70u9cmo OF _MSYSMENU ACTIVATE POPUP utilities
ON PAD _qc70u9coc OF _MSYSMENU ACTIVATE POPUP databases
ON SELECTION PAD _qc70u9cow OF _MSYSMENU ;
    DO _qc70u9cr7 ;
    IN LOCFILE("MAIN" ,"MPX;MPR;FXP;PRG" ,"Where is MAIN?")

DEFINE POPUP utilities MARGIN RELATIVE SHADOW COLOR SCHEME 4
DEFINE BAR _MST_CALCU OF utilities PROMPT "\<Calculator"
DEFINE BAR _MST_DIARY OF utilities PROMPT "Calendar/\<Diary"

DEFINE POPUP databases MARGIN RELATIVE SHADOW COLOR SCHEME 4
DEFINE BAR 1 OF databases PROMPT "\<Aircraft"
ON SELECTION BAR 1 OF databases DO AIRCRAFT.SPR


PROCEDURE _qc70u9cr7
Done = .T.
CLEAR READ ALL
SET SYSMENU TO DEFAULT
```

Summary

Seems a bit roundabout, doesn't it? Well, I suppose it is. This simple case doesn't show all the variations that can occur, and those are what the READ VALID control mechanism is meant to handle.

In the next chapter, you'll add in another screen and see what complications arise. I think you'll agree that doubling the number of screens increases the amount of coding by much, much more than a factor of two.

3
Event-driven
multiscreen models

In the last chapter, you built a simple application with one screen, and added a menu to control the process. What happens with the addition of another screen? As you'll see, all sorts of complications arise. Happily, FoxPro is entirely up to the challenge.

Adding another screen

Build a screen for aircraft owners, and then go in and do the same things that you did to the Aircraft screen. In fact, you can copy pretty much verbatim from the Aircraft screen code snippets. The resulting screen appears in Fig. 3-1, and its code in Listing 3-1.

Now add the new screen to the menu as a second database, with the command DO OWNERS SPR. Also, go into both Screen Layout dialogs and turn off the option to CLEAR WINDOWS so neither one will stay on the screen when you run the other. Then edit MAIN.PRG and include one line to open the OWNERS database, and rebuild the project. (If you're following on the source code disk, look for SKYKINGB.PJX. Note that, in this project file, all of the components' names have a B added to the end of their names so you can have two versions of everything in the CHAPTER 3 directory. That's why the OWNERS screen is called OWNERSB.) Then run it, and you'll get a lot of unpleasant surprises.

If you pick applications from the menu, they run as expected. And if you click on a window that's underneath, it comes to the foreground. But it doesn't *do* anything. Clicking on windows doesn't awaken their related code or change databases.

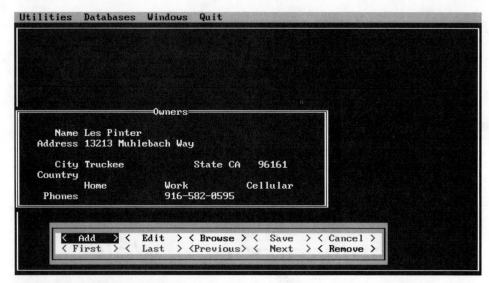

Figure 3-1 The Owners screen.

Listing 3-1 OWNERS.SPR.

```
*
*     01/24/93              OWNERSB.SPR              16:44:45
*


#REGION 0

IF NOT WEXIST("owners") ;
   OR UPPER(WTITLE("OWNERS")) == "OWNERS.PJX" ;
   OR UPPER(WTITLE("OWNERS")) == "OWNERS.SCX" ;
   OR UPPER(WTITLE("OWNERS")) == "OWNERS.MNX" ;
   OR UPPER(WTITLE("OWNERS")) == "OWNERS.PRG" ;
   OR UPPER(WTITLE("OWNERS")) == "OWNERS.QPR"
   DEFINE WINDOW owners ;
     FROM INT((SROW()-13)/2),INT((SCOL()-67)/2) ;
     TO INT((SROW()-13)/2)+12,INT((SCOL()-67)/2)+66 ;
     TITLE "Owners" FLOAT CLOSE SHADOW NOMINIMIZE COLOR SCHEME 1
ENDIF

#REGION 1
SELECT OWNERS
SCATTER MEMVAR
Adding = .F.
```

3-1 Continued.

```
*
*                    ┌──────────────────────────────────────────────────┐
*                    │              OWNERSB/MS-DOS Screen Layout          │
                     └──────────────────────────────────────────────────┘

#REGION 1
IF WVISIBLE("owners")
   ACTIVATE WINDOW owners SAME
ELSE
   ACTIVATE WINDOW owners NOSHOW
ENDIF

@ 1, 6 SAY "Name"        SIZE 1,4, 0
@ 4, 6 SAY "City"        SIZE 1,4, 0
@ 5, 3 SAY "Country"     SIZE 1,7, 0
@ 2, 3 SAY "Address"     SIZE 1,7, 0
@ 4,30 SAY "State"       SIZE 1,5, 0
@ 7, 4 SAY "Phones"      SIZE 1,6, 0
@ 6,11 SAY "Home"        SIZE 1,4, 0
@ 6,25 SAY "Work"        SIZE 1,4, 0
@ 6,39 SAY "Cellular"    SIZE 1,8, 0

@ 1,11 GET m.name        SIZE 1,40 DEFAULT " " DISABLE
@ 2,11 GET m.address1    SIZE 1,40 DEFAULT " " DISABLE
@ 3,11 GET m.address2    SIZE 1,40 DEFAULT " " DISABLE
@ 4,11 GET m.city        SIZE 1,17 DEFAULT " " DISABLE
@ 4,36 GET m.state       SIZE 1, 3 DEFAULT " " DISABLE
@ 4,41 GET m.zip         SIZE 1,10 DEFAULT " " DISABLE
@ 5,11 GET m.country     SIZE 1, 3 DEFAULT " " DISABLE
@ 7,11 GET m.homephone   SIZE 1,12 DEFAULT " " DISABLE
@ 7,25 GET m.workphone   SIZE 1,12 DEFAULT " " DISABLE
@ 7,39 GET m.cellphone   SIZE 1,12 DEFAULT " " DISABLE

@ 9,0 GET m.What2Do ;
   PICTURE "@*HN Next;Prev;Edit;Add;Find;Exit" ;
   SIZE 1,10,1 DEFAULT 1 WHEN DisableAll() VALID _qcr0zw5j6()
IF NOT WVISIBLE("owners")
   ACTIVATE WINDOW owners
ENDIF

READ CYCLE

RELEASE WINDOW owners
```

```
*
*        ╔══════════════════════════════════════════════════════╗
*        ║    OWNERSB/MS-DOS Supporting Procedures and Functions ║
*        ╚══════════════════════════════════════════════════════╝

* CLEANUP code:

#REGION 1
FUNCTION EnableAll
SHOW GET m.name              ENABLE
SHOW GET m.address1          ENABLE
SHOW GET m.address2          ENABLE
SHOW GET m.City              ENABLE
SHOW GET m.state             ENABLE
SHOW GET m.zip               ENABLE
SHOW GET m.country           ENABLE
SHOW GET m.homephone         ENABLE
SHOW GET m.workphone         ENABLE
SHOW GET m.cellphone         ENABLE


FUNCTION DisableAll
SHOW GET m.name              DISABLE
SHOW GET m.address1          DISABLE
SHOW GET m.address2          DISABLE
SHOW GET m.City              DISABLE
SHOW GET m.state             DISABLE
SHOW GET m.zip               DISABLE
SHOW GET m.country           DISABLE
SHOW GET m.homephone         DISABLE
SHOW GET m.workphone         DISABLE
SHOW GET m.cellphone         DISABLE


FUNCTION _qcr0zw5j6                  && m.What2Do VALID
#REGION 1
IF Adding
   INSERT INTO OWNERS    FROM MEMVAR
ENDIF
Adding = .F.
IF RECCOUNT() > 0
   GATHER MEMVAR
ENDIF
DO CASE
   CASE What2Do = 1              && Next
      IF NOT EOF()
         SKIP
      ENDIF
```

```
      IF EOF()
         ?? CHR(7)
         GO BOTTOM
      ENDIF
      SCATTER MEMVAR
      =DisableAll()
   CASE What2Do = 2            && Previous
      IF NOT BOF()
         SKIP -1
      ENDIF
      IF BOF()
         ?? CHR(7)
         GO TOP
      ENDIF
      SCATTER MEMVAR
      =DisableAll()
   CASE What2Do = 3            && Edit
      =EnableAll()
      _CurObj = 1
   CASE What2Do = 4            && Add
      Adding = .T.
      SCATTER MEMVAR BLANK
      =EnableAll()
      _CurObj = 1
   CASE What2Do = 5            && Search
      DEFINE WINDOW VIEWER FROM 2,19 TO 21,62 SHADOW
      BROWSE WINDOW VIEWER NOMODIFY FIELDS NAME
      RELEASE WINDOW VIEWER
      SCATTER MEMVAR
      =DisableAll()
   CASE What2Do = 6            && Quit
      CLEAR READ
ENDCASE
```

This is an ugly surprise. I looked at some published sources for ideas on how to deal with this problem. I consulted books by Tom Rettig, Alan Griver, Randy Brown, Dick Bard, and Tapani Isoranta. Sure enough, in every case there was a fair amount of code related to simply finding out what window had been clicked and running the appropriate program. If these smart guys can't avoid doing some serious coding, you and I won't be able to, either.

The trick, as it turns out, is the READ DEACTIVATE snippet. When you click on a window, FoxPro evaluates the DEACTIVATE clause of the window that you're about to leave to determine whether to let you out. In the process, you tell it to find out the name of the program it's supposed to run next.

The technique for finding out what was clicked is less than obvious. If you go into the code and add the line ON KEY LABEL F9 SET SYSMENU TO DE-FAULT to the MAIN program, you can see what happens as you change windows using the mouse. Use the menu to run AIRCRAFT.SPR and OWNERS.SPR, and then press F9; the normal FoxPro menu will appear. Press Alt to activate it, and then select Windows. As you can see in Fig. 3-2, the Aircraft window is the last window in the list. Click on the Owners window, and then press Alt and select Windows again, and Owners has become the last window in the list (Fig. 3-3).

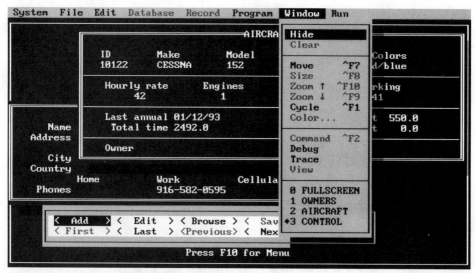

Figure 3-2 The WINDOWS list with AIRCRAFT on top.

Figure 3-3 The WINDOWS list with OWNERS on top.

60 Event-driven multiscreen models

I wrote a pair of functions to find and return the name of the last window and the name of the associated .SPR, as shown in Listing 3-2. Both use the FoxPro function WChild( ). With a null as the first parameter and a second parameter of 0, it returns the name of the first window in the window list. Each successive call with the second parameter of 1 finds the next name in the list, until it returns a null string.

Listing 3-2 UDFs to get the top window and related .SPR names.

```
FUNCTION FindSPR
PRIVATE m.Program, m.Window
***************************************
** Find the current screen program **
***************************************
m.Program = ""
m.Window = WCHILD("",0)
DO WHILE NOT EMPTY(m.Window)
    IF NOT UPPER ( m.Window ) $ [CONTROL/FULLSCREEN/COMMAND]
        m.Program = m.Window
        m.Program = m.Program+".SPR"
    ENDIF
        m.Window = WCHILD("",1)
ENDDO
RETURN m.Program


FUNCTION FindWin
PRIVATE m.Window, m.ReadWind
***********************************
** Find the current READ window **
***********************************
m.Window = WCHILD("",0)
DO WHILE NOT EMPTY(m.Window)
    IF NOT UPPER ( m.Window ) $ [CONTROL/FULLSCREEN/COMMAND]
        m.ReadWind = m.Window
    ENDIF
        m.Window = WCHILD("",1)
ENDDO
RETURN m.ReadWind
```

IF NOT *name* $ *namelist* is to exclude nonapplication windows. I named the sign-on/logo screen FULLSCREEN, but I don't want the program to try to run FULLSCREEN.SPR if the user clicks somewhere off of the two applications windows. Similarly, under some circumstances the FoxPro Command window stays on the screen during a READ; I don't want to try to execute COMMAND.SPR, either. And you're going to be moving the controls to a window of their own, and the Control window will require special handling.

Now you can test which window was clicked and run the associated program name. But first, let's add a separate Control window that works with both application screens. Associating the Control window with that of each application is a little tricky.

Consolidating controls

Because you have the same controls in both windows, it makes sense to consolidate them and add a few other buttons of interest. Add buttons for Top, Bottom, Save, and Cancel—these last two in the event you'll come from editing or adding a screen of data. In addition, you want to be able to add a record and view the data in the form of a BROWSE. This last option will also serve as a sort of visual Find, making it easy for users to look for a record in the context of its immediate neighborhood.

Lo and behold, the screen isn't wide enough for a push-button variable that has all of these controls, and there's no wrap feature. But you can use 10 individual push-button variables. The resulting window is shown in Fig. 3-4.

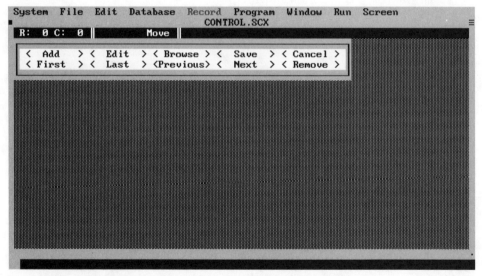

Figure 3-4 The CONTROL window and push buttons.

The original source code for this single-variable control-window VALID clause is pretty short. With 10 push-button variables, you need to attach a valid clause to each one. Still, if you can consolidate the validation code in the CONTROL.SPR file, it'll be a lot easier to read. So I'll have you use the technique Alan Griver used in his *CodeBook*. For each push-button memvar, there's a valid clause that calls a function named Controls located in the CONTROL.SPR cleanup code, passing it a string to indicate what to do. The CONTROL.SPR is shown in Listing 3-3.

Listing 3-3 CONTROL.SPR.

```
*
*    ┌──────────────────────────────────────────────────────────┐
*    │ 01/16/93              CONTROL.SPR              14:34:37    │
*    └──────────────────────────────────────────────────────────┘
#REGION 0
*
*    ┌──────────────────────────────────────────────────────────┐
*    │                 MS-DOS Window definitions                 │
*    └──────────────────────────────────────────────────────────┘

IF NOT WEXIST("CONTROL")
   DEFINE WINDOW CONTROL ;
      FROM 15, 8 TO 18,65 FLOAT NOCLOSE NOMINIMIZE COLOR SCHEME 8
ENDIF


*
*    ┌──────────────────────────────────────────────────────────┐
*    │           CONTROLS-DOS Setup Code - SECTION 2             │
*    └──────────────────────────────────────────────────────────┘


#REGION 1
REGIONAL LastButton
PRIVATE Done
STORE SPACE(6) TO LastButton      && used by Save when Adding
Done    = .F.
Editing = .F.


*
*    ┌──────────────────────────────────────────────────────────┐
*    │              CONTROL/MS-DOS Screen Layout                 │
*    └──────────────────────────────────────────────────────────┘


#REGION 1
IF WVISIBLE("CONTROL")
   ACTIVATE WINDOW CONTROL SAME
ELSE
   ACTIVATE WINDOW CONTROL NOSHOW
ENDIF
@ 0,1  GET m.Add              ;
   PICTURE "@*HN Add"         ;
   SIZE 1,10,2 DEFAULT 1 VALID _qcj0v8skd() ;
   MESSAGE "Add a new record to the file"
@ 0,12 GET m.Edit            ;
   PICTURE "@*HN Edit"        ;
   SIZE 1,10,2 DEFAULT 1 VALID _qcj0v8soe() ;
   MESSAGE "Enable editing of the current record"
@ 0,23 GET m.Browse          ;
   PICTURE "@*HN Browse"      ;
   SIZE 1,10,2 DEFAULT 1 VALID _qcj0v8ss1() ;
```

3-3 Continued.

```
   MESSAGE "List all available records."
@ 0,34 GET m.Save              ;
   PICTURE "@*HN Save"          ;
   SIZE 1,10,2 DEFAULT 1 VALID _qcj0v8sv8() ;
   MESSAGE "Save the current record"
@ 0,45 GET m.Cancel            ;
   PICTURE "@*HN Cancel"        ;
   SIZE 1,10,2 DEFAULT 1 VALID _qcj0v8sz8() ;
   MESSAGE "Cancel all modifications."
@ 1,1  GET m.First             ;
   PICTURE "@*HN First"         ;
   SIZE 1,10,2 DEFAULT 1 VALID _qcj0v8t2e() ;
   MESSAGE "Go to the first available record"
@ 1,12 GET m.Last              ;
   PICTURE "@*HN Last"          ;
   SIZE 1,10,2 DEFAULT 1 VALID _qcj0v8t5k() ;
   MESSAGE "Show the last available record"
@ 1,23 GET m.Previous          ;
   PICTURE "@*HN Previous"      ;
   SIZE 1,10,2 DEFAULT 1 VALID _qcj0v8t8p() ;
   MESSAGE "Show the previous record"
@ 1,34 GET m.Next              ;
   PICTURE "@*HN Next"          ;
   SIZE 1,10,2 DEFAULT 1 VALID _qcj0v8tco() ;
   MESSAGE "Show the next record"
@ 1,45 GET m.Remove            ;
  PICTURE "@*HN Remove"         ;
   SIZE 1,10,2 DEFAULT 1 VALID _qcj0v8tfw() ;
   MESSAGE "Remove this window from the screen"

IF NOT WVISIBLE("CONTROL")
   ACTIVATE WINDOW CONTROL
ENDIF

READ CYCLE WHEN _qcj0v8tit()

RELEASE WINDOW CONTROL

#REGION 0

*
*        ┌─────────────────────────────────────────────────────┐┃
*        │   CONTROL/MS-DOS Supporting Procedures and Functions ┃┃
*        └─────────────────────────────────────────────────────┘┃

#REGION 1
```

```
PROCEDURE Controls

PARAMETER Choice
PRIVATE    Prog2Run

DO CASE
   CASE m.Choice = "Add"
      Prog2Run = FindSpr()
      IF NOT EMPTY( Prog2Run )
         DO Startup IN ( Prog2Run )
      ENDIF
      Editing = .T.
      _CUROBJ = 1
   CASE m.Choice = "Edit"
      Editing = .T.
      _CUROBJ = 1
   CASE m.Choice = "Save"
      Prog2Run   = Findspr()
      IF NOT EMPTY( Prog2Run )
        IF LastButton = "Add"
           DO add IN ( Prog2Run )
        ELSE
           DO save IN ( Prog2Run )
        ENDIF
      ENDIF
      IF OkToSave
        WAIT WINDOW NOWAIT "Saving"
        Editing = .F.
      ENDIF
   CASE m.Choice = "Cancel"
      OkToSave = .T.
      Prog2Run = FindSpr()
      IF NOT EMPTY( Prog2Run )
         DO Cancel IN ( Prog2Run )
      ENDIF
      WAIT WINDOW NOWAIT "Changes ignored"
      Editing = .F.
   CASE m.Choice = "Browse"
      Prog2Run   = Findspr()
      IF NOT EMPTY( Prog2Run )
         DO Browser IN ( Prog2Run )
      ENDIF
      Editing = .F.
   CASE m.Choice = "First"
      GO TOP
```

```
        SCATTER MEMVAR MEMO
   CASE m.Choice = "Previous"
        SKIP -1
        SCATTER MEMVAR MEMO
   CASE m.Choice = "Next"
        SKIP
        SCATTER MEMVAR MEMO
   CASE m.Choice = "Last"
        GO BOTTOM
        SCATTER MEMVAR MEMO
   CASE m.Choice = "Remove"
        Done = .T.
        CLEAR READ
   CASE m.Choice = "Delete"
        Prog2Run    = FindSpr()
        IF NOT EMPTY( Prog2Run )
            DO delete IN ( Prog2Run )
            GO TOP
            SCATTER MEMVAR MEMO
        ENDIF
ENDCASE

DO PushButtons

LastButton = m.Choice

RETURN

PROCEDURE PushButtons
PRIVATE SaveRec
SaveRec = RECNO()
COUNT TO RecCount
IF RecCount > 0
   GO SaveRec
   IF NOT Editing
        SHOW GET m.Add        ENABLE
        SHOW GET m.Edit       ENABLE
        SHOW GET m.Save       DISABLE
        SHOW GET m.Cancel     DISABLE
        SHOW GET m.Remove     ENABLE
        SHOW GET m.Browse     ENABLE
        SKIP -1
        IF BOF()
            SHOW GET m.First    DISABLE
            SHOW GET m.Previous DISABLE
```

3-3 Continued.

```
        ELSE
            SHOW GET m.First      ENABLE
            SHOW GET m.Previous ENABLE
        ENDIF
        GO SaveRec
        SKIP
        IF EOF()
            SHOW GET m.Next      DISABLE
            SHOW GET m.Last      DISABLE
        ELSE
            SHOW GET m.Next      ENABLE
            SHOW GET m.Last      ENABLE
        ENDIF
        GO SaveRec
    ELSE
        SHOW GET m.Add       DISABLE
        SHOW GET m.Edit      DISABLE
        SHOW GET m.Save      ENABLE
        SHOW GET m.Cancel    ENABLE
        SHOW GET m.Remove    DISABLE
        SHOW GET m.First     DISABLE
        SHOW GET m.Previous  DISABLE
        SHOW GET m.Next      DISABLE
        SHOW GET m.Last      DISABLE
        SHOW GET m.Browse    DISABLE
    ENDIF
ELSE
    SHOW GET m.First     DISABLE
    SHOW GET m.Previous  DISABLE
    SHOW GET m.Next      DISABLE
    SHOW GET m.Last      DISABLE
    SHOW GET m.Browse    DISABLE
    SHOW GET m.Edit      DISABLE
    IF Editing
        SHOW GET m.Add       DISABLE
        SHOW GET m.Remove    DISABLE
        SHOW GET m.Save      ENABLE
        SHOW GET m.Cancel    ENABLE
    ELSE
        SHOW GET m.Add       ENABLE
        SHOW GET m.Remove    ENABLE
        SHOW GET m.Save      DISABLE
        SHOW GET m.Cancel    DISABLE
    ENDIF
ENDIF
```

Now that you've moved the controls to a separate window, you can use a powerful FoxPro command to simplify the code. The SHOW GETS command has a parameter, WINDOW *windowname*, that allows you to enable or disable all of the GETs in a single window. Before you moved the controls to a separate window, this wasn't too practical. But now that the windows are separated, this is exactly what the doctor ordered. Add the following code to the end of the Controls function in CONTROL.SPR, and erase the EnableAll/DisableAll functions from the cleanup code of the Application screens:

```
ReadWind = currwr()
IF NOT Editing
   SHOW GETS WINDOW (ReadWind) DISABLE
ELSE
   SHOW GETS WINDOW (ReadWind) ENABLE ONLY
 ENDIF
RETURN
```

The 10 controls in the Control window each has its own VALID clause, but in each case the code has been consolidated into the Controls function in the cleanup code. Simply pass the appropriate parameter, and then look into Controls function to determine precisely what to do. This is shown in Listing 3-4 (a continuation of the code shown in Listing 3-3).

Listing 3-4 CONTROL.SPR, continued.

```
FUNCTION _qcj0v8skd      &&  m.Add VALID
#REGION 1
DO Controls WITH "Add"


FUNCTION _qcj0v8soe      &&  m.Edit VALID
#REGION 1
DO Controls WITH "Edit"


FUNCTION _qcj0v8ss1      &&  m.Browse VALID
#REGION 1
DO Controls WITH "Browse"


FUNCTION _qcj0v8sv8      &&  m.Save VALID
#REGION 1
DO Controls WITH "Save"


FUNCTION _qcj0v8sz8      &&  m.Cancel VALID
#REGION 1
DO Controls WITH "Cancel"


FUNCTION _qcj0v8t2e      &&  m.First VALID
#REGION 1
DO Controls WITH "First"
```

```
FUNCTION _qcj0v8t5k        && m.Last VALID
#REGION 1
DO Controls WITH "Last"

FUNCTION _qcj0v8t8p        && m.Previous VALID
#REGION 1
DO Controls WITH "Previous"

FUNCTION _qcj0v8tco        && m.Next VALID
#REGION 1
DO Controls WITH "Next"

FUNCTION _qcj0v8tfw        && m.Remove VALID
#REGION 1
DO Controls WITH "Remove"

FUNCTION _qcj0v8tit        && Read Level When
*
* When Code from screen: CONTROL
*
#REGION 1
DO PushButtons
```

Now, whenever you click on or select one of the push buttons by highlighting it and pressing Enter, the VALID clause calls the larger procedure Controls in the CONTROL.SPR cleanup code. The code is written so it doesn't matter which database is open.

Notice the PushButtons function. Remember the code used in the previous chapter when you selected the Next or Previous control? You specified SKIP or SKIP −1, checked for EOF( ) or BOF( ), and then GO BOTTOM or GO TOP if you'd gone a SKIP too far. Well, the PushButtons function avoids the issue entirely by dimming the buttons that don't apply. Now, you can't select Next if there isn't a next record. The controls communicate additional information before users try to do something that wouldn't work anyway.

Although I won't deal with it in this chapter, you can use an analogous mechanism for your menus. When you add a Record Menu popup, you can include all of the controls found in the Control window, plus a few more. You can also use a parallel set of memvars to dim inappropriate menu choices, using the DEFINE BAR...SKIP FOR memvar command. It's actually very easy to do, now that you have the PushButtons function to prime the process.

Looking at the code, you'll see that you just went from 27 lines of code to about 150, mostly because the push-button PICTURE clause contains too much text to display on one line of the screen. That's one of the tradeoffs of using event-driven code. You get more capabilities, but there's more coding. The question is, of course, whether it's cost-effective.

What would be perfect is to list each of the accommodations required by the event-driven model and assign it a value relating the benefit to the cost. Then you could see which features produced the most "bang for the buck." Unfortunately, that's probably not possible. With event-driven programming, you have to deal with *all* the issues it raises, not just some. Still, I was surprised by how much additional code was required when all I did was go beyond one line of push buttons.

Application screen cleanup code

When a READ is terminated, control of the program drops through to the next statement following the READ. In screen programs, that's the cleanup code. Take a look at the code shown in Listing 3-5, which is the cleanup code for each of your application screens.

Listing 3-5 The screen cleanup code (both applications).

```
IF End_App
    RELEASE WINDOW OWNERS
    DO EraseCtrl
    IF NOT EMPTY ( WindChck )
        Prog = WindChck + [.SPR]
        DO ( Prog )
    ENDIF
ENDIF

#REGION 1

FUNCTION Save
    OKtoSave = .T.
    GATHER MEMVAR MEMO
RETURN

FUNCTION Browser
    BROWSE LAST NORMAL TITLE " Table View "
    IF LASTKEY() <> 27
        SCATTER MEMVAR MEMO
    ENDIF
RETURN

FUNCTION Startup
    SCATTER MEMVAR MEMO BLANK
RETURN

FUNCTION Add
```

3-5 Continued.

```
    APPEND BLANK
    GATHER MEMVAR MEMO
RETURN

FUNCTION Cancel
    SCATTER MEMVAR MEMO
RETURN

FUNCTION Delete
IF CONFIRM ( ' Delete this record? ')
    DELETE
    IF NOT BOF()
        SKIP -1
        ELSE
        GO TOP
        SKIP
    ENDIF
    SCATTER MEMVAR MEMO
ENDIF
RETURN
```

In this example, the functions are identical for each of the applications screens. Because the Controls function in CONTROL.SPR is written to:

```
    DO Init IN ( CurrentProgram )
```

These functions for each screen can be customized as needed—without rewriting the CONTROLS routines! This is referred to by some writers as *encapsulation*, one of the three characteristics of object-oriented programming, but it looks to me like using subroutines in a clever way and, again, I'm not sure it requires a new name.

CONFIRM is a general-purpose Yes/No function that uses DEFINE POPUP, and appears in Listing 3-6.

Listing 3-6 CONFIRM.PRG.

```
* Program-ID...: Confirm.PRG
* Purpose......: Displays a confirming dialogue using the title
*                passed to it when called; defaults to 'Yes'
PARAMETERS ctitle
currwind = WOUTPUT()
PRIVATE length,where,choice
length = LEN ( ctitle )
where  = 40 - length / 2
DEFINE POPUP CONFIRM FROM 13, where ;
    COLOR N/W,N/W,N/W,N/W,N/W,W+/R
DEFINE BAR 1 OF CONFIRM PROMPT [\] + PADC ( ctitle , length )
```

```
DEFINE BAR 2 OF CONFIRM PROMPT [\-]
DEFINE BAR 3 OF CONFIRM PROMPT        PADC ( [\<Yes] , length )
DEFINE BAR 4 OF CONFIRM PROMPT        PADC ( [\<No ] , length )
ON SELECTION POPUP CONFIRM DEACTIVATE POPUP CONFIRM
SaveConf = SET ( [CONFIRM] )
SET CONFIRM OFF
ACTIVATE SCREEN
ACTIVATE POPUP CONFIRM
choice = PROMPT()
RELEASE POPUP CONFIRM
SET CONFIRM &SaveConf
IF LEN(TRIM(currwind)) > 0
   ACTIVATE WINDOW (currwind)
ENDIF
RETURN IIF ( [Yes] $ choice , .T. , .F. )
```

Linking screens

To link the AIRCRAFT and CONTROL screens together into a screen set, you have to be in the Project Manager. FoxPro remembers a number of things about screens and screen sets by storing parameters in the project file. In fact, there are some things you can't do with screens unless you're in a project file. Linking several screens is one of them.

This time when you go into the Project Manager and select the Aircraft screen, stop short of clicking Edit, and click on Add. Now you're looking for the CONTROL screen. If necessary, change the POPUP box to display screens, and change to the \SCREENS directory. Then highlight CONTROL and press Enter. The selection process is shown in Fig. 3-5, and the result in Fig. 3-6.

What FoxPro does with screen sets

When FoxPro generates code for a screen set, it:

- Generates DEFINE WINDOW code for window.
- Generates the GETs for each window while the appropriate window is activated with the NOSHOW parameter.
- Issues a single READ. READ knows which GETs are a part of the READ, and which window each GET is in.

With a screen set, you *always* check the READ CYCLE box on the Screen Builder dialog box. FoxPro will automatically activate the appropriate window when you leave the last GET on one of the screens. Also, pressing PgDn will flip you from one window to the next.

You want to make sure to arrange the windows so that the Control window is the last one in the list. That's because the normal sequence of

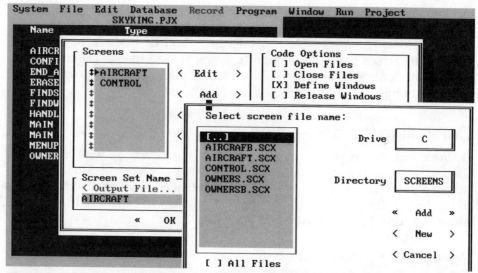

Figure 3-5 Looking for screens in the \SCREENS subdirectory.

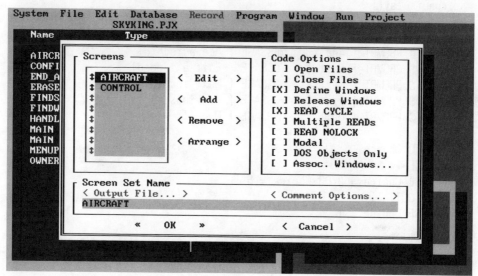

Figure 3-6 A screen set.

events will be to use the controls to find what you want, and then select Edit if you want to make any changes. So you want the Control window to be "on top," and the Application window to be showing just above it. You can also use the Arrange feature to control the relative positions of the Application and Control screen so that they don't overlap.

The CurrWind and CurrSPR functions will continue to work, even though Control is now usually the last window in the WChild list, because you told the two functions to ignore Control.

You might want to generate the .SPR for this screen set and take a look at it. Go into the Application screen for Aircraft, select Program and Generate, and then look at SCREENS\AIRCRAFT.SPR. You can DO SCREENS\AIR-CRAFT.SPR to see how PgDn, cursor movement, and mouse clicking will affect the windows. Edit out all the DISABLE statements to get a clear picture of what's happening.

Controlling the application

Before event-driven programming, you had to use a loop with a menu at the top, as shown in Listing 3-7. It's clear that the very idea of an event-driven application is that choosing from a menu is only one of several ways to run one of the programs in the application. So what you use is any event handler to do what we want when you want it.

Listing 3-7 Traditional menu-controlled program.

```
* Program-ID....: Standard.PRG


=ScreenDisplay()


DO WHILE .T.
        @ 24, 0 PROMPT [ Add  ]    MESSAGE [ Add a record]
        @ 24, $ PROMPT [ Edit ]    MESSAGE [ Edit a record]
        @ 24, $ PROMPT [ Next ]    MESSAGE [ Next record]
        @ 24, $ PROMPT [ Prev ]    MESSAGE [ Previous record]
        @ 24, $ PROMPT [ Quit ]    MESSAGE [ Done ]


    MENU TO Choice
    DO CASE
        CASE Choice = 0 OR Choice = 5
            QUIT
        CASE Choice = 1
            ...
    ENDCASE
ENDDO
```

FoxPro's answer is FOUNDATION READ. With this technique, your application is started by a main program—that's what the Set Main option in the Project Menu is for—that redefines the FoxPro system menu and then goes into a wait state. The precise mechanism for accomplishing this is the READ VALID clause, an example of which might be as simple as:

```
READ VALID .F.
```

When FoxPro initiates a READ with a VALID clause, the READ stays active until the VALID clause returns a value of .True. This line says *Don't EVER terminate the read while in FoxPro.* If you attach QUIT to a menu selection, you can use this simplest case to wait for events.

For multiscreen applications, you'll need a more powerful event handler. But let's defer the details for a few pages, and see what limitations this approach poses.

I added a MAIN program that simply defined a few global variables, called my MENU.SPR to redefine the FoxPro menu, and dropped in a READ VALID .T. to give control to the menu. The resulting MAIN.PRG and MENU.MPR appear in Listing 3-8 (the .SPRs are the same as in chapter 2).

Listing 3-8 The simplest cases of MAIN.PRG and MAIN.MPR.

```
* Program-ID.....: Main.PRG
* Purpose........: Controls SKY KING application

SET TALK    OFF
SET CONFIRM OFF
SET SAFETY  OFF
SET COLOR OF SCHEME 1 TO ,,,,,,,,,GR+/B

CLOSE DATABASES

USE DBFS\AIRCRAFT IN 1 ORDER 1
USE DBFS\OWNERS   IN 2 ORDER 1

DO MAIN.MPR

READ VALID .F.

CLEAR WINDOWS
CLEAR

CLOSE DATABASES
SET SYSMENU TO DEFAULT

RETURN        && QUIT in production

*
*
*
*
```

```
01/22/93              MAIN.MPR              19:48:48
This program was automatically generated by GENMENU.
```

```
SET SYSMENU TO
SET SYSMENU AUTOMATIC

DEFINE PAD _qcp16gt51 OF _MSYSMENU PROMPT "\<Utilities" COLOR SCHEME 3
```

```
DEFINE PAD _qcp16gt5q OF _MSYSMENU PROMPT "\<Databases" COLOR SCHEME 3
DEFINE PAD _qcp16gt68 OF _MSYSMENU PROMPT "\<Windows" COLOR SCHEME 3
DEFINE PAD _qcp16gt6h OF _MSYSMENU PROMPT "\<Quit" COLOR SCHEME 3
ON PAD _qcp16gt51 OF _MSYSMENU ACTIVATE POPUP utilities
ON PAD _qcp16gt5q OF _MSYSMENU ACTIVATE POPUP databases
ON PAD _qcp16gt68 OF _MSYSMENU ACTIVATE POPUP windows
ON SELECTION PAD _qcp16gt6h OF _MSYSMENU QUIT

DEFINE POPUP utilities MARGIN RELATIVE SHADOW COLOR SCHEME 4
DEFINE BAR _MST_CALCU OF utilities PROMPT "\<Calculator"
DEFINE BAR _MST_DIARY OF utilities PROMPT "Calendar/\<Diary"

DEFINE POPUP databases MARGIN RELATIVE SHADOW COLOR SCHEME 4
DEFINE BAR 1 OF databases PROMPT "\<Aircraft"
DEFINE BAR 2 OF databases PROMPT "\<Owners"
ON SELECTION BAR 1 OF databases DO AIRCRAFT.SPR
ON SELECTION BAR 2 OF databases DO OWNERS.SPR

DEFINE POPUP windows MARGIN RELATIVE SHADOW COLOR SCHEME 4
DEFINE BAR _MWI_TRACE OF windows PROMPT "\<Trace"
DEFINE BAR _MWI_DEBUG OF windows PROMPT "\<Debug"
```

Well, it worked. You could click on the appropriate database selection from the menu, and it would run the associated screen program. But a few things are missing. Once both the Aircraft and the Owners windows are showing on the screen, you would think you could click on the window that isn't on top to bring it to the top. Well, clicking on a window in FoxPro *does* put it on top of any other windows on the screen, but that's all it does. There's nothing in FoxPro to make it run the correct screen program when you click on a window. So, you can run your programs from the menu, but you can't "click to activate."

Window functions

That's where the FindSPR and FindWind functions come in handy. Find-SPR returns the name of the last application window in FoxPro's window list with the extension .SPR tacked onto the end, while FindWind returns just the window's name.

The READ DEACTIVATE clause for the application window is going to do the work for you. READ DEACTIVATE is like a VALID clause for a window; it answers the question "Do I deactivate this window ?". You want to invoke this clause if the user does any of the things that would remove the window: Clicking on another window or issuing CLEAR READ are the two principal events that will cause this.

Ask yourself the following questions. Did the user remove an application window and, if so, was it the only application window on the screen? That's important because, if it was and if he did, you have to remove the Control window too. It wouldn't make much sense to leave it out there on the screen by itself. Finally, is the window being deactivated in favor of the Calendar or Calculator, neither of which is your application? If you're editing, don't end the application just to select one of the utilities.

The Deactivate code snippet for each Application window consists of a one-line call to a routine that tests whether to terminate that application. In Aircraft, it's:

```
RETURN End_app ( "AIRCRAFT" )
```

and in Owners, it's:

```
RETURN End_app ( "OWNERS" )
```

The code for End_app function is shown in Listing 3-9. This last RETURN statement uses the logical OR function in a way you might not be familiar with. UtilTest will be .True. if the Calendar or Calculator windows were on top. NOT WindTest will be true if they weren't.

Listing 3-9 The READ DEACTIVATE clause for application windows.

```
FUNCTION End_App      && End read for the current window?
PARAMETER m.window    && Yes if another APPLICATION window was chosen

End_App = .F.
PRIVATE m.WindName

* IF they clicked on the background screen, put it back on the bottom.
IF WONTOP() = [FULLSCREEN]
   ACTIVATE WINDOW FULLSCREEN BOTTOM
   RETURN .F.
ENDIF

IF NOT WVISIBLE(m.window)    && Did window get closed manually?
   m.WindName = WCHILD("",0)
   DO WHILE NOT EMPTY(m.WindName)
      IF m.WindName = "CONTROL"
         SHOW WINDOW (m.WindName) TOP
      ENDIF
      m.WindName = WCHILD("",1)
   ENDDO
   End_App = .T.
ENDIF

CurrProg = FindSPR()
```

```
CurrWind = FindWIN()

*--- Test for a return from the Calculator/Calendar
UtilTest = WREAD()
IF NOT WREAD()
   IF LEFT(WONTOP(),8) $ "Calculator/Calendar"
      UtilTest = .T.
      ELSE
      UtilTest = IIF ( Editing, .T. , .F. )
      IF Editing
         m.WindName = WLAST()
         SHOW WINDOW ( m.WindName ) TOP
      ENDIF
   ENDIF
ENDIF

* Force READ to end
IF NOT EMPTY ( NextProg ) AND NOT ( CurrWind $ NextProg )
   End_App = .T.
ENDIF

RETURN End_App OR NOT UtilTest
```

Recall that this function is called if you try to deactivate an application window (it's called in the READ DEACTIVATE clauses of both screens). Now, when you use logical operators, A OR B is .True. if either A is true or B is true. So if the user closed the window from which this function was called *or* if a CLEAR READ was issued, the function is called.

A related issue is that, if you want to change windows, how do you know which one is next and which program to run? The following function attempts to deal with each of these issues. Note the global variable End_App, which is set in this function.

The READ ACTIVATE clause

READ ACTIVATE adds one more piece of the puzzle. In order for your controls to work smoothly, you must ensure that the windows are presented in the correct order. Remember how the FindSPR and FindWind functions work. So when you activate a screen program, you'll force the windows to appear in the correct order, which is the applications window followed by the control window. Each application screen, therefore, will have a READ ACTIVATE clause that looks like this:

```
FUNCTION _qcsOs9mlx          && Read-Level Activate
* Activate code from screen: OWNERS
#REGION 1
```

```
ACTIVATE WINDOW OWNERS TOP
ACTIVATE WINDOW CONTROL TOP
```

Modifications to MAIN.PRG and MENU.MPR

A few changes are needed in the MAIN program, and MENU as well. In order to have the event handler HANDLER( ) manage all events, you'll have to change the Database Menu popup commands in MENU.MPR as follows:

```
DO AIRCRAFT.SPR becomes DO MenuPick WITH "AIRCRAFT.SPR"
DO OWNERS.SPR becomes DO MenuPick WITH "OWNERS.SPR"
```

MenuPick is as follows:

```
FUNCTION MENUPICK
PARAMETERS ScreenName
IF RDLEVEL() > 1
    NextProg = ScreenName
    CLEAR READ
    ELSE
    DO ( ScreenName )
ENDIF
```

This points out a very important fact about reusable code. If RDLEVEL is greater than 1, there's already another program running. So if you want to run a new program—which is probably the case, because the user just picked it from the menu—you need to terminate the program that's currently running. You know one's currently running because RDLEVEL( ) is greater than 1. By stuffing the passed screen name into NextProg and doing a CLEAR READ, you force the event handler to become active, and give it the name of the program you want to run. If RDLEVEL( ) = 1, nothing else is running, so just crank 'er up.

New global variables for MAIN.PRG

Add several global variable declarations in MAIN.PRG:

```
NextProg = ""  && Tells program if app was chosen from menu
End_App  = .T. && Set to .T. if Remove was clicked
Done     = .F. && Terminates this program
Editing  = .F. && .True. if application edit is in progress
OKtoSave = .T. && .True. if edit/add data is to be saved
WindChck = []  && App window top after another is removed.
```

Look them up in the code. Once you understand why each one's there, you'll have a pretty good handle on this entire process.

Changes to the event handler

In the HANDLER function, add the code in Listing 3-10. The menu program calls the event handler directly. It passes the name of the program that is

Listing 3-10 Modifications to the event handler.

```
FUNCTION HANDLER
PRIVATE Prog
IF Done
   RETURN .T.
ENDIF
DO CASE
   CASE NOT EMPTY ( NextProg )      && set in MENUPICK.PRG!
      Prog = NextProg
      NextProg = ""
      DO ( Prog )
      RETURN .F.
   CASE   UPPER(WONTOP()) <> [CONTROL]    ;
      AND UPPER(WONTOP()) <> [COMMAND]    ;
      AND UPPER(WONTOP()) <> [FULLSCREEN]
      Prog = FindSPR()
      DO (Prog)
      RETURN .F.
ENDCASE
RETURN .F.
```

to be run. To terminate the READ, set Done to .True. and then issue a CLEAR READ ALL, thus ensuring that control will be passed through the READ VALID clause.

Controlling the controls

If the last application window was just removed, you need to remove the Control window as well. That's done with the EraseCtl function (shown in Listing 3-11).

Listing 3-11 ERASECTL.PRG to manage the Control window.

```
PROCEDURE EraseCtl

* This loops through all window names:
* WCHILD("",0) finds first window; WCHILD("",1) finds next window.
* Exit with no action if CONTROL isn't on top.
* If any name appears before CONTROL, we're done.

m.WindChck = WCHILD("",0)
DO WHILE NOT EMPTY(m.WindChck)
   IF  WindChck <> [CONTROL]    ;
   AND WindChck <> [FULLSCREEN] ;
   AND WindChck <> [Command]
      RETURN
   ENDIF
```

```
   m.WindChck = WCHILD("",1)
ENDDO
* No APP window on top; set to null value and release the control box
WindChck = []
IF NOT EMPTY(WONTOP())
   RELEASE WINDOW CONTROL
ENDIF
```

The project file

The project screen in its final form appears in Fig. 3-7. All of the program files could be included in MAIN.PRG. I left them outside for clarity, but because MAIN is the top program FoxPro would have found all the others if they were simply included at the end of MAIN.

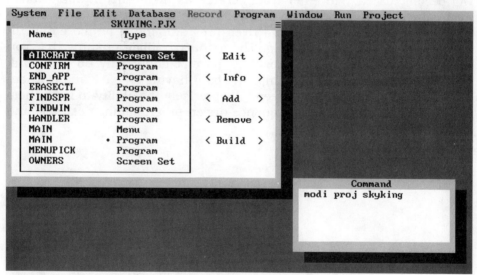

Figure 3-7 The project file for SKYKING.PJX.

This format is the one I use for event-driven applications. To use it for your prototypes, substitute your screens for mine, make each one into a screen set that includes CONTROL.SCX, and modify the Databases menu pop-up to call your screen programs. Remember to change the second line of the cleanup code for each screen to refer to its own screen name, and make sure the Remove Window box on the Screen Setup dialog isn't checked. It should work exactly the way this model does, with about five minutes' worth of work.

There are more features in most commercial applications. You might have noticed that there's a DELETE function in the cleanup code, but it isn't called anywhere. That's because you're going to do so using a menu choice from a Record menu pop-up, which you'll add in the next chapter.

Probably the single capability that most distinguishes simplistic applications from those in the "real world" is the handling of parent-child records. In the flying-club application, you'll want to schedule rentals, bill members, and log payments. Each of these functions requires a transaction database, which we haven't dealt with yet. In FoxPro's event-driven scheme of things, creating such a database requires using BROWSE, and integrating it into an application entails a number of complications, as you'll also see in the next chapter.

Conclusion

I hope you were able to follow every step of this chapter. If you can commit the elements required to manage an event-driven application to memory, you should be able to generate this whole thing from memory. In time, it will become as easy to enter from scratch as menu-driven applications might already be for you.

That's not to say that event-driven programming is no more difficult than menu-driven programming. The menu paradigm ensures that you can control what your users have or haven't done. Why do you think menu-driven software users complain about having to "save and exit" before they can go to another screen? It's precisely the ability to force them to save and exit that makes sequence-driven programming desirable and relatively simple.

4

Enhancing
the event-driven model

In the previous chapter, you built a model for event-driven applications with several screens. Using this model, it's relatively simple to add more screens. But you still haven't dealt with several of FoxPro's other important features: menus and BROWSEs. In this chapter, you'll add both capabilities. Menus are easy, especially now that the event-driven engine is in place. BROWSE, on the other hand, is a little more eccentric. You can do a lot with a little programming, but you'll do it BROWSE's way.

Adding another screen

Before you tackle these two features, however, let's find out how easy it is to add a screen. The original purpose of this exercise was to rent airplanes to club members, but you still don't have a MEMBERS screen. You could use QuickScreen to pull in the field names and then complete the design, as shown in Fig. 4-1.

Recall that you have to duplicate the setup and CLEANUP code in each screen. Rather than type them in, you can copy them from another screen. Use Ctrl–F2 to go to the command window, and then type MODIFY SCREEN SCREENS\AIRCRAFT. Then pull down the Screen Layout dialog, click on Cleanup, and then click on Ok. Hold down the Shift key, press PgDn until the entire snippet is highlighted, and press Ctrl–C. This will copy the highlighted code into the paste buffer.

Now press Esc to exit the screen, Ctrl–F1 to cycle back to your original screen, and the same keystrokes to bring up the MEMBERS window's CLEANUP code. Press Ctrl–V, and the code will be magically pasted into

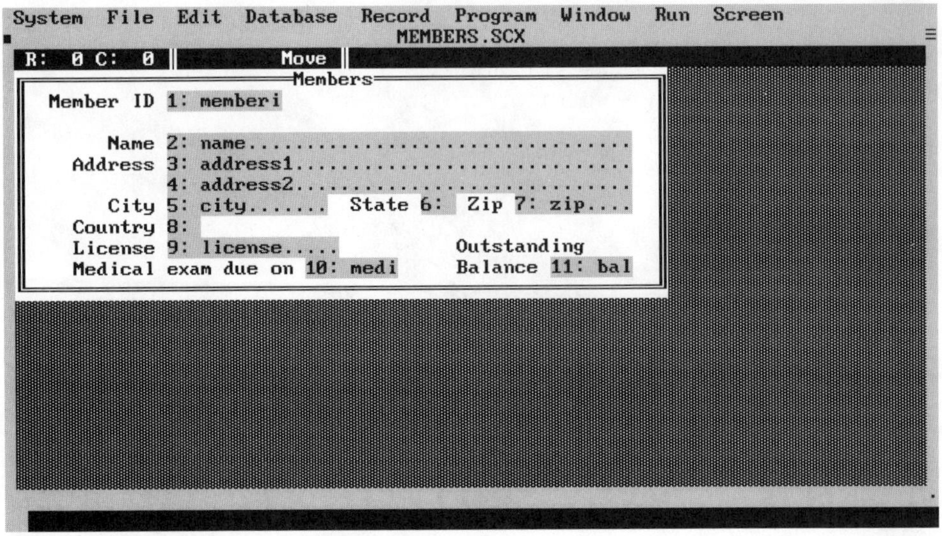
System File Edit Database Record Program Window Run Screen
MEMBERS.SCX
R: 0 C: 0
Move
Members
Member ID 1: memberi
Name 2: name
Address 3: address1
4: address2
City 5: city
State 6:
Zip 7: zip
Country 8:
License 9: license
Outstanding
Medical exam due on 10: medi
Balance 11: bal

Figure 4-1 The Members screen.

the snippet. Do the same with the screen setup code, changing the `SELECT AIRCRAFT` to `SELECT MEMBERS`. In MAIN.PRG, add a line to:

```
USE MEMBERS  IN C ORDER 1
```

There are three changes that have to be made to the screen code. First, go to the second line of the CLEANUP snippet and change:

```
RELEASE WINDOW AIRCRAFT
```

to:

```
RELEASE WINDOW MEMBERS
```

Now enter the READ ACTIVATE snippet and change:

```
ACTIVATE WINDOW AIRCRAFT TOP
```

to:

```
ACTIVATE WINDOW MEMBERS TOP
```

Then enter the READ DEACTIVATE snippet and change:

```
RETURN End_App ( "AIRCRAFT" )
```

to:

```
RETURN End_App ( "MEMBERS" )
```

Finally, go to the MAIN menu and add the line:

```
DO MENUPICK WITH "MEMBERS.SPR"
```

as the third choice in the DATABASE popup. Rebuild the application and give it a test drive. It took me about four minutes to add the MEMBERS screen, and everything works as advertised.

Adding a menu popup

Besides controls, there are two additional ways to navigate around the database: shortcut hotkeys and menu popups.

When you press F10 (or Alt) to activate the FoxPro system menu—or your redefinition—you can pull down a panel of choices, and then highlight one and press Enter. If the choices have a designated hotkey within the menu bar (e.g., if you typed \<Add, the letter A is a menu hotkey), then pressing A will execute the Add option.

But there's another type of hotkey. It's what FoxPro calls a "shortcut keystroke combination"—typically Ctrl or Alt plus a letter—and you can use it at any time, whether the menu popup is showing or not. Such shortcuts appear to the right of the menu pad on the popup, as seen in Fig. 4-2.

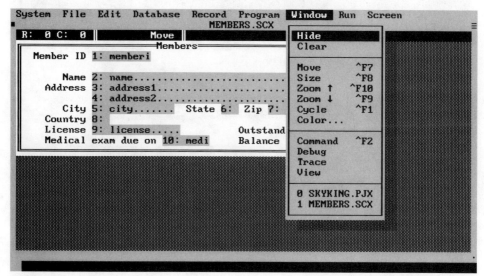

Figure 4-2 The Windows menu popup.

FoxPro uses menu popups to do the same things you do with control windows. There are several reasons for duplicating control functions in a pull-down menu, or for putting additional commands on a menu that aren't on-screen controls. For one thing, you might want to do things that are potentially dangerous (delete a record), or you might simply want to leave infrequently used commands out of the control window. Also, controls are often designed for use with a mouse, but many DOS users don't have a mouse or don't like using them. To nonmouse users, a control box won't seem natural. Finally, you might simply *like* menus. That's a valid reason, too.

I replaced the \<Windows menu bar with \<Record, as shown in Fig. 4-3. Then I added the menu bars shown in Fig. 4-4. Notice that there's a field for giving this menu bar a name. I've entered the name *Record*, which will make the code a lot easier to read. If you don't name the bars, FoxPro

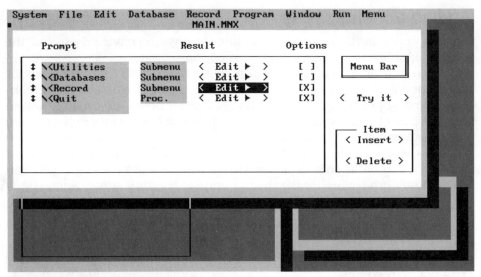

Figure 4-3 Adding the Record menu popup.

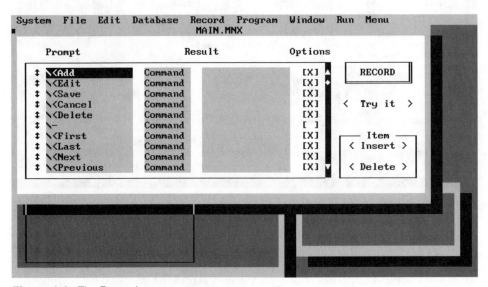

Figure 4-4 The Record menu popup menu prompts.

will assign its own odd little names. By the way, for the rest of the book you'll be using the #NAME directive in screen snippets to assign names that are easier to follow in the code. Just remember that conflicts are possible when you assign unique snippet names.

These screens are where you assign global hotkeys, which work at any time, even if the menu popup isn't showing. It's also where you enter the conditions under which the menu pad, or a bar of a menu popup, is disabled.

Disabling menu options

In the old days before FoxPro, you let users choose things from a menu, and then beeped at them if the choice made no sense. If they picked Next and were already at the end of the file, they might get a *You're already at the end, doofus* message. I think this might have contributed to some user hostility. It seems kinder and gentler simply to dim the option, thus letting them know that they shouldn't even try. And even if they do try, nothing happens.

I don't know how often FoxPro evaluates menu bars and pads to determine whether or not they're disabled, but it must be pretty darned often. If you set up the condition `SKIP FOR Editing` on a menu bar and then change the value of Editing to .T. in your program, the menu prompt will instantly dim.

You can dim individual bars or the entire menu pad. In each case, find the Skip For checkbox in the appropriate screen and then enter a condition (typically a global memory variable created just for that purpose) that, if it evaluates to .True., means you want the menu pad or menu bar to be dimmed and unselectable.

Before you begin this, I should point out something about FoxPro's VALID clauses: They can consist of several logical variables, logical expressions, and user-defined functions (UDFs). So, an expression like `Editing AND NOT IsPrinterOn()` is typical in the case of SKIP FOR snippets. You can concatenate as many of these expressions as is consistent with your personal value system.

Disabling the Quit menu pad

As an example, let's prevent the user from quitting while editing. You might have read articles about some of the special problems attendant to event-driven programming. One such complication involves users who try to back out of partially completed multiscreen transactions. How can you compel them to cancel the edit, thus enforcing your transaction cleanup procedure? Well, brute force sounds pretty good. If Quit is dimmed, then pulling down the system menu won't get them into trouble, because they can't select Quit.

So go into the screen shown in Fig. 4-5 and select Skip For. When the snippet window appears, enter the condition Editing (Fig. 4-6). Editing is one of my global variables, and it's .True. during a screen edit. Rebuild the application and see what happens. If yours did what mine did, you now have a goof-proof Quit option on your menu. Not bad for two minutes' work!

In this case, the Record menu pad shouldn't be active until there's a record to edit. So you'll want to use a condition to test whether one of the applications' windows is on top. Select the Skip For option and enter the condition into the snippet window, as shown in Fig. 4-7.

If the Command or FullScreen windows are on top, there's no application running, so the Record menu pad is dimmed and inactive.

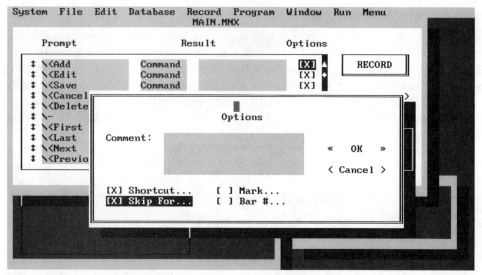

Figure 4-5 Selecting the Skip For option.

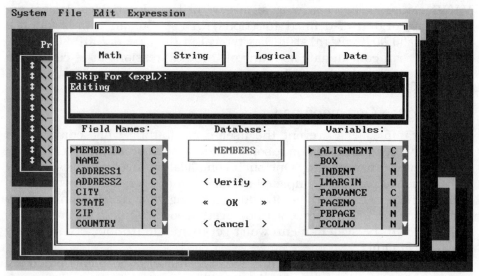

Figure 4-6 Entering the Skip For condition.

Disabling Record menu choices

The choices on your menu are shown back in Fig. 4-4. If you're at the first record in the file, Previous and Top are irrelevant. Similarly, Next and Bottom don't have meaning if your user is looking at the last record in the file. You already have the LightsOut function to determine which push-buttons to dim, so just add two global variables, AtTop and AtBottom.

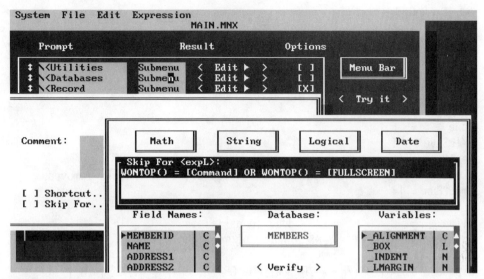

Figure 4-7 Disabling the Record menu pad.

You can force the user to either save or cancel an edit. Then skipping to the next record in the file in the middle of an edit without asking to save or cancel means you have to assume one or the other. In some heads-down data-entry applications, I might permit an automatic save, but in this case, you can force the user to choose by dimming all other options while editing. If you use the global variable Editing, the clause SKIP FOR Editing would do exactly what it looks like it should do. The Next option would read SKIP FOR Editing OR AtBottom, meaning "dim the Next menu prompt if the user's editing or if the current record is the last one in the selected file."

Listing 4-1, MAIN.PRG, shows the new global variables and the Lights-Out function from the previous chapter (modified to update these two new variables). Listing 4-2 is MAIN.MPR with the Record pad added.

Listing 4-1 MAIN.PRG and the LightsOut function.

```
* Program-ID.....: Main.PRG
* Purpose........: Controls SKY KING application

Counter = 0

SET TALK    OFF
SET CONFIRM OFF
SET SAFETY  OFF
SET DELETED ON

SET COLOR OF SCHEME 1 TO ,,,,,,,,,GR+/B

CLOSE DATABASES
```

4-1 Continued.

```
USE DBFS\AIRCRAFT IN 1 ORDER aircraftid
USE DBFS\OWNERS   IN 2 ORDER name
USE DBFS\MEMBERS  IN 3 ORDER memberid
USE DBFS\CHARGES  IN 4 ORDER memberid

End_App  = .T.
Done     = .F.
OKtoSave = .T.
NextProg = []
WindChck = []              && App window top after another is removed.
Prog2Run = []
Editing  = .F.
AtTop    = .F              && Added to assist in
AtBottom = .F.             && dimming of menu choices.

BrowseColor = [ GR+/B, W+/R,  W+/BG, GR+/B, GR+/B, W+/R, W+/R ]

DO MAIN.MPR

DEFINE   WINDOW FULLSCREEN FROM 1,0 TO 24, 79
ACTIVATE WINDOW FULLSCREEN
WTITLE = [ Sky King Flying Club ]
@ WROWS()/2, WCOLS()/2 - LEN(WTITLE)/2 SAY WTITLE
WTITLE = [ Press F10 for Menu ]
@ WROWS()-1, WCOLS()/2 - LEN(WTITLE)/2 SAY WTITLE

READ VALID HANDLER()

CLEAR TYPEAHEAD
CLEAR WINDOWS
CLEAR

CLOSE DATABASES
SET SYSMENU TO DEFAULT

RETURN          && or QUIT
```

Listing 4-2 MAIN.MPR with the Record menu added.

```
*
*      ┌──────────────────────────────────────────────────┐
*      │  02/08/93              MAIN.MPR            10:37:23 │
       └──────────────────────────────────────────────────┘
```

4-2 Continued.

```
SET SYSMENU TO
SET SYSMENU AUTOMATIC

DEFINE PAD _qd60mrp9x OF _MSYSMENU PROMPT "\<Utilities" COLOR SCHEME 3
DEFINE PAD _qd60mrpbm OF _MSYSMENU PROMPT "\<Databases" COLOR SCHEME 3
DEFINE PAD _qd60mrpcm OF _MSYSMENU PROMPT "\<Record" COLOR SCHEME 3 ;
SKIP FOR WONTOP() = [Command] OR WONTOP() = [FULLSCREEN]
DEFINE PAD _qd60mrpcy OF _MSYSMENU PROMPT "\<Quit" COLOR SCHEME 3 ;
KEY CTRL+Q, "CTRL+Q" ;
SKIP FOR Editing
ON PAD _qd60mrp9x OF _MSYSMENU ACTIVATE POPUP utilities
ON PAD _qd60mrpbm OF _MSYSMENU ACTIVATE POPUP databases
ON PAD _qd60mrpcm OF _MSYSMENU ACTIVATE POPUP record
ON SELECTION PAD _qd60mrpcy OF _MSYSMENU ;
DO _qd60mrper ;
IN LOCFILE("MENUS\MAIN" ,"MPX;MPR¦FXP;PRG" ,"Where is MAIN?")

DEFINE POPUP utilities MARGIN RELATIVE SHADOW COLOR SCHEME 4
DEFINE BAR _MST_CALCU OF utilities PROMPT "\<Calculator"
DEFINE BAR _MST_DIARY OF utilities PROMPT "Calendar/\<Diary"

DEFINE POPUP databases MARGIN RELATIVE SHADOW COLOR SCHEME 4
DEFINE BAR 1 OF databases PROMPT "\<Aircraft"
DEFINE BAR 2 OF databases PROMPT "\<Owners"
DEFINE BAR 3 OF databases PROMPT "\<Members"
ON SELECTION BAR 1 OF databases DO MenuPick WITH "AIRCRAFT.SPR"
ON SELECTION BAR 2 OF databases DO MenuPick WITH "OWNERS.SPR"
ON SELECTION BAR 3 OF databases DO MenuPick WITH "MEMBERS.SPR"

DEFINE POPUP record MARGIN RELATIVE SHADOW COLOR SCHEME 4
DEFINE BAR 1 OF record PROMPT "\<Add" ;
KEY CTRL+INS, "^INS" ;
SKIP FOR Editing
DEFINE BAR 2 OF record PROMPT "\<Edit" ;
KEY CTRL+E, "^E" ;
SKIP FOR Editing
DEFINE BAR 3 OF record PROMPT "\<Save" ;
KEY CTRL+S, "^S" ;
```

```
SKIP FOR NOT Editing
DEFINE BAR 4 OF record PROMPT "\<Cancel" ;
KEY CTRL+K, "^K" ;
SKIP FOR NOT Editing
DEFINE BAR 5 OF record PROMPT "\<Delete" ;
KEY CTRL+DEL, "^-Del" ;
SKIP FOR Editing
DEFINE BAR 6 OF record PROMPT "\-"
DEFINE BAR 7 OF record PROMPT "\<First" ;
KEY CTRL+F, "^F" ;
SKIP FOR Editing OR AtTop
DEFINE BAR 8 OF record PROMPT "\<Last" ;
KEY CTRL+L, "^L" ;
SKIP FOR Editing OR AtBottom
DEFINE BAR 9 OF record PROMPT "\<Next" ;
KEY CTRL+UPARROW, "^↑" ;

SKIP FOR Editing or AtBottom
DEFINE BAR 10 OF record PROMPT "\<Previous" ;
KEY CTRL+DNARROW, "^↓" ;

SKIP FOR Editing or AtTop


*
*        ║                Cleanup Code & Procedures                ║
*        ║                                                         ║


ON SELECTION POPUP RECORD DO CONTROLS WITH PROMPT()

PROCEDURE _qd60mrper

End_App  = .T.
Done     = .T.
CLEAR READ ALL
KEYBOARD [{Ctrl+W}]+↑{Ctrl+W}]
```

Menu hotkeys

I've added a global hotkey to each menu prompt. Some of them are more intuitive than others. Next, for *next record*, is Ctrl–N. The first letter of Next is also highlighted. If the menu is pulled down, the letter N is "hot," and pressing it will select the choice whether that menu bar is highlighted or not. But Ctrl–N, shown at the right of the bar, is active any time the option is available, whether the menu is pulled down or not.

This last feature is very, very handy. If you do menu-driven programming, you spend a certain amount of your time pushing and popping hotkeys to avoid recursive calls—running a program that's already running. When you use FoxPro's menu system to enable your hotkeys, the mechanism that you use to dim menu choices and menu pads will automatically handle the associated hotkeys in an analogous fashion.

I hope this has encouraged you to do interesting things with your menus. It's easier than it's ever been, and the payoff is considerable.

Adding BROWSE to an event-driven system

BROWSE is FoxPro's table manager. It allows you to view any file as a table of records, up to the maximum that will fit on the screen or in the BROWSE window. The program shown in Listing 4-3, which relates members and their history of charges, will serve to demonstrate some of BROWSE's characteristics. The result is shown in Fig. 4-8.

Listing 4-3 A sample BROWSE.

```
* Program-ID.....: BROWSE1.PRG

USE DBFS\MEMBERS IN A ORDER MemberID       && memberid
USE DBFS\CHARGES IN B ORDER MemberID DESC && memberid + DTOC ( date )

*        Browse color scheme (#10):
*        Color Pair              Applied to:
*        ----------      --------------------
*        1                       Other records
*        2                       Current field
*        3                       Border
*        4                       Title (when active)
*        5                       Title (when inactive)
*        6                       Highlighted text
*        7                       Current record
*        8                       Shadow
*        9                       -
*        10                      -

BrowseColor = [ GR+/B, W+/R,  W+/BG, GR+/B, GR+/B, W+/R, W+/R ]
*              Bkgrnd,CurFld,Border,Title1,Title2,Text, CurRec
```

4-3 Continued.

```
*                  1      2      3      4      5      6     7

SELECT MEMBERS
SET RELATION TO memberid INTO CHARGES

DEFINE  WINDOW members FROM  1,3 TO  8,76 DOUBLE SHADOW FLOAT GROW
BROWSE                              ;
  COLOR ( BrowseColor )             ;
  NOWAIT                            ;
  TITLE [Membership Roster]         ;
  WINDOW members
RELEASE WINDOW members

SELECT  CHARGES

DEFINE  WINDOW charges FROM 10,3 TO 16,76 DOUBLE SHADOW FLOAT GROW
BROWSE                              ;
  COLOR ( BrowseColor )             ;
  NOWAIT                            ;
  TITLE [Related Charges]           ;
  WINDOW charges                    ;
  FOR memberid = MEMBERS.memberid
RELEASE WINDOW charges

SELECT MEMBERS
ACTIVATE WINDOW Membership
```

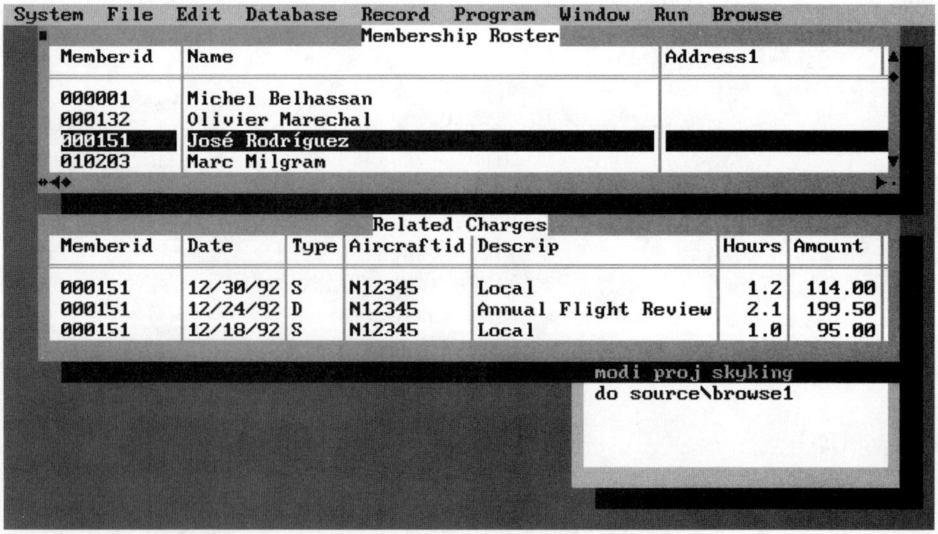

Figure 4-8 A BROWSE example.

What's NOWAIT?

When you issue a BROWSE from the command window, you go right into the function. But your programs can use BROWSE as a display tool if you use the NOWAIT parameter. NOWAIT leaves the BROWSE on the screen. Any time you move the file pointer for that BROWSE's file, the data in the BROWSE is automatically redisplayed. To remove it, use the RELEASE command to get rid of the window that contains the BROWSE.

Coordinating a pair of BROWSEs

A pair of BROWSEs lets the user scroll through the top window, and repositions the bottom window of related charges as the cursor moves from member to member. This is done using two tools. The first is `SET RELATION TO memberid INTO charges`, which forces repositioning the record pointer in the CHARGES file every time the key in the MEMBERS file changes. The second is the KEY subcommand of the CHARGES BROWSE, which limits the display of records to those records whose memberid matches with that of the current MEMBERS record. There's a SET SKIP command that does something like this in a single BROWSE, but, like many "off the shelf" tools, it has advantages and disadvantages.

The BROWSE color scheme

I explicitly defined the BROWSE colors because I have my own preferences, and the FoxPro defaults aren't even close. (You can also specify `SET COLOR OF SCHEME 10 TO &Browsecolor`.) Note that if you `SET BLINK OFF`, you can use some of the bright colors as background colors. Press Ctrl–W, then L for Color Picker, and then examine the available choices. BROWSE is the 10th scheme in the pull-down list at the upper right corner of the screen; that's how I know it's color scheme 10.

Coordinating files

Before you browse the child records, you need to force the BROWSE to co-operate. In the MEMBERS screen setup code, add the following new lines:

```
SELECT  CHARGES                              <==== NEW!
SET ORDER TO memberid                        <==== NEW!
SELECT  MEMBERS
SCATTER MEMVAR
SET RELATION TO memberid INTO charges        <==== NEW!
Adding = .F.
```

Your BROWSE will use the KEY statement to display only the charges that relate to this member, so the memberid index tag is required (KEY is a little faster than FOR, but it needs an index). SET RELATION is used in a co-ordinated BROWSE to reposition the child-file record pointer every time the key in the primary file changes. That's why the child-file BROWSE "follows" the MEMBERS record. The BROWSE window for this example is shown in Fig. 4-9.

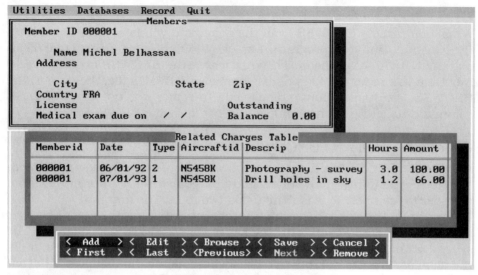

```
Utilities  Databases  Record  Quit
                          ─Members─
  Member ID 000001

      Name Michel Belhassan
  Address

      City                   State      Zip
  Country FRA
  License                          Outstanding
  Medical exam due on    /  /      Balance    0.00
```
```
                          Related Charges Table
  ┌─────────┬─────────┬────┬─────────┬───────────────────┬─────┬───────┐
  │ Memberid│ Date    │Type│Aircraftid│Descrip           │Hours│ Amount│
  │─────────┼─────────┼────┼─────────┼───────────────────┼─────┼───────│
  │ 000001  │06/01/92 │2   │N5458K   │Photography - survey│ 3.0 │ 180.00│
  │ 000001  │07/01/93 │1   │N5458K   │Drill holes in sky │ 1.2 │  66.00│
  └─────────┴─────────┴────┴─────────┴───────────────────┴─────┴───────┘
```
```
  < Add    > < Edit   > < Browse > < Save   > < Cancel >
  < First  > < Last   > <Previous> < Next   > < Remove >
```

Figure 4-9 The Members screen with a CHARGES browse.

Window names

You might have seen the lines RELEASE WINDOW charges and RELEASE WIN
DOW members and wondered why they were there. This is one of the slightly
odd things about BROWSE: When you browse in a window, FoxPro gives
BROWSE another window with the name taken from your BROWSE title.
While BROWSE1 is running, Press Alt–W and look at the names of the
windows. Comment out the two RELEASE WINDOW lines and run BROWSE1
again, and you'll see four window names in the list.

This isn't really so odd. BROWSE needs a window anyway because of
the way it's designed. But where it gets its name from is a little odd. If you
just issue a BROWSE from the command window, it takes its window name
from the name of the current database. If you include a title, it uses the title. Referring to the first word of the title is sufficient in commands, for example, RELEASE WINDOW This for a window entitled This is a window.

It's common to define a window of a given size, and then activate
BROWSE within that window. This causes BROWSE to appear with the
desired dimensions. What you might not have known, however, is that
once BROWSE has been activated (with NOWAIT), you can release the window in which it was activated; it used it only to get its attributes.

Two alternatives

The addition of a BROWSE window name to the window list that FINDSPR
and FINDWIN read to return application screen names will cause a problem: How do these two functions know that a BROWSE window isn't an
application? Most other approaches to event-driven programming suggest
the use of prefixes for window names, so that a BROWSE window might
have a name like WBPAYMENTS.

Because you've gotten this far without window naming conventions, let's try to continue to avoid them. But it isn't easy. Your generic program code isn't going to know the titles of all of your BROWSEs, so you're going to have to make some compromises. In particular, the FINDWIN and FIND-SPR programs need to know that a BROWSE window isn't an application.

If you want your BROWSE to stay on the screen under its parent, even when you bring forward another application, the simplest way is to use a naming convention in your BROWSE titles and rewrite your window functions to accommodate them. In the example, any BROWSE windows must contain the word *table*. Then the modifications to FINDSPR and FINDWIN shown in Listing 4-4 won't try to run TABLE OF CHARGES SPR.

Listing 4-4 Modifications to treat Browse windows properly.

```
FUNCTION FindSPR
PRIVATE m.Program, m.Window
**********************************************
** Find the current screen program name: **
**********************************************
m.Program = ""
m.Window = WCHILD("",0)
DO WHILE NOT EMPTY(m.Window)
   IF  NOT UPPER ( m.Window ) $ [CONTROL/FULLSCREEN/COMMAND] ;
   AND NOT "TABLE" $ UPPER ( m.Window )      <====== modification
      m.Program = m.Window
      m.Program = m.Program+".SPR"
   ENDIF
   m.Window = WCHILD("",1)
ENDDO
RETURN m.Program


FUNCTION FindWin
PRIVATE m.Window, m.ReadWind
**********************************************
** Find the current READ window:        **
** In FoxPro, the LAST window in the     **
** window list is the current window.    **
**********************************************
m.Window = WCHILD("",0)
DO WHILE NOT EMPTY(m.Window)
   IF  NOT UPPER ( m.Window ) $ [CONTROL/FULLSCREEN/COMMAND] ;
   AND NOT "TABLE" $ UPPER ( m.Window )      <====== modification
      m.ReadWind = m.Window
   ENDIF
   m.Window = WCHILD("",1)
ENDDO
RETURN m.ReadWind
```

Notice the two added lines (with the required semicolon for continuation). Now the BROWSE window names won't be returned as the name of the window to activate and the program to run.

Some people will have the same objections to this approach that they have to window naming conventions. I'm afraid that you're pretty much boxed in. BROWSE window names will appear in the window list, and you have to have some mechanism for identifying the ones that aren't application names.

Another way to skin a cat

If you think about it, it isn't often necessary to show the BROWSE of child records at all times; you need to see them only when the related parent window is foremost. I prefer to write my applications so that BROWSEs appear and disappear with the windows that use them. The ACTIVATE and DEACTIVATE code for the window that has a BROWSE of child records can display the BROWSE when activated, and release it when deactivated. See Listing 4-5 for the changes I made to the READ ACTIVATE and READ DEACTIVATE for the MEMBERS screen. (Note that I was able to give these snippets my own names using the #NAME directive in each snippet.)

Listing 4-5 The READ ACTIVATE and DEACTIVATE clauses.

```
FUNCTION MEMBRACT       && Read-Level Activate
*
* Activate Code from screen: MEMBERS
*
#REGION 1
IF NOT WEXIST('Related Charges Table')
    DEFINE  WINDOW charges FROM 12,3 TO 20,76 DOUBLE SHADOW FLOAT GROW CLOSE
    SELECT  CHARGES
    BROWSE                          ;
      COLOR ( BrowseColor )         ;
      NOWAIT                        ;
      TITLE [Related Charges Table] ;
      WINDOW charges                ;
      FOR memberid = MEMBERS.memberid
    RELEASE WINDOW charges
    SELECT MEMBERS
ENDIF

ACTIVATE SCREEN MEMBERS TOP
ACTIVATE SCREEN Related TOP         <===== NEW
ACTIVATE SCREEN CONTROL TOP

FUNCTION MEMBRDEACT     && Read-Level Deactivate
```

```
*
* Deactivate Code from screen: MEMBERS
*
#REGION 1
RELEASE WINDOW Related              <====== NEW
RETURN End_App ( "MEMBERS" )
```

This compromise avoids many, many problems. The BROWSE window appears only when the MEMBERS window is activated, either by menu selection or by clicking on the window to bring it forward.

The End_App function, which is run when the application shuts down, needs to do two things: release both the MEMBERS and the RELATED CHARGES TABLE windows, and specify SET RELATION OFF INTO CHARGES. The reason for the latter is that another application might need to view the charges in a different order; for example, AIRCRAFT profitability is determined by looking at charges for each individual airplane. See the following for the changes to the MEMBERS CLEANUP code:

```
IF End_App
    RELEASE WINDOW MEMBERS
    RELEASE WINDOW Related               <====== NEW
    SET RELATION OFF INTO CHARGES        <====== NEW
    DO EraseCtl
    IF NOT EMPTY ( WindChck )
        Prog = WindChck + [.SPR]
        DO ( Prog )
    ENDIF
ENDIF
```

Notice also (function MEMBRACT) that I force the windows to be redisplayed in a precise order: MEMBERS, related child records, CONTROLS. This is important because FINDSPR and FINDWIN look for the last window in the window list.

Finally, the READ DEACTIVATE clause RELEASES the child window RELATED. Remember, this is an either/or deal: If you don't mind if the BROWSE window comes and goes, release it with the READ DEACTIVATE clause; to leave the BROWSE on the screen when another application is run, include a key word (e.g., *table*) in the BROWSE TITLE of each BROWSE window, and add the line "TITLE" $ UPPER (m Window) in FINDSPR and FINDWIN.

Referential integrity

Now that you've added child records under a MEMBER, you need to look briefly at a related issue: If you delete a member who's no longer with the club, what happens to his charges? In this simple example, simply delete both. Deleting the charges is less appropriate in some cases than in others—in fact, it's not really a great idea in this case—but it demonstrates a point. See the DELETE function in the CLEANUP code for this "referential integrity" test.

The final version of the MEMBERS screen with the CHARGES BROWSE appears in Listing 4-6. Note that I made the MEMBERS screen a little smaller to allow more CHARGES lines to fit.

Listing 4-6 The MEMBERS screen with a CHARGES browse added.

```
*
*   ||                      MEMBERS.SPR                      ||
*   ||                                                       ||


*
*   ||                  MS-DOS Window Definitions            ||
*   ||                                                       ||


IF NOT WEXIST("members") ;
OR UPPER(WTITLE("MEMBERS")) == "MEMBERS.PJX" ;
OR UPPER(WTITLE("MEMBERS")) == "MEMBERS.SCX" ;
OR UPPER(WTITLE("MEMBERS")) == "MEMBERS.MNX" ;
OR UPPER(WTITLE("MEMBERS")) == "MEMBERS.PRG" ;
OR UPPER(WTITLE("MEMBERS")) == "MEMBERS.QPR"
DEFINE WINDOW members ;
        FROM 1, 0 TO 11,55 TITLE "Members" ;
        FLOAT NOCLOSE SHADOW NOMINIMIZE DOUBLE COLOR SCHEME 1
ENDIF

IF NOT WEXIST("control") ;
OR UPPER(WTITLE("CONTROL")) == "CONTROL.PJX" ;
OR UPPER(WTITLE("CONTROL")) == "CONTROL.SCX" ;
OR UPPER(WTITLE("CONTROL")) == "CONTROL.MNX" ;
OR UPPER(WTITLE("CONTROL")) == "CONTROL.PRG" ;
OR UPPER(WTITLE("CONTROL")) == "CONTROL.QPR"

DEFINE WINDOW control ;
        FROM 21, 8 TO 24,65 FLOAT NOCLOSE NOMINIMIZE COLOR SCHEME 8
ENDIF

*
*   ||            MEMBERS/MS-DOS Setup Code - SECTION 2       ||
*   ||                                                       ||
```

4-6 Continued.

```
#REGION 1
SELECT   CHARGES
SET ORDER TO memberid
SELECT   MEMBERS
SCATTER MEMVAR
SET RELATION TO memberid INTO charges
Adding = .F.
```

```
*
*         ┌─────────────────────────────────────────────────┐
          │     CONTROL/MS-DOS Setup Code - SECTION 2       ║
*         └─────────────────────────────────────────────────┘
```

```
#REGION 2
REGIONAL LastButton
PRIVATE  End_App
STORE    SPACE(6) TO LastButton
End_App  = .F.
Editing  = .F.
```

```
*
*         ┌─────────────────────────────────────────────────┐
          │        MEMBERS/MS-DOS Screen Layout             ║
*         └─────────────────────────────────────────────────┘
```

```
#REGION 1
IF WVISIBLE("members")

   ACTIVATE WINDOW members SAME
 ELSE
   ACTIVATE WINDOW members NOSHOW
ENDIF

@ 0, 2 SAY "Member ID"          SIZE 1,9, 0
@ 2, 7 SAY "Name"               SIZE 1,4, 0
@ 3, 4 SAY "Address"            SIZE 1,7, 0
@ 5, 7 SAY "City"               SIZE 1,4, 0
@ 5,28 SAY "State"              SIZE 1,5, 0
@ 5,38 SAY "Zip"                SIZE 1,3, 0
@ 7, 4 SAY "License"            SIZE 1,7, 0
```

```
@ 6, 4 SAY "Country"                SIZE 1,7, 0
@ 7,37 SAY "Outstanding "           SIZE 1,12, 0
@ 8,37 SAY "Balance"                SIZE 1,7, 0
@ 8, 4 SAY "Medical exam due on"    SIZE 1,19, 0

@ 0,12 GET m.memberid               SIZE 1,10 DEFAULT " "
@ 2,12 GET m.name                   SIZE 1,40 DEFAULT " "
@ 3,12 GET m.address1               SIZE 1,40 DEFAULT " "
@ 4,12 GET m.address2               SIZE 1,40 DEFAULT " "
@ 5,12 GET m.city                   SIZE 1,14 DEFAULT " "
@ 5,34 GET m.state                  SIZE 1,3  DEFAULT " "
@ 5,42 GET m.zip                    SIZE 1,10 DEFAULT " "
@ 6,12 GET m.country                SIZE 1,3  DEFAULT " "
@ 7,12 GET m.license                SIZE 1,15 DEFAULT " "
@ 8,24 GET m.medicaldat             SIZE 1,8  DEFAULT {  /  / }
@ 8,45 GET m.balancedue             SIZE 1,7  DEFAULT 0

*
*           ┌─────────────────────────────────────────────┐
*           │          CONTROL/MS-DOS Screen Layout        │
            └─────────────────────────────────────────────┘


#REGION 2


IF WVISIBLE("control")
   ACTIVATE WINDOW control SAME
ELSE
   ACTIVATE WINDOW control NOSHOW
ENDIF


@ 0,1  GET m.Add PICTURE "@*HN \<Add"        SIZE 1,10,2 DEFAULT 1 ;
       VALID Controls( "Add" )               MESSAGE "Add a record"
@ 0,12 GET m.Edit PICTURE "@*HN \<Edit"      SIZE 1,10,2 DEFAULT 1 ;
       VALID Controls ( "Edit" )             MESSAGE "Edit this record"
@ 0,23 GET m.Browse PICTURE "@*HN \<Browse"  SIZE 1,10,2 DEFAULT 1 ;
       VALID Controls ( "Browse" )           MESSAGE "Display table of records"
@ 0,34 GET m.Save PICTURE "@*HN \<Save"      SIZE 1,10,2 DEFAULT 1 ;
       VALID Controls ( "Save" )             MESSAGE "Save on-screen data"
@ 0,45 GET m.Cancel PICTURE "@*HN \<Cancel"  SIZE 1,10,2 DEFAULT 1 ;
       VALID Controls ( "Cancel" )           MESSAGE "Cancel add/change"
@ 1,1 GET m.First PICTURE "@*HN \<First"     SIZE 1,10,2 DEFAULT 1 ;
       VALID Controls ( "First" )            MESSAGE "Top of file"
@ 1,12 GET m.Last PICTURE "@*HN \<Last"      SIZE 1,10,2 DEFAULT 1 ;
       VALID Controls ( "Last" )             MESSAGE "Bottom of file"
@ 1,23 GET m.Previous ;
       PICTURE "@*HN \<Previous"             SIZE 1.10.2 DEFAULT 1 :
```

```
          VALID Controls ( "Previous" )              MESSAGE "Previous record"
@ 1,34 GET m.Next PICTURE "@*HN \<Next"              SIZE 1,10,2 DEFAULT 1 ;
          VALID Controls ( "Next" )                  MESSAGE "Next record"
@ 1,45 GET m.Remove PICTURE "@*HN \<Remove" SIZE 1,10,2 DEFAULT 1 ;
          VALID Controls ( "Remove" )                MESSAGE "Remove this window"


IF NOT WVISIBLE("control")
   ACTIVATE WINDOW control
ENDIF


IF NOT WVISIBLE("members")
   ACTIVATE WINDOW members
ENDIF


READ CYCLE ;
    WHEN          CTRLWHEN() ;
    ACTIVATE      MEMBRACT() ;                 <===== NEW
    DEACTIVATE    MEMBRDEACT()                 <===== NEW


#REGION 1
IF End_App
   RELEASE WINDOW MEMBERS
   RELEASE WINDOW Related                      <===== NEW
   SET RELATION OFF INTO CHARGES              <===== NEW
   DO EraseCtl
   IF NOT EMPTY ( WindChck )
      Prog = WindChck + [.SPR]
      DO ( Prog )
   ENDIF
ENDIF


*
*      ┌────────────────────────────────────────────┐
*      │      MEMBERS CLEANUP code                   │
       └────────────────────────────────────────────┘


#REGION 1
FUNCTION Save
   Oktosave = .T.
   GATHER MEMVAR MEMO
RETURN



FUNCTION Browser
   BROWSE LAST NORMAL TITLE " Table View "
   IF LASTKEY() <> 27
```

```
        SCATTER MEMVAR MEMO
    ENDIF
RETURN

FUNCTION Startup
   SCATTER MEMVAR MEMO BLANK
RETURN

FUNCTION Add
   APPEND BLANK
   GATHER MEMVAR MEMO
RETURN

FUNCTION Cancel
   SCATTER MEMVAR MEMO
RETURN

FUNCTION Delete

IF  CONFIRM ( ' Delete this record? ' )

* New code for 'Referential integrity'          <==== NEW
   HasKids = SEEK ( MEMBERS.memberid, "CHARGES" )
     GoAhead = .T.
     IF HasKids
        IF NOT CONFIRM ( ' Delete related charges also? ' )
           GoAhead = .F.
        ENDIF
     ENDIF
     IF NOT GoAhead
        RETURN
     ENDIF
     IF HasKids
        SELECT Charges
        DELETE FOR memberid = MEMBERS.memberid
        SELECT MEMBERS
     ENDIF                                  <==== NEW code ends here
     DELETE
     IF NOT BOF()
        SKIP -1
     ELSE
        GO TOP
        SKIP
     ENDIF
     SCATTER MEMVAR MEMO
```

```
 ENDIF
RETURN


*
*         ┌─────────────────────────────────────────────┐
*         │     CONTROL CLEANUP                          │
          └─────────────────────────────────────────────┘

#REGION 2

PROCEDURE Controls

PARAMETER Choice
PRIVATE   Prog2Run

DO CASE

   CASE m.Choice = "Add"

      Prog2Run = FindSPR( )
      IF NOT EMPTY( Prog2Run )
         DO Startup IN ( Prog2Run )
      ENDIF
      Editing = .T.
      _CUROBJ = 1


   CASE m.Choice = "Edit"

      Editing = .T.
      _CUROBJ = 1


   CASE m.Choice = "Save"

      Prog2Run = FindSPR( )
      IF NOT EMPTY( Prog2Run )
        IF LastButton = "Add"
           DO add IN ( Prog2Run )
        ELSE
           DO save IN ( Prog2Run )
        ENDIF
      ENDIF
      IF OkToSave
        WAIT WINDOW NOWAIT "Saving"
        Editing = .F.
      ENDIF
```

4-6 Continued.

```
CASE m.Choice = "Cancel"

   OkToSave = .T.
   Prog2Run = FindSPR()
   IF NOT EMPTY( Prog2Run )
     DO Cancel IN ( Prog2Run )
   ENDIF
   WAIT WINDOW NOWAIT "Changes ignored"
   Editing = .F.

CASE m.Choice = "Browse"

   Prog2Run = FindSPR()
   IF NOT EMPTY( Prog2Run )
     DO Browser IN ( Prog2Run )
   ENDIF
   Editing = .F.

CASE m.Choice = "First"

   GO TOP
   SCATTER MEMVAR MEMO

CASE m.Choice = "Previous"

   SKIP -1
   SCATTER MEMVAR MEMO

CASE m.Choice = "Next"

   SKIP
   SCATTER MEMVAR MEMO

CASE m.Choice = "Last"

   GO BOTTOM
   SCATTER MEMVAR MEMO

CASE m.Choice = "Remove"

   End_App = .T.
   CLEAR READ

CASE m.Choice = "Delete"
```

4-6 Continued.

```
      Prog2Run = FindSPR()
      IF NOT EMPTY( Prog2Run )
        DO delete IN ( Prog2Run )
        GO TOP
        SCATTER MEMVAR MEMO
      ENDIF

ENDCASE

DO PushButtons

LastButton = m.Choice

RETURN

PROCEDURE PushButtons

PRIVATE SaveRec

SaveRec = RECNO()
COUNT TO RecCount

IF RecCount > 0
  GO SaveRec
  IF NOT Editing
    SHOW GET m.Add        ENABLE
    SHOW GET m.Edit       ENABLE
    SHOW GET m.Save       DISABLE
    SHOW GET m.Cancel     DISABLE
    SHOW GET m.Remove     ENABLE
    SHOW GET m.Browse     ENABLE
    SKIP -1
    IF BOF()
      SHOW GET m.First    DISABLE
      SHOW GET m.Previous DISABLE
      AtTop     = .T.
      AtBottom  = .F.
    ELSE
      SHOW GET m.First    ENABLE
      SHOW GET m.Previous ENABLE
      AtTop     = .F.
    ENDIF
    GO SaveRec
    SKIP
```

```
   IF EOF()
      SHOW GET m.Next      DISABLE
      SHOW GET m.Last      DISABLE
      AtTop     = .F.
      AtBottom  = .T.
   ELSE
      SHOW GET m.Next      ENABLE
      SHOW GET m.Last      ENABLE
      AtBottom  = .F.
   ENDIF
   GO SaveRec
 ELSE
    SHOW GET m.Add         DISABLE
    SHOW GET m.Edit        DISABLE
    SHOW GET m.Save        ENABLE
    SHOW GET m.Cancel      ENABLE
    SHOW GET m.Remove      DISABLE
    SHOW GET m.First       DISABLE
    SHOW GET m.Previous    DISABLE
    SHOW GET m.Next        DISABLE
    SHOW GET m.Last        DISABLE
    SHOW GET m.Browse      DISABLE
  ENDIF
ELSE
  AtBottom  = .T.
  AtTop     = .T.
  SHOW GET m.First         DISABLE
  SHOW GET m.Previous      DISABLE
  SHOW GET m.Next          DISABLE
  SHOW GET m.Last          DISABLE
  SHOW GET m.Browse        DISABLE
  SHOW GET m.Edit          DISABLE
  IF Editing
    SHOW GET m.Add         DISABLE
    SHOW GET m.Remove      DISABLE
    SHOW GET m.Save        ENABLE
    SHOW GET m.Cancel      ENABLE
  ELSE
    SHOW GET m.Add         ENABLE
    SHOW GET m.Remove      ENABLE
    SHOW GET m.Save        DISABLE
    SHOW GET m.Cancel      DISABLE
  ENDIF
ENDIF
```

```
* Disable all GETS in the current READ Window if not in EDIT mode
ReadWind = FindWin()
IF NOT Editing
   SHOW GETS WINDOW (ReadWind) DISABLE
ELSE
   SHOW GETS WINDOW (ReadWind) ENABLE ONLY
ENDIF

RETURN

FUNCTION CTRLWHEN              && Read-Level When
*
* When Code from screen: CONTROL
*
#REGION 2
DO PushButtons

FUNCTION MEMBRACT             && Read-Level Activate
*
* Activate Code from screen: MEMBERS
*
#REGION 1
IF NOT WEXIST('Related Charges Table')
   DEFINE  WINDOW charges FROM 12,3 TO 20,76 DOUBLE SHADOW FLOAT GROW CLOSE
   SELECT   CHARGES
   BROWSE                            ;
     COLOR ( BrowseColor )           ;
     NOWAIT                          ;
     TITLE [Related Charges Table] ;
     WINDOW charges                  ;
     FOR memberid = MEMBERS.memberid
   RELEASE WINDOW charges
   SELECT MEMBERS
ENDIF

                          <=== Everything above here is new
ACTIVATE SCREEN MEMBERS TOP
ACTIVATE SCREEN Related TOP    <=== NEW
ACTIVATE SCREEN CONTROL TOP

FUNCTION MEMBRDEACT          && Read-Level Deactivate
*
* Deactivate Code from screen: MEMBERS
*
#REGION 1
RELEASE WINDOW Related          <===== NEW
RETURN End_App ( "MEMBERS" )
```

READ MODAL

Now I'd like you to try something. Go into the SKYKING application, select the MEMBERS screen, and check the MODAL checkbox. Now rebuild the application and run it. Select AIRCRAFT, then OWNERS, then MEMBERS. Now try to click on other windows or pull down the menu. You can't. That's what *modal* means.

Think for a minute about what you're looking at. You have several application screens, linked by a menu. You go into each one, do your thing, and leave. What MODAL does is disable everything you spent the last two chapters developing.

This mode of operation is exactly how many, many database applications ought to work—not for lack of alternative techniques, but because it's the best way to do the job.

Summary

That's how you add additional screens, a Record menu with dimmed options, and child browse windows to the basic model. If you've committed these techniques to memory, you now have a powerful arsenal for designing event-driven code for a variety of applications. In case you don't need it all, use READ MODAL, or read the next chapter.

5
A menu-driven example

In the previous two chapters, you built a model for event-driven applications with multiple screens, added a menu, and incorporated BROWSEs into a screen. In this chapter, the same screens are linked with a menu, so you can compare the two approaches (menu-driven and event-driven) for functionality and ease of programming.

Theory of operation

Event-driven programming in FoxPro—or in C, for that matter—can be complex. The reasons for that complexity are based, not on FoxPro's deficiencies, but on the nature of the event-driven model. The work done by Dick Bard, Alan Griver, Tapani Isoranta, Phil Neufeld, Tom Rettig, and others consists largely of contingencies to deal with potential complications. Backing out of complex transactions is one; building an "event queue" to guide the program once the current operation finishes is another. And there are many, many other potential problems that must be considered.

Before event-driven programming, we used menus to control software. At each step of the way, users got a menu of choices. If it was on the menu, they could do it. In order to get back to the menu and pick another application, they had to exit the screen they were in. If the menu wasn't showing, they couldn't pick from it.

Menu-driven software is called simplistic by some; I just call it simple. Using this technique, you no longer have to deal with saving and restoring the states of environments last exited. Menu-driven applications, however, won't let you run other applications unless they're explicitly written to do

111

so internally—for example, with an included hotkey or an additional internal menu option.

What can go wrong

Not that there's no danger in menu-driven software. You have to write what's usually called *structured* or "top-down" code. If you write something like this:

```
FUNCTION A
DO B
FUNCTION B
DO C
FUNCTION C
DO A
```

you'll eventually get a message that says:

```
DO NESTING TOO DEEP
```

This is called *recursion*. FoxPro won't stop you from calling a function that calls itself, and sometimes recursive calls are handy. But you can only DO programs to a depth of 32 calls. Practically speaking, that's a huge number of levels, so you'll get the *nesting too deep* message only if you engage in inadvertent recursion.

A case in point

I gave a seminar for *Point DBF*, a French magazine, in Paris a while back. I studied French for five months to get ready for that class, which lasted for eight hours. I was pretty satisfied with the day's lecture fee, until I factored in the 500 hours of French classes; I actually earned only about three dollars an hour for my one-day class. But I got to relearn one of the fundamental lessons in top-down programming, and it provided me with this case in point.

At my seminar, a charming American expatriate couple asked me to look at their program, which they'd written in FoxPro as their first-ever programming effort. They write restaurant guides, and had a lot of gastronomic wisdom to keep track of. They needed a pair of screens to store their data, but hadn't yet discovered screen sets. So at the end of SCREEN1 they used DO SCREEN2, and at the end of SCREEN2 they had a DO SCREEN1. They could flip screens about 30 times before it blew up.

The error is obvious, once you know what to look for. This particular problem is easy to avoid using screen sets. But the lesson is a larger one. In structured programming, you must *always* return from the terminal function in a series of calls, and you must *never* permit a program to call a program that's in its own calling sequence. (That's a requirement of top-down programming, not something that FoxPro won't let you do. FoxPro will cheerfully let you shoot yourself in the foot—but don't feel that you've been recklessly endangered; assembler or C will erase your hard disk if you just use a single bad pointer.)

A menu-driven application

Let's look at the application developed in the previous chapters as a menu-driven program. Note that such programs are called *sequence-driven* of late. You can use that as your new buzzword if you're burned out on *object-oriented*.

The application will now be a loop, with the menu at the top. That's done using a variation on the theme shown in the following listing:

```
DO WHILE .T.
   * Show menu and get a selection
   DO CASE
      CASE selection = 1
         DO choice1
      CASE selection = 2
         DO choice2
      ...
   ENDCASE
ENDDO
```

Each of the programs, represented by *choice1* and *choice2* in this example, starts, does what it was designed to do, and returns to the calling program before another program can start. There's no need to keep track of duplicated variable names, changed settings for FoxPro's SET commands, and window names or relative window locations. It's simple.

To run an application, select it from the Databases menu pad. As soon as the application starts up, the Databases menu pad will dim. That's because you can't run another program without exiting the current one. This forces you to clean up one environment before you move to another one. It is, in fact, what makes the interactions among constituent applications so predictable. When you enter function B, you can rest assured that function A won't be harmed because it's already finished. But that's not a drawback in accounting packages, inventory control systems, and a whole range of other types of applications. It's actually the way you want them to work.

Compromises

This isn't to say that there aren't some shortcomings to this technique—ones that even I regret. First, the bad news. There are aspects of FoxPro that were designed to work within the event-driven framework. The Calendar and Calculator are such creatures. Type:

```
ACTIVATE WINDOW CALCULATOR
```

from the command window, and you'll get a functioning calculator. Put the same statement into one of your programs, however, and you'll just get a picture of a calculator on the screen. Your program won't stop for you to use the calculator; it just "activates" it.

It turns out that the Calculator and Calendar are expected to be involved in a READ; they need another screen to hang with. So you can use SET SKIP on the menu to permit use of these two utilities only when another application is running. Come to think of it, that's probably not a huge compromise because that's when users would probably need them.

Modifications to the menu

Because this is a menu-driven application, start with the menu: MAIN.MPR. Use a variable name (Prog in this example) to store the name of the program to execute. When an application ends, use `Prog = ""` to reset the name of the currently executing program to nulls (blank).

Why bother to do this? After all, in this model, you're going to let only one program run at a time. The reason is that you're going to use the contents of Prog to tell the menu what options are valid. If Prog isn't empty, you're running a program. So:

```
SKIP FOR EMPTY ( Prog )
```

is the SKIP FOR condition for menu pads and bars that aren't supposed to be available unless a program is running, and:

```
SKIP FOR NOT EMPTY ( Prog )
```

will disable options that you can select only when a program isn't running—like, for example, another program.

Another way to determine whether a program is running is the WONTOP() function. If `WONTOP("FULLSCREEN")` is .True., then the "wallpaper" is showing instead of one of the application screens, so you can use that to determine whether to enable the Utilities menu pad. Similarly, the Record menu isn't meaningful until an application window is on top. You don't want to list the names of the application windows, because that can change if you decide to add another window. Instead, disable the Record menu pad if a nonapplication command window or FullScreen are on top. The rest of the SKIP FOR clauses are the same as before. The modified code appears in Listing 5-1.

Listing 5-1 The menu code for the menu-driven application.

```
*
*                 |                    MAIN.MPR                    |
*                 |                                                |


SET SYSMENU TO
SET SYSMENU AUTOMATIC
DEFINE PAD _qdd0nxhrm OF _MSYSMENU ;
```

```
PROMPT "\<Utilities" ;
COLOR SCHEME 3 ;
SKIP FOR WONTOP([FULLSCREEN])
DEFINE PAD _qdd0nxhsm OF _MSYSMENU ;
PROMPT "\<Databases" ;
COLOR SCHEME 3 ;
KEY ALT+D, "ALT+D" ;
SKIP FOR NOT EMPTY ( Prog )
DEFINE PAD _qdd0nxhtd OF _MSYSMENU ;
PROMPT "\<Record" COLOR SCHEME 3 ;
SKIP FOR WONTOP() = [Command] OR WONTOP() = [FULLSCREEN]
DEFINE PAD _qdd0nxhto OF _MSYSMENU PROMPT "\<Quit" COLOR SCHEME 3 ;
KEY CTRL+Q, "CTRL+Q" ;
SKIP FOR Editing

ON PAD _qdd0nxhrm OF _MSYSMENU ACTIVATE POPUP utilities
ON PAD _qdd0nxhsm OF _MSYSMENU ACTIVATE POPUP databases
ON PAD _qdd0nxhtd OF _MSYSMENU ACTIVATE POPUP record
ON SELECTION PAD _qdd0nxhto OF _MSYSMENU DO Finisher

DEFINE POPUP utilities MARGIN RELATIVE SHADOW COLOR SCHEME 4
DEFINE BAR 1 OF utilities PROMPT "\<Calculator"
DEFINE BAR 2 OF utilities PROMPT "Calendar/\<Diary"
ON SELECTION BAR 1 OF utilities ACTIVATE WINDOW Calculator
ON SELECTION BAR 2 OF utilities ACTIVATE WINDOW Calendar

DEFINE POPUP databases MARGIN RELATIVE SHADOW COLOR SCHEME 4
DEFINE BAR 1 OF databases PROMPT "\<Aircraft"
DEFINE BAR 2 OF databases PROMPT "\<Owners"
DEFINE BAR 3 OF databases PROMPT "\<Members"

ON SELECTION BAR 1 OF databases Prog = "AIRCRAFT.SPR"
ON SELECTION BAR 2 OF databases Prog = "OWNERS.SPR"
ON SELECTION BAR 3 OF databases Prog = "MEMBERS.SPR"
```

```
DEFINE POPUP record MARGIN RELATIVE SHADOW COLOR SCHEME 4
DEFINE BAR 1 OF record PROMPT "\<Add" ;
KEY CTRL+INS, "^Ins" ;
SKIP FOR Editing
DEFINE BAR 2 OF record PROMPT "\<Edit" ;
KEY CTRL+E, "^E" ;
SKIP FOR Editing
DEFINE BAR 3 OF record PROMPT "\<Save" ;
KEY CTRL+S, "^S" ;
SKIP FOR NOT Editing
DEFINE BAR 4 OF record PROMPT "\<Cancel" ;
KEY CTRL+K, "^K" ;
SKIP FOR NOT Editing
DEFINE BAR 5 OF record PROMPT "\<Delete" ;
KEY CTRL+DEL, "^-Del" ;
SKIP FOR Editing
DEFINE BAR 6 OF record PROMPT "\-"

DEFINE BAR 7 OF record PROMPT "\<First" ;
KEY CTRL+F, "^F" ;
SKIP FOR Editing OR AtTop
DEFINE BAR 8 OF record PROMPT "\<Last" ;
KEY CTRL+L, "^L" ;
SKIP FOR Editing OR AtBottom
DEFINE BAR 9 OF record PROMPT "\<Next" ;
KEY CTRL+DNARROW, "^↓" ;
SKIP FOR Editing or AtBottom
DEFINE BAR 10 OF record PROMPT "\<Previous" ;
KEY CTRL+UPARROW, "^↑" ;
SKIP FOR Editing or AtTop
ON SELECTION POPUP RECORD DO CONTROLS WITH PROMPT()


PROCEDURE Finisher
Done = .T.
CLEAR READ ALL
KEYBOARD [{Ctrl+W}]
```

Modifications to MAIN.PRG

What does it take to make MAIN.PRG in SKYKING function as a menu-driven program? Well, you need a menu loop to repeatedly display the menu and take action based on what is chosen. Other than that, there aren't many changes.

The traditional approach to the menu loop uses either of two approaches. The first emulates a Lotus-style menu, as seen in Listing 5-2. This technique is still very useful, and quite applicable in many cases. A variation on this approach uses a POPUP, as seen in Listing 5-3.

Listing 5-2   The Lotus-style menu loop.

```
DO WHILE .T.

    =DispScrn()

    @ 23, 0    PROMPT [ \<Add ]       MESSAGE [ Add a record]
    @ 23, $+1 PROMPT [ \<Edit ]       MESSAGE [ Edit this record]
    @ 23, $+1 PROMPT [ \<Delete ]     MESSAGE [ Delete this record]
    @ 23, $+1 PROMPT [ \<Next ]       MESSAGE [ Next record]
    @ 23, $+1 PROMPT [ \<Previous ] MESSAGE [ Previous record]
    @ 23, $+1 PROMPT [ \<Search ]     MESSAGE [ Search for a record]
    @ 23, $+1 PROMPT [ E\<xit ]       MESSAGE [ Exit this screen]
    . . .
    Choice = 1
    MENU TO Choice
    Choice = IIF ( Choice = 0 , [X] , SUBSTR ( [AEDNPSX] , Choice , 1 )

DO CASE

    Case Choice = [X]
        EXIT
    Case Choice = [A]
        =AddRec()
    Case Choice = [E]
        =EditRec()
```

```
     Case Choice = [D]
           =DelRec()
     Case Choice = [N]
           IF NOT EOF()
              SKIP
              IF EOF()
                 ?? CHR(7)
                 GO BOTTOM
              ENDIF
           ENDIF
     Case Choice = [P]
           IF NOT BOF()
              SKIP -1
              IF EOF()
                 ?? CHR(7)
                 GO TOP
              ENDIF
           ENDIF
     Case Choice = [S]
           =FindRec()
   ENDCASE


ENDDO
```

Listing 5-3 A variation on the MENU LOOP.
```
DEFINE POPUP MENUPOP FROM 6,30
DEFINE BAR 1 OF MENUPOP PROMPT [\]+PADC([Menu],20)
DEFINE BAR 2 OF MENUPOP PROMPT [\-]
DEFINE BAR 3 OF MENUPOP PROMPT PADC([\<Add a record]        ,20)
DEFINE BAR 4 OF MENUPOP PROMPT PADC([\<Edit this record]    ,20)
DEFINE BAR 5 OF MENUPOP PROMPT PADC([\<Delete this record] ,20)
DEFINE BAR 6 OF MENUPOP PROMPT PADC([\<Next record]         ,20)
DEFINE BAR 7 OF MENUPOP PROMPT PADC([\<Search for a record],20)
DEFINE BAR 8 OF MENUPOP PROMPT PADC([E\<xit this screen]    ,20)
ON SELECTION POPUP MENUPOP DEACTIVATE POPUP MENUPOP

DO WHILE .T.

   =DispScrn()

   ACTIVATE POPUP MENUPOP       && deactivated upon selection

   mPrompt = PROMPT()           && saves the selected bar text

   DO CASE
```

```
     CASE EMPTY ( mPrompt ) OR [Exit] $ mPrompt
          RELEASE POPUP MENUPOP
          EXIT
     CASE [Add] $ mPrompt
          =AddRec()
     CASE [Edit] $ mPrompt
          =EditRec()
     CASE [Next] $ mPrompt
          =NextRec()
     CASE [Prev] $ mPrompt
          =PrevRec()
     CASE [Search] $ mPrompt
          =FindRec()

  ENDCASE

ENDDO
```

Although both of these approaches work exactly as advertised and are very easy to understand, FoxPro has gone out of its way to provide you with a really excellent menu system, and it would be a shame not to avail yourself of its many features, especially the ability to disable menu options.

As it would happen, it's very easy to implement the type of generated menu program that Menu Builder constructs without losing any of the pad and bar-dimming features. Look at Listing 5-4. The menu is defined using DO MAIN.MPR, just as in the event-driven case. But this time, you specify ACTIVATE MENU _MSYSMENU explicitly within the loop, and then pick something from the menu.

The signs that a menu has been activated in FoxPro can be subtle. Typically, the first menu choice changes from black on gray to black on light blue. I prefer to force the menu to appear with one of its menu pop-ups showing. The ACTIVATE MENU subcommand 'BAR (barname) lets you do just that. I used a variable name here, which you could change to the name of the last popup chosen if you wanted to, and if the menu had enough popups to warrant it.

Rather than simply call the program that was chosen, you can borrow from the event-driven approach. If one of the applications is picked, the menu code stuffs the name of the application into the memvar Prog:

```
ON SELECTION BAR 1 OF databases Prog = "AIRCRAFT.SPR"
ON SELECTION BAR 2 OF databases Prog = "OWNERS.SPR"
ON SELECTION BAR 3 OF databases Prog = "MEMBERS.SPR"
```

When you drop through to the next line of code, if one of the database bars was chosen, Prog contains the name of the program to run. If not, Prog is empty.

Listing 5-4 Changes to MAIN.PRG.

```
* Program -ID.....: Main.PRG
* Purpose........: Controls SKY KING application

Counter = 0

SET TALK     OFF
SET CONFIRM OFF
SET SAFETY   OFF
SET DELETED ON

SET COLOR OF SCHEME 1 TO ,,,,,,,,,GR+/B

CLOSE DATABASES

USE DBFS\AIRCRAFT IN 1 ORDER aircraftid
USE DBFS\OWNERS    IN 2 ORDER name
USE DBFS\MEMBERS   IN 3 ORDER memberid
USE DBFS\CHARGES   IN 4 ORDER memberid

Done     = .F.
OKtoSave = .T.
Prog     = []
Editing  = .F.
AtTop    = .F.        && Added to assist in
AtBottom = .F.        && dimming of menu choices.

BrowseColor = [ GR+/B, W+/R,  W+/BG, GR+/B, GR+/B, W+/R, W+/R ]

DO MAIN.MPR

DEFINE    WINDOW FULLSCREEN FROM 1,0 TO WROWS(-2, 79
ACTIVATE WINDOW FULLSCREEN
WTITLE = [ Sky King Flying Club ]
@ WROWS()/2, WCOLS()/2 - LEN(WTITLE)/2 SAY WTITLE
WTITLE = [ Press F10 for Menu ]
@ WROWS()-1, WCOLS()/2 - LEN(WTITLE)/2 SAY WTITLE

LastPad = "Databases"

DO WHILE NOT Done
   ACTIVATE MENU _MSYSMENU PAD ( LastPad )        <=== Call to menu
   IF Done
      LOOP
   ENDIF
   DO ( Prog )
```

```
ENDDO

CLEAR TYPEAHEAD
CLEAR WINDOWS
CLEAR

CLOSE DATABASES
SET SYSMENU TO DEFAULT
RETURN              && or QUIT
```

The user might also have pressed Quit. The three lines after AC
TIVATE MENU _MSYSMENU PAD (LastPad) are used to exit the loop. Again, I
set the value of the logical variable Done to .True. You could have easily said:

```
IF Done
    EXIT
ENDIF
```

Perhaps I read one too many of Yourdon's books on structured programming back when I was doing time in COBOL on mainframes. But this approach actually has another benefit: It lets you allow exit points in other
parts of your application, just by including the lines:

```
Done = .t.
RETURN
```

The instant the control returns, the loop condition DO WHILE NOT DONE
will be evaluated.

Modifications to the screens

Listings 5-5 through 5-7 contain the modified screen programs. The screens
require several changes, but they generally need to have something taken
out, rather than more code added. Notably, you no longer need the READ DE-
ACTIVATE clause, which was used to find the next "on top" window, redisplay
it, and prepare to execute its .SPR. What you do have to do, however, is clear
out the variable Prog, so that the menu's SKIP FOR variables will know that
the program is no longer running. The dimmed menu is shown in Fig. 5-1.

General observations

The above screens, menu, and MAIN program are the entirety of the menu-
driven model. The approach is simpler to code because fewer things can go
wrong.

I've worked on menu-driven programs with dozens of screens, however, and things can get very complex. If your clients are sophisticated
users, they'll probably understand what's easy and what isn't. But if they
don't know anything at all about software, their demands are likely to be
much, much greater.

Listing 5-5 OWNERS.SPR.

```
*
*                           ┌──────────────────────────────────────────┐
*                           ║              OWNERS.SPR                   ║
                            └──────────────────────────────────────────┘

#REGION 0

IF NOT WEXIST("owners") ;
OR UPPER(WTITLE("OWNERS")) == "OWNERS.PJX" ;
OR UPPER(WTITLE("OWNERS")) == "OWNERS.SCX" ;
OR UPPER(WTITLE("OWNERS")) == "OWNERS.MNX" ;
OR UPPER(WTITLE("OWNERS")) == "OWNERS.PRG" ;
OR UPPER(WTITLE("OWNERS")) == "OWNERS.FRX" ;
OR UPPER(WTITLE("OWNERS")) == "OWNERS.QPR"
DEFINE WINDOW owners FROM 6, 0 TO 15,53 TITLE "Owners" ;
        FLOAT NOCLOSE SHADOW NOMINIMIZE DOUBLE COLOR SCHEME 1
ENDIF

IF NOT WEXIST("control") ;
OR UPPER(WTITLE("CONTROL")) == "CONTROL.PJX" ;
OR UPPER(WTITLE("CONTROL")) == "CONTROL.SCX" ;
OR UPPER(WTITLE("CONTROL")) == "CONTROL.MNX" ;
OR UPPER(WTITLE("CONTROL")) == "CONTROL.PRG" ;
OR UPPER(WTITLE("CONTROL")) == "CONTROL.FRX" ;
OR UPPER(WTITLE("CONTROL")) == "CONTROL.QPR"
DEFINE WINDOW control FROM 20, 6 TO 23,63 ;
        FLOAT NOCLOSE NOMINIMIZE COLOR SCHEME 8
ENDIF

*
*                           ┌──────────────────────────────────────────┐
*                           ║    OWNERS/MS-DOS Setup Code - SECTION 2   ║
*                           └──────────────────────────────────────────┘

#REGION 1
SELECT OWNERS
SCATTER MEMVAR
Adding = .F.
```

5-5 Continued.

```
*
*           ┌────────────────────────────────────────────────────────┐
*           │           CONTROL/MS-DOS Setup Code - SECTION 2        ║
*           └────────────────────────────────────────────────────────┘


#REGION 2
REGIONAL LastButton
STORE SPACE(6) TO LastButton
Editing = .F.


*
*           ┌────────────────────────────────────────────────────────┐
*           │           OWNERS/MS-DOS Screen Layout                  ║
*           └────────────────────────────────────────────────────────┘


#REGION 1
IF WVISIBLE("owners")
   ACTIVATE WINDOW owners SAME
   ELSE
   ACTIVATE WINDOW owners NOSHOW
ENDIF
@ 1, 6 SAY "Name"       SIZE 1,4,0
@ 4, 6 SAY "City"       SIZE 1,4,0
@ 5, 3 SAY "Country"    SIZE 1,7,0
@ 2, 3 SAY "Address"    SIZE 1,7,0
@ 4,30 SAY "State"      SIZE 1,5,0
@ 7, 4 SAY "Phones"     SIZE 1,6,0
@ 6,11 SAY "Home"       SIZE 1,4,0
@ 6,25 SAY "Work"       SIZE 1,4,0
@ 6,39 SAY "Cellular"   SIZE 1,8,0


@ 1,11 GET m.name       SIZE 1,40        DEFAULT " " DISABLE
@ 2,11 GET m.address1   SIZE 1,40        DEFAULT " " DISABLE
@ 3,11 GET m.address2   SIZE 1,40        DEFAULT " " DISABLE
@ 4,11 GET m.city       SIZE 1,17        DEFAULT " " DISABLE
@ 4,36 GET m.state      SIZE 1,3         DEFAULT " " DISABLE
```

```
@ 4,41 GET m.zip                    SIZE 1,10        DEFAULT " " DISABLE
@ 5,11 GET m.country    SIZE 1,3        DEFAULT " " DISABLE
@ 7,11 GET m.homephone  SIZE 1,12       DEFAULT " " DISABLE
@ 7,25 GET m.workphone  SIZE 1,12       DEFAULT " " DISABLE
@ 7,39 GET m.cellphone  SIZE 1,12       DEFAULT " " DISABLE
```

```
*
*          ┌────────────────────────────────────────────┐
*          │            CONTROL/MS-DOS Screen Layout      ║
*          └────────────────────────────────────────────┘
```

```
#REGION 2

IF WVISIBLE("control")
   ACTIVATE WINDOW control SAME
  ELSE
   ACTIVATE WINDOW control NOSHOW
ENDIF


@ 0,1 GET m.Add ;
PICTURE "@*HN \<Add"    SIZE 1,10,2     DEFAULT 1
VALID Controls( "Add" )         MESSAGE "Add a record"
@ 0,12 GET m.Edit ;
PICTURE "@*HN \<Edit"   SIZE 1,10,2     DEFAULT 1 ;
VALID Controls ( "Edit" )       MESSAGE "Edit this record"
@ 0,23 GET m.Browse ;
PICTURE "@*HN \<Browse" SIZE 1,10,2     DEFAULT 1 ;
VALID Controls ( "Browse" )     MESSAGE "Display table of records"
@ 0,34 GET m.Save ;
PICTURE "@*HN \<Save"   SIZE 1,10,2     DEFAULT 1 ;
VALID Controls ( "Save" )       MESSAGE "Save on-screen data"
@ 0,45 GET m.Cancel ;
PICTURE "@*HN \<Cancel" SIZE 1,10,2     DEFAULT 1 ;
VALID Controls ( "Cancel" )     MESSAGE "Cancel any changes or addi-
tions"
@ 1,1 GET m.First ;
PICTURE "@*HN \<First"  SIZE 1,10,2     DEFAULT 1 ;
VALID Controls ( "First" )      MESSAGE "Top of file"
@ 1,12 GET m.Last
PICTURE "@*HN \<Last"   SIZE 1,10,2     DEFAULT 1 ;
VALID Controls ( "Last" )       MESSAGE "Bottom of file"
@ 1,23 GET m.Previous ;
```

5-5 Continued.

```
PICTURE "@*HN \<Previous" SIZE 1,10,2    DEFAULT 1 ;
VALID Controls ( "Previous" )    MESSAGE "Previous record"
@ 1,34 GET m.Next ;
PICTURE "@*HN \<Next"    SIZE 1,10,2    DEFAULT 1 ;
VALID Controls ( "Next" )        MESSAGE "Next record"
@ 1,45 GET m.Remove ;

PICTURE "@*HN \<Remove" SIZE 1,10,2    DEFAULT 1 ;
VALID Controls ( "Remove" )      MESSAGE "Remove this window"


IF NOT WVISIBLE("control")
   ACTIVATE WINDOW control
ENDIF
IF NOT WVISIBLE("owners")
   ACTIVATE WINDOW owners
ENDIF


READ CYCLE                    ;
   WHEN        CTRLWHEN()      ;
   ACTIVATE    OWNERACT()


#REGION 0

*
*              ┌──────────────────────────────────────────┐
*              │        OWNERS/MS-DOS Cleanup Code         │
*              └──────────────────────────────────────────┘


#REGION 1

RELEASE WINDOW OWNERS
RELEASE WINDOW CONTROL
```

```
Prog = []          && Reactivate the 'Database' pad on the menu

RETURN

*
*                        CONTROL/MS-DOS Cleanup Code
*

#REGION 2

IF DBF() = [CHARGES]
    SELECT MEMBERS
ENDIF

RETURN

*
*            OWNERS/MS-DOS Supporting Procedures and Functions
*

#REGION 1
FUNCTION Save
OKtoSave = .T.
GATHER MEMVAR MEMO

FUNCTION Browser
BROWSE LAST NORMAL TITLE " Table View "
IF LASTKEY() <> 27
    SCATTER MEMVAR MEMO
ENDIF

FUNCTION Startup
SCATTER MEMVAR MEMO BLANK

FUNCTION Add
APPEND BLANK
GATHER MEMVAR MEMO

FUNCTION Cancel
SCATTER MEMVAR MEMO

FUNCTION Delete
IF CONFIRM ( ' Delete this record? ')
    DELETE
    IF NOT BOF()
```

```
      SKIP -1
    ELSE
      GO TOP
      SKIP
  ENDIF
  SCATTER MEMVAR MEMO
ENDIF
RETURN


*
*           CONTROL/MS-DOS  Supporting  Procedures  and  Functions
*


#REGION 2

PROCEDURE Controls

PARAMETER Choice

DO CASE

  CASE m.Choice = "Add"

      SCATTER MEMVAR BLANK MEMO
      Editing = .T.
      _CUROBJ = 1

  CASE m.Choice = "Edit"

      Editing = .T.
      _CUROBJ = 1

  CASE m.Choice = "Save"

      IF LastButton = "Add"
        DO add IN ( Prog )
       ELSE
        DO save IN ( Prog )
      ENDIF
      IF OkToSave
        WAIT WINDOW NOWAIT "Saving"
        Editing = .F.
      ENDIF

  CASE m.Choice = "Cancel"
```

```
      DO Cancel IN ( Prog )
      WAIT WINDOW NOWAIT "Changes ignored"
      Editing = .F.
   CASE m.Choice = "Browse"

      DO Browser IN ( Prog )
      Editing = .F.

   CASE m.Choice = "First"

      GO TOP
      SCATTER MEMVAR MEMO

   CASE m.Choice = "Previous"

      SKIP -1
      SCATTER MEMVAR MEMO
   CASE m.Choice = "Next"

      SKIP
      SCATTER MEMVAR MEMO

   CASE m.Choice = "Last"

      GO BOTTOM
      SCATTER MEMVAR MEMO

   CASE m.Choice = "Remove"

      CLEAR READ

   CASE m.Choice = "Delete"

      DO delete IN ( Prog )
      GO TOP
      SCATTER MEMVAR MEMO

ENDCASE

DO PushButtons

LastButton = m.Choice

RETURN
```

```
PROCEDURE PushButtons
PRIVATE SaveRec
SaveRec = RECNO()
COUNT TO RecCount
IF RecCount > 0
  GO SaveRec
  IF NOT Editing
    SHOW GET m.Add          ENABLE
    SHOW GET m.Edit         ENABLE
    SHOW GET m.Save         DISABLE
    SHOW GET m.Cancel       DISABLE
    SHOW GET m.Remove       ENABLE
    SHOW GET m.Browse       ENABLE
    SKIP -1
    IF BOF()
      SHOW GET m.First      DISABLE
      SHOW GET m.Previous   DISABLE
      AtTop     = .T.
      AtBottom  = .F.
    ELSE
      SHOW GET m.First      ENABLE
      SHOW GET m.Previous   ENABLE
      AtTop     = .F.
    ENDIF
    GO SaveRec
    SKIP
    IF EOF()
      SHOW GET m.Next       DISABLE
      SHOW GET m.Last       DISABLE
      AtTop     = .F.
      AtBottom  = .T.
    ELSE
      SHOW GET m.Next       ENABLE
      SHOW GET m.Last       ENABLE
      AtBottom  = .F.
    ENDIF
    GO SaveRec
  ELSE
    SHOW GET m.Add          DISABLE
    SHOW GET m.Edit         DISABLE
    SHOW GET m.Save         ENABLE
    SHOW GET m.Cancel       ENABLE
    SHOW GET m.Remove       DISABLE
    SHOW GET m.First        DISABLE
    SHOW GET m.Previous     DISABLE
```

5-5 Continued.

```
      SHOW GET m.Next          DISABLE
      SHOW GET m.Last          DISABLE
      SHOW GET m.Browse        DISABLE
   ENDIF
ELSE
  AtBottom  = .T.
  AtTop     = .T.
   SHOW GET m.First            DISABLE
   SHOW GET m.Previous         DISABLE
   SHOW GET m.Next             DISABLE
   SHOW GET m.Last             DISABLE
   SHOW GET m.Browse           DISABLE
   SHOW GET m.Edit             DISABLE
   IF Editing
      SHOW GET m.Add           DISABLE
      SHOW GET m.Remove        DISABLE
      SHOW GET m.Save          ENABLE
      SHOW GET m.Cancel        ENABLE
   ELSE
      SHOW GET m.Add           ENABLE
      SHOW GET m.Remove        ENABLE
      SHOW GET m.Save          DISABLE
      SHOW GET m.Cancel        DISABLE
   ENDIF
ENDIF


* Disable all GETS in the current READ Window if not in EDIT mode
ReadWind = LEFT ( Prog , AT ( '.' , Prog ) -1 )

IF NOT Editing
  SHOW GETS WINDOW (ReadWind) DISABLE
 ELSE
  SHOW GETS WINDOW (ReadWind) ENABLE ONLY
ENDIF


RETURN


FUNCTION CTRLWHEN      && Read Level When
* When Code from screen: CONTROL
#REGION 2

DO PushButtons
```

5-5 Continued.

```
FUNCTION OWNERACT        && Read Level Activate
* Activate Code from screen: OWNERS
#REGION 1


ACTIVATE WINDOW OWNERS  TOP
ACTIVATE WINDOW CONTROL TOP
```

Listing 5-6 AIRCRAFT.SPR.

```
*
*     ┌─────────────────────────────────────────────────────────┐
*     │                     AIRCRAFT.SPR                          │
*     └─────────────────────────────────────────────────────────┘

#REGION 0

IF NOT WEXIST("aircraft") ;
OR UPPER(WTITLE("AIRCRAFT")) == "AIRCRAFT.PJX" ;
OR UPPER(WTITLE("AIRCRAFT")) == "AIRCRAFT.SCX" ;
OR UPPER(WTITLE("AIRCRAFT")) == "AIRCRAFT.MNX" ;
OR UPPER(WTITLE("AIRCRAFT")) == "AIRCRAFT.PRG" ;
OR UPPER(WTITLE("AIRCRAFT")) == "AIRCRAFT.FRX" ;
OR UPPER(WTITLE("AIRCRAFT")) == "AIRCRAFT.QPR"

DEFINE WINDOW aircraft FROM 2, 10 TO 14,76 TITLE "AIRCRAFT" ;

        FLOAT NOCLOSE SHADOW NOMINIMIZE DOUBLE COLOR SCHEME 1
ENDIF

IF NOT WEXIST("control") ;
OR UPPER(WTITLE("CONTROL")) == "CONTROL.PJX" ;
OR UPPER(WTITLE("CONTROL")) == "CONTROL.SCX" ;
OR UPPER(WTITLE("CONTROL")) == "CONTROL.MNX" ;
OR UPPER(WTITLE("CONTROL")) == "CONTROL.PRG" ;
OR UPPER(WTITLE("CONTROL")) == "CONTROL.FRX" ;
OR UPPER(WTITLE("CONTROL")) == "CONTROL.QPR"

DEFINE WINDOW control FROM 20, 7 TO 23,64 ;
        FLOAT NOCLOSE NOMINIMIZE COLOR SCHEME 8
ENDIF
```

```
*
*                    AIRCRAFT/MS-DOS Setup Code - SECTION 2
*
```

#REGION 1

```
SELECT AIRCRAFT
SCATTER MEMVAR
Adding = .F.
```

```
*
*                    CONTROL/MS-DOS Setup Code - SECTION 2
*
```

#REGION 2

```
REGIONAL LastButton
STORE SPACE(6) TO LastButton
Editing = .F.
```

```
*
*                    AIRCRAFT/MS-DOS Screen Layout
*
```

#REGION 1

```
IF WVISIBLE("aircraft")
   ACTIVATE WINDOW aircraft SAME
 ELSE
   ACTIVATE WINDOW aircraft NOSHOW
ENDIF
```

```
@  1,13 SAY "Make"              SIZE 1,4, 0
@  1,25 SAY "Model"             SIZE 1,5, 0
@  1,50 SAY "Colors"            SIZE 1,6, 0
@  4,48 SAY "Parking"           SIZE 1,7, 0
@  4,21 SAY "Engines"           SIZE 1,7, 0
@  4,36 SAY "Seats"             SIZE 1,5, 0
@ 10, 4 SAY "Owner"             SIZE 1,5, 0
@  1, 3 SAY "ID"                        SIZE 1,2, 0
@  7, 4 SAY "Last annual"       SIZE 1,11, 0
@  8, 5 SAY "Total time"        SIZE 1,10, 0
@  4, 4 SAY "Hourly rate"       SIZE 1,11, 0
@  7,47 SAY "Left"              SIZE 1,4, 0
```

```
@  7,34 SAY "Hours since"        SIZE 1,11, 0
@  8,35 SAY "major O/H:"         SIZE 1,10, 0
@  8,46 SAY "Right"             SIZE 1,5, 0
@  3,0 TO 3,64
@  6,0 TO 6,64
@  9,0 TO 9,64
@  1,38 SAY "Year"             SIZE 1,4,0
@  2, 3 GET m.aircraftid        SIZE 1,6 DEFA " " WHEN StuffID() DISABLE
@  2,13 GET m.make             SIZE 1,8  DEFA " " FUNC "!" VALID ACTYPE() DISABLE
@  2,25 GET m.model            SIZE 1,6  DEFA " " DISABLE
@  2,38 GET m.Year             SIZE 1,4  DEFA " " PICTURE "####" DISABLE
@  2,48 GET m.colors           SIZE 1,10 DEFA " " DISABLE
@  5, 8 GET m.hourlyrate        SIZE 1,3 DEFA 0    DISABLE
@  5,24 GET m.engines          SIZE 1,1  DEFA " " DISABLE
@  5,37 GET m.seats            SIZE 1,3  DEFA " " DISABLE
@  5,48 GET m.parking          SIZE 1,4  DEFA " " DISABLE
@  7,16 GET m.lastannual        SIZE 1,8 DEFA {  /  / } DISABLE
@  7,52 GET m.smoh             SIZE 1,6  DEFA 0    DISABLE
@  8,16 GET m.totaltime         SIZE 1,6  DEFA 0    DISABLE
@  8,52 GET m.smohright         SIZE 1,6  DEFA 0    DISABLE
@ 10,10 GET m.owner            SIZE 1,40 DEFA " " DISABLE

*
*            ┌──────────────────────────────────────────────┐
*            │         CONTROL/MS-DOS Screen Layout         │
             └──────────────────────────────────────────────┘


#REGION 2

IF WVISIBLE("control")
   ACTIVATE WINDOW control SAME
   ELSE
   ACTIVATE WINDOW control NOSHOW
ENDIF

@ 0,1 GET m.Add ;
PICTURE "@*HN \<Add"    SIZE 1,10,2    DEFAULT 1
VALID Controls( "Add" )         MESSAGE "Add a record"
@ 0,12 GET m.Edit ;
PICTURE "@*HN \<Edit"   SIZE 1,10,2    DEFAULT 1 ;
VALID Controls ( "Edit" )       MESSAGE "Edit this record"
@ 0,23 GET m.Browse ;
PICTURE "@*HN \<Browse" SIZE 1,10,2    DEFAULT 1 ;
```

```
VALID Controls ( "Browse" )        MESSAGE "Display table of records"
@ 0,34 GET m.Save ;
PICTURE "@*HN \<Save"   SIZE 1,10,2    DEFAULT 1 ;
VALID Controls ( "Save" )          MESSAGE "Save on-screen data"
@ 0,45 GET m.Cancel ;
PICTURE "@*HN \<Cancel" SIZE 1,10,2    DEFAULT 1 ;
VALID Controls ( "Cancel" )        MESSAGE "Cancel any changes or additions"
@ 1,1 GET m.First ;
PICTURE "@*HN \<First"  SIZE 1,10,2    DEFAULT 1 ;
VALID Controls ( "First" )         MESSAGE "Top of file"
@ 1,12 GET m.Last ;
PICTURE "@*HN \<Last"   SIZE 1,10,2    DEFAULT 1 ;
VALID Controls ( "Last" )          MESSAGE "Bottom of file"
@ 1,23 GET m.Previous ;
PICTURE "@*HN \<Previous" SIZE 1,10,2   DEFAULT 1 ;
VALID Controls ( "Previous" )    MESSAGE "Previous record"
@ 1,34 GET m.Next ;
PICTURE "@*HN \<Next"   SIZE 1,10,2    DEFAULT 1 ;
VALID Controls ( "Next" )          MESSAGE "Next record"
@ 1,45 GET m.Remove ;
PICTURE "@*HN \<Remove" SIZE 1,10,2    DEFAULT 1 ;

VALID Controls ( "Remove" )        MESSAGE "Remove this window"


IF NOT WVISIBLE("control")
   ACTIVATE WINDOW control
ENDIF
IF NOT WVISIBLE("aircraft")
   ACTIVATE WINDOW aircraft
ENDIF

READ CYCLE                          ;

WHEN      CTRLWHEN() ;

ACTIVATE PLANEACT()

#REGION 0


*
*     ┌──────────────────────────────────────────────┐
*     │          AIRCRAFT/MS-DOS Cleanup Code          │
*     └──────────────────────────────────────────────┘
```

5-6 Continued.

```
#REGION 1

RELEASE WINDOW AIRCRAFT
RELEASE WINDOW CONTROL

Prog = []        && Reactivate the 'Database' pad on the menu

*
*              CONTROL/MS-DOS Cleanup Code
*

#REGION 2

IF DBF() = [CHARGES]
    SELECT MEMBERS
ENDIF
*
*          AIRCRAFT/MS-DOS Supporting Procedures and Functions
*

#REGION 1

FUNCTION Save
OKtoSave = .T.
GATHER MEMVAR MEMO

FUNCTION Browser
BROWSE LAST NORMAL TITLE " Table View "
IF LASTKEY() <> 27
    SCATTER MEMVAR MEMO
ENDIF
```

5-6 Continued.

```
FUNCTION Startup
SCATTER MEMVAR MEMO BLANK

FUNCTION Add
APPEND BLANK
GATHER MEMVAR MEMO

FUNCTION Cancel
SCATTER MEMVAR MEMO

FUNCTION Delete
IF CONFIRM ( ' Delete this record? ' )
   DELETE
   IF NOT BOF()
      SKIP -1
    ELSE
      GO TOP
      SKIP
   ENDIF
   SCATTER MEMVAR MEMO
ENDIF

*
*        CONTROL/MS-DOS Supporting Procedures and Functions
*


#REGION 2
PROCEDURE Controls

*** SAME AS IN PREVIOUS SCREEN ***

PROCEDURE PushButtons

*** SAME AS IN PREVIOUS SCREEN ***

*
*        STUFFID              m.aircraftid WHEN
*


FUNCTION STUFFID    && m.aircraftid WHEN
#REGION 1
IF EMPTY ( m.AircraftID )
   KEYBOARD "N"
ENDIF
```

5-6 Continued.

```
*
*    ┌─────────────────────────────────────────────────────┐
*    │  ACTYPE                     m.make VALID             │
*    │                                                       │
     └─────────────────────────────────────────────────────┘

FUNCTION ACTYPE     && m.make VALID
#REGION 1
IF TRIM(m.Make) $ [CESSNA/MOONEY/PIPER /BEECH /]
    RETURN
ENDIF
DEFINE POPUP MAKES FROM $,$+10 SHADOW
DEFINE BAR 1 OF MAKES PROMPT [CESSNA  ]
DEFINE BAR 2 OF MAKES PROMPT [PIPER   ]
DEFINE BAR 3 OF MAKES PROMPT [MOONEY  ]
DEFINE BAR 4 OF MAKES PROMPT [BEECH   ]
ON SELECTION POPUP MAKES DEACTIVATE POPUP MAKES
ACTIVATE POPUP MAKES
m.Make = PROMPT()
RELEASE POPUP MAKES
RETURN IIF ( EMPTY ( m.Make ) , .F. , .T. )    && Can't leave empty

*
*    ┌─────────────────────────────────────────────────────┐
*    │  CTRLWHEN                Read-Level When             │
*    │                                                       │
     └─────────────────────────────────────────────────────┘

FUNCTION CTRLWHEN     && Read-Level When
* When Code from screen: CONTROL
#REGION 2

DO PushButtons

*
*    ┌─────────────────────────────────────────────────────┐
*    │  PLANEACT                Read-Level Activate         │
*    │                                                       │
     └─────────────────────────────────────────────────────┘

FUNCTION PLANEACT     && Read-Level Activate
* Activate Code from screen: AIRCRAFT
#REGION 1

ACTIVATE WINDOW AIRCRAFT TOP
ACTIVATE WINDOW CONTROL  TOP
```

Listing 5-7 MEMBERS.SPR.

```
*
*                                  MEMBERS.SPR
*

#REGION 0

*
*                             MS-DOS Window definitions
*

IF NOT WEXIST("members") ;
OR UPPER(WTITLE("MEMBERS")) == "MEMBERS.PJX" ;
OR UPPER(WTITLE("MEMBERS")) == "MEMBERS.SCX" ;
OR UPPER(WTITLE("MEMBERS")) == "MEMBERS.MNX" ;
OR UPPER(WTITLE("MEMBERS")) == "MEMBERS.PRG" ;
OR UPPER(WTITLE("MEMBERS")) == "MEMBERS.FRX" ;
OR UPPER(WTITLE("MEMBERS")) == "MEMBERS.QPR"
DEFINE WINDOW members FROM 1, 0 TO 11,55 TITLE "Members" ;

        FLOAT NOCLOSE SHADOW NOMINIMIZE DOUBLE COLOR SCHEME 1
ENDIF

IF NOT WEXIST("control") ;
OR UPPER(WTITLE("CONTROL")) == "CONTROL.PJX" ;
OR UPPER(WTITLE("CONTROL")) == "CONTROL.SCX" ;
OR UPPER(WTITLE("CONTROL")) == "CONTROL.MNX" ;
OR UPPER(WTITLE("CONTROL")) == "CONTROL.PRG" ;
OR UPPER(WTITLE("CONTROL")) == "CONTROL.FRX" ;
OR UPPER(WTITLE("CONTROL")) == "CONTROL.QPR"

DEFINE WINDOW control FROM 20, 7 TO 23,64 ;

        FLOAT NOCLOSE NOMINIMIZE COLOR SCHEME 8
ENDIF

*
*                      MEMBERS/MS-DOS Setup Code - SECTION 2
*

#REGION 1
```

5-7 Continued.

```
SELECT  CHARGES
SET ORDER TO memberid

SELECT  MEMBERS
SCATTER MEMVAR

SET RELATION TO memberid INTO charges

Adding = .F.

*
*                    CONTROL/MS-DOS Setup Code - SECTION 2
*


#REGION 2

REGIONAL LastButton
STORE SPACE(6) TO LastButton
Editing = .F.

*
*                    MEMBERS/MS-DOS Screen Layout
*


#REGION 1

IF WVISIBLE("members")
   ACTIVATE WINDOW members SAME
  ELSE
   ACTIVATE WINDOW members NOSHOW
ENDIF

@ 0,12 GET m.memberid    SIZE 1,10 DEFAULT " "
@ 2,7 SAY "Name"         SIZE 1,4, 0
@ 2,12 GET m.name        SIZE 1,40 DEFAULT " "
@ 3,12 GET m.address1    SIZE 1,40 DEFAULT " "
```

```
@ 4,12 GET m.address2    SIZE 1,40 DEFAULT " "
@ 5,7 SAY "City"         SIZE 1,4, 0
@ 5,12 GET m.city        SIZE 1,14 DEFAULT " "
@ 5,28 SAY "State"       SIZE 1,5, 0
@ 5,34 GET m.state       SIZE 1,3  DEFAULT " "
@ 5,38 SAY "Zip"         SIZE 1,3, 0
@ 5,42 GET m.zip         SIZE 1,10 DEFAULT " "
@ 6,4 SAY "Country"      SIZE 1,7, 0
@ 6,12 GET m.country     SIZE 1,3  DEFAULT " "
@ 7,4 SAY "License"      SIZE 1,7, 0
@ 7,12 GET m.license     SIZE 1,15 DEFAULT " "
@ 8,24 GET m.medicaldat  SIZE 1,8  DEFAULT {  /  / }
@ 8,45 GET m.balancedue  SIZE 1,7  DEFAULT 0
@ 3,4 SAY "Address"      SIZE 1,7, 0
@ 7,37 SAY "Outstanding" SIZE 1,12, 0
@ 8,37 SAY "Balance"     SIZE 1,7, 0
@ 8,4 SAY "Medical exam due on" SIZE 1,19, 0
@ 0,2 SAY "Member ID"    SIZE 1,9, 0


*
*              ┌──────────────────────────────────────────┐
*              │        CONTROL/MS-DOS Screen Layout        │
               └──────────────────────────────────────────┘


#REGION 2

IF WVISIBLE("control")
   ACTIVATE WINDOW control SAME
  ELSE
   ACTIVATE WINDOW control NOSHOW
ENDIF


@ 0,1 GET m.Add ;
PICTURE "@*HN \<Add"    SIZE 1,10,2    DEFAULT 1
VALID Controls( "Add" )          MESSAGE "Add a record"
@ 0,12 GET m.Edit ;
PICTURE "@*HN \<Edit"   SIZE 1,10,2    DEFAULT 1 ;
VALID Controls ( "Edit" )        MESSAGE "Edit this record"
@ 0,23 GET m.Browse ;
PICTURE "@*HN \<Browse" SIZE 1,10,2    DEFAULT 1 ;
VALID Controls ( "Browse" )      MESSAGE "Display table of records"
@ 0,34 GET m.Save ;
PICTURE "@*HN \<Save"   SIZE 1,10,2    DEFAULT 1 ;
VALID Controls ( "Save" )        MESSAGE "Save on-screen data"
```

```
@ 0,45 GET m.Cancel ;
PICTURE "@*HN \<Cancel" SIZE 1,10,2     DEFAULT 1 ;
VALID Controls ( "Cancel" )     MESSAGE "Cancel any changes or additions"
@ 1,1 GET m.First ;
PICTURE "@*HN \<First"  SIZE 1,10,2     DEFAULT 1 ;
VALID Controls ( "First" )      MESSAGE "Top of file"
@ 1,12 GET m.Last ;
PICTURE "@*HN \<Last"   SIZE 1,10,2     DEFAULT 1 ;
VALID Controls ( "Last" )       MESSAGE "Bottom of file"
@ 1,23 GET m.Previous ;
PICTURE "@*HN \<Previous" SIZE 1,10,2   DEFAULT 1 ;
VALID Controls ( "Previous" )   MESSAGE "Previous record"
@ 1,34 GET m.Next ;
PICTURE "@*HN \<Next"   SIZE 1,10,2     DEFAULT 1 ;
VALID Controls ( "Next" )       MESSAGE "Next record"
@ 1,45 GET m.Remove ;
PICTURE "@*HN \<Remove" SIZE 1,10,2     DEFAULT 1 ;
VALID Controls ( "Remove" )     MESSAGE "Remove this window"


IF NOT WVISIBLE("control")
    ACTIVATE WINDOW control
ENDIF

IF NOT WVISIBLE("members")
    ACTIVATE WINDOW members
ENDIF

READ CYCLE ;

WHEN            CTRLWHEN() ;

ACTIVATE        MEMBRACT()

#REGION 0

*
*       ┌──────────────────────────────────────────────────────┐
*       │            MEMBERS/MS-DOS Cleanup Code                │
        └──────────────────────────────────────────────────────┘

#REGION 1
RELEASE WINDOW MEMBERS
RELEASE WINDOW Related
RELEASE WINDOW Control
```

```
Prog = []          && Reactivate the 'Database' pad on the menu
```

```
*
*    ┌──────────────────────────────────────────────────────────┐
*    │               CONTROL/MS-DOS Cleanup Code                │
*    └──────────────────────────────────────────────────────────┘
```

```
#REGION 2
IF DBF() = [CHARGES]
   SELECT MEMBERS
ENDIF
```

```
RETURN
```

```
*
*    ┌──────────────────────────────────────────────────────────┐
*    │       MEMBERS/MS-DOS Supporting Procedures and Functions  │
*    └──────────────────────────────────────────────────────────┘
```

```
#REGION 1
FUNCTION Save
```

```
OKtoSave = .T.
```

```
GATHER MEMVAR MEMO
RETURN
```

```
FUNCTION Browser
   BROWSE LAST NORMAL TITLE " Table View "
   IF LASTKEY() <> 27
      SCATTER MEMVAR MEMO
   ENDIF
RETURN
```

```
FUNCTION Startup
   SCATTER MEMVAR MEMO BLANK
RETURN
```

```
FUNCTION Add
```

```
APPEND BLANK
```

```
GATHER MEMVAR MEMO
RETURN
```

```
FUNCTION Cancel
```

```
SCATTER MEMVAR MEMO
RETURN

FUNCTION Delete

IF CONFIRM ( ' Delete this record? ' )
* New code for "Referential integrity"
   HasKids = SEEK ( MEMBERS.memberid, "CHARGES" )
   GoAhead = .T.
   IF HasKids
      IF NOT CONFIRM ( ' Delete related charges also? ' )
         GoAhead = .F.
      ENDIF
   ENDIF
   IF NOT GoAhead
      RETURN
   ENDIF
   IF HasKids
      SELECT Charges
      DELETE FOR memberid = MEMBERS.memberid
      SELECT MEMBERS
   ENDIF

   DELETE
   IF NOT BOF()
      SKIP -1
    ELSE
      GO TOP
      SKIP
   ENDIF
   SCATTER MEMVAR MEMO
ENDIF


*
*     ┌─────────────────────────────────────────────────────┐
*     │  CONTROL/MS-DOS Supporting Procedures and Functions  │
*     └─────────────────────────────────────────────────────┘

#REGION 2
PROCEDURE Controls

*** SAME AS IN PREVIOUS SCREENS ***

PROCEDURE PushButtons
```

5-7 Continued.

*** SAME AS IN PREVIOUS SCREENS ***

```
*
*   ┌─┬───────────────────────────────────────────────────┬─┐
*   │ │ CTRLWHEN            Read Level When                │ │
*   └─┴───────────────────────────────────────────────────┴─┘


FUNCTION CTRLWHEN
* When Code from screen: CONTROL
#REGION 2

DO PushButtons

*
*   ┌─┬───────────────────────────────────────────────────┬─┐
*   │ │ MEMBRACT            Read Level Activate            │ │
*   └─┴───────────────────────────────────────────────────┴─┘


FUNCTION MEMBRACT      && Read Level Activate
* Activate Code from screen: MEMBERS
#REGION 1

IF NOT WEXIST('Related Charges Table')
    DEFINE  WINDOW charges FROM 12,3 TO 20,76 DOUBLE SHADOW FLOAT GROW CLOSE
    SELECT   CHARGES
    BROWSE                          ;
      COLOR ( BrowseColor )         ;
      NOWAIT                        ;
      TITLE [Related Charges Table] ;
      WINDOW charges                ;
      FOR memberid = MEMBERS.memberid
    RELEASE WINDOW charges
    SELECT MEMBERS
ENDIF


* Note that the word TABLE is required in the title of each BROWSE window

ACTIVATE SCREEN MEMBERS TOP
ACTIVATE WINDOW Related TOP
ACTIVATE SCREEN CONTROL TOP
```

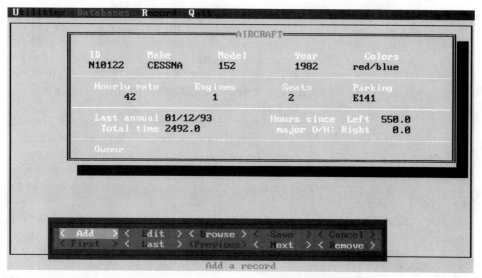

Figure 5-1 Dimmed Databases menu pad when AIRCRAFT.SPR is active.

Remember the film *Star Trek XXXIV* or whatever, where they go back in time to the 20th century. Scotty needs a computer, so his host points to a Macintosh. "Computer," Scotty intones in his best brogue. Nothing. Embarrassed, his host points to the mouse. Sheepishly, Scotty picks up the mouse like a microphone and repeats the command, "Computer." That's what some of my clients are like.

I've sacrificed hours of my life to people who asked in an offhanded manner, "Can you make it do such-and-such?" Of course I can. I take it as a personal challenge. But when they get the bill two days later, they're shocked. I guess what they meant was, "Can you make it do such-and-such at no cost whatsoever?"

Menu-driven programming is one of your defenses against this kind of environment and this kind of computer user. If you spend two days writing a prototype that your client decides not to pay for, you're out two days. If you spend two months writing it, you lose your house. I've been there. Literally.

Summary

Menu control, especially when you have access to FoxPro's elegant system menu, is a clean, straightforward way to manage applications. Coding is simple and relatively inexpensive, and many of the complications of event-driven programming simply can't happen.

I'm afraid that avoidance of menu-driven programming has become an emotional issue. I've even read that you should never, *ever* write menu-driven programs because they're always in hard execution, instead of being in a wait state. That particular comment was in the official FoxPro documentation for version 2. I spent six months feeling guilty about writing programs that were always in hard execution, until I figured out that I *wanted* my programs to be in hard execution.

Wait states are for interrupting. Interrupting means saving and restoring states. Saving and restoring states means more things can go wrong. And more possible mistakes means more time and more money. Some of my customers are—how do I put it delicately?—cheap. Menu-driven applications are cheaper. Methodological elegance is not the sole criterion for the choice of technique.

The option to write menu-driven code instead of event-driven code is yours. If you have to develop event-driven programs, either because users request them or because the application demands that you do so, the model presented in chapters 3 and 4 will provide a foundation. If you need additional insights into dealing with the complications that the event-driven approach can lead to, I recommend the work of any of the gurus mentioned earlier in this chapter. But please consider the menu-driven model. It acknowledges Murphy's Law.

6
List management
in screen design

Now that you have two ways to control software, let's focus for a while on a few other topics common to database applications. The most important issue in many applications is the look and feel of the screen. I've had clients whose principal goal was to see their personal design ideas implemented. I mean, if you've built a successful business, why can't you design software? I've been asked to do things that were nearly impossible, but sometimes the ideas are quite interesting. They just don't happen to coincide with FoxPro's command and function list.

New design ideas sometimes compel you to do things in a different way, so you start down the path, not always sure of what you'll end up with. In some cases, you reach a dead end; other times, you strike gold.

Designing your own screen-display functions

Sometimes I write functions that work in a particular context, using hard-coded field names and text. Occasionally, such functions can be rewritten in a generic form so they can be reused in other contexts with no recoding. This chapter contains one of each: The first is a hard-coded password system with a unique twist on scrolled detail lines that you code specifically for your environment. The second is a generic, multiline pick-list function that you can use in any of your applications. The former looks a lot like BROWSE, and the latter a little like DEFINE POPUP...MULTISELECT. With FoxPro's excellent BROWSE and DEFINE POPUP functions, you wouldn't think you'd have to write your own tools. Well, you don't—unless you want complete control over the result.

Scrolling lists

FoxPro's @ GET FROM (*list*) function, which continuously displays part of an array-based list for editing, can be used to develop a number of interesting screen designs. It scrolls an array or popup you can build with a WHEN clause and process with a VALID clause.

Scrolling lists can be incorporated into many designs besides simple BROWSEs. Order entry, with a header and footer area and a scrolling list in the middle, is one such application. Many significant vertical market database applications begin with an operator standing by to take your order. Data thus collected turns into invoices, inventory pull tickets, shipping memos, and so on. So this is the starting point for a lot of custom programming. Order-entry screens have detail lines, and detail lines have to be entered and edited. BROWSE looks like just the ticket, but sometimes it is and sometimes it isn't.

In my last book, *FoxPro 2.0 Applications*, @ GET FROM (*list*) provided the basis for an easy way to use Screen Builder to write an order-entry system. In this chapter, you'll use some of the same concepts to develop a complete password system. If you're interested in the order-entry application, give me a call.

A password system

Password systems are a common request. Unfortunately, clients often have unbelievably complex ideas about how a computer should control access to information. Their requirements get a lot simpler when they find out how much it's going to cost.

I think Hollywood might have romanticized this password business somewhat. When I watch 15-year-olds get into Cheyenne Mountain's computers, I start to doubt that I can keep a determined snooper out of the most accessible database in the world. Computer security systems are sometimes as successful as car-door locks, keeping out everyone except the thieves. Still, it turns out to be relatively easy to build an inexpensive security system that makes it a little harder for employees to dip into the cash register. Surely peace of mind is worth an hour's programming. And that's about how long it should take to modify this set of functions to fit your application.

Access functions

I needed a pair of functions to either allow or deny access to various parts of my application. Those functions look in a table of users, in which each functional area is represented by a field name that contains a Y if the users have access and is blank if they don't. I needed two functions because, although you don't want users to have to enter their passwords each time they enter a function, some cases require a password (such as month-end closings or changing a password). Except for the fact that one requires a password, the two functions are similar in other respects. They're shown in Listings 6-1 and 6-2.

Listing 6-1 FUNCTION GetAcces (requires a password).

```
* Program -ID.....: HasAccess
* Purpose........: Ensure that user has access to requested area
PARAMETERS Function        && name of one of the fields in PASSWORD.DBF

Passed = .T.
Failed = NOT Passed

IF NOT TRIM(UPPER(Function)) $ ;
    "CASHREG,NONSALES,VOID,BACKROOM,REPORTS,CLOSE"
    WAIT WINDOW function + ' - invalid functional area ID' TIMEOUT 1
    SUSPEND
ENDIF

IF NOT USED ( [PASSWORD] )
    SELECT 0
    fil = [PASSWORD]
    USE ( fil )
 ELSE
    SELECT PASSWORD
ENDIF
    m.UserID = mUserID       && Use copy of active UserID
IF m.UserID = [SUPER]        && Supervisor has access to everything
    RETURN Passed
ENDIF
IF EMPTY ( m.UserID )
    =Alarm()
    WAIT WINDOW [ ** No user logged in - cancelled ** ]  TIMEOUT 2
    RETURN Failed
ENDIF
LOCATE FOR PASSWORD.UserID = m.UserID
IF NOT FOUND()
    IF mUserID <> [SUPER]
       =Alarm()
       WAIT WINDOW [ ** User ID not on file - cancelled ** ] TIMEOUT 2
       RETURN Failed
    ENDIF
ENDIF
IF EMPTY ( &Function )
    =Alarm()
```

6-1 Continued.

```
     WAIT WINDOW [Access denied]  TIMEOUT 1
     RETURN Failed
ENDIF


RETURN Passed              && Default
```

Listing 6-2 FUNCTION HasAcces (doesn't require a password).

```
* Program -ID.....: GetAccess
* Purpose........: Ensure that user knows password for his ID

PARAMETERS Function          && name of one of the fields in PASSWORD.DBF

Passed = .T.
Failed = NOT Passed


* PROGRAMMER TRAP - REMOVE IN PRODUCTION...
IF NOT TRIM(UPPER(Function)) $ ;
  "CASHREG,NONSALES,VOID,BACKROOM,REPORTS,CLOSE,NEWUSER"
    WAIT WINDOW function + ' - invalid functional area ID' TIMEOUT 2
    SUSPEND
ENDIF

m.UserID = mUserID            && Use copy of active UserID

IF Function <> 'NEWUSER' AND Function <> 'CASHREG'
    IF m.UserID = [SUPER]     && Supervisor has access to everything
       RETURN Passed
    ENDIF
ENDIF

IF NOT USED ( [PASSWORD] )
    SELECT 0
    fil = [PASSWORD]
    USE ( fil )
 ELSE
    SELECT PASSWORD
ENDIF

LOCATE FOR PASSWORD.USERID = m.UserID

IF     NOT EMPTY ( Function ) ;
   AND Function <> 'CASHREG'  ;
   AND Function <> 'NEWUSER'  ;
   AND FOUND()
```

```
    RETURN Passed
ENDIF


*******  NOT FOUND - ASK FOR USERID AND PASSWORD  ********

DEFINE    WINDOW PASSWORD FROM 14,29 TO 17,51 IN SCREEN DOUBLE SHADOW
ACTIVATE WINDOW PASSWORD

@ 0,1 SAY [   UserID: ] GET m.UserID DEFAULT SPACE(5) FUNCTION [!]
SET  CONFIRM ON
READ COLOR ,W+/R TIMEOUT 30
SET  CONFIRM OFF

IF READKEY(1) = 6
   WAIT WINDOW [ *** Timeout - logging ] + mUserID + [ out *** ] TIMEOUT 2
   mUserID = SPACE(5)
   RELEASE WINDOW PASSWORD
   RETURN TO MASTER
ENDIF


IF m.UserID = [SUPER]
   mUserID  = SPACE(5)
ENDIF


IF EMPTY ( m.UserID )
   =Alarm( )
   RELEASE WINDOW PASSWORD
   RETURN Failed
ENDIF


IF Function <> 'NEWUSER'

   IF m.UserID = mUserID          && no change since last access
      RELEASE WINDOW PASSWORD
      RETURN
   ENDIF

   LOCATE FOR PASSWORD.USERID = m.UserID

   IF NOT FOUND( )
      IF mUserID <> [SUPER]
         =Alarm( )
         WAIT WINDOW [ ** Requires supervisor access - cancelled ** ] ;
```

```
            TIMEOUT 2
         RELEASE WINDOW PASSWORD
         RETURN Failed
      ENDIF
      RELEASE WINDOW PASSWORD
      DO Security
      RETURN Passed
   ENDIF

 ELSE

   LOCATE FOR PASSWORD.USERID = m.UserID

ENDIF

SET CURSOR OFF
@ 1,1 SAY [Password: ]
m.PassWord = []

DO WHILE LEN(m.PassWord) < 8

*-Wait for a keystroke
   a=inkey(0)

*-If backspace, remove any available trailing character
   IF a=127 OR a=19
      IF LEN(m.Password) > 0
         m.PassWord = LEFT ( m.PassWord , LEN ( m.PassWord )  2D 1 )
         =Stars()
         LOOP
      ENDIF
   ENDIF

*-RETURN or ESCAPE exits
   IF a = 13 OR a = 27
      EXIT
   ENDIF

*-Alpha only
  IF a < ASC([A]) OR a > ASC([z])
     ?? CHR(7)
     LOOP
  ENDIF

*-Convert to uppercase
```

6-2 Continued.

```
   IF a > 96                          && uppercase conversion
      a = a - 32
   ENDIF

   m.PassWord = m.PassWord + CHR(a)

   =Stars()

   IF LEN ( m.PassWord ) = 8
      EXIT
   ENDIF

ENDDO

IF EMPTY ( m.PassWord )
   =Alarm()
   RELEASE WINDOW PASSWORD
   RETURN Failed
ENDIF

SET CURSOR ON

Left  = LEN(ALLTRIM(m.Password))
Right = 8 - Left
m.PassWord = m.PassWord + SPACE(Right)

IF ENCRYPT ( m.PassWord ) <> PASSWORD.Password
   =Alarm()
   RELEASE WINDOW PASSWORD
   RETURN Failed
ENDIF

IF EMPTY ( &Function )
   =Alarm()
   WAIT WINDOW [Access denied] TIMEOUT 1
   RELEASE WINDOW PASSWORD
   RETURN Failed
ENDIF

mUserID = m.UserID

RELEASE WINDOW PASSWORD

RETURN Passed                        && okay to continue
```

```
FUNCTION ENCRYPT
PARAMETERS n
sw=0
a=1
str=[]
DO WHILE a <= LEN(n)
    IF sw  = 0
        str = str+CHR(ASC(SUBSTR(n,a,1))+10+a)
        sw  = 1
    ELSE
        str = str+CHR(ASC(SUBSTR(n,a,1))+5 -a)
        sw  = 0
    ENDIF
    a = a+1
ENDDO
RETURN str


FUNCTION Stars
Left  = LEN(ALLTRIM(m.Password))
Right = 8 - Left
@ 1,12 SAY REPLICATE(CHR(254),Left) + SPACE(Right) COLOR W+/B
```

Principles of operation

The key to this application is the use of field names in the password file to correspond exactly to functional areas in your application. In this example, there's a cash register, nonsales functions, voiding, "back room" functions (e.g., customer file maintenance), reports, and month-end closing. When the password functions are called, they pass a parameter indicating which functional area the user is trying to get into. If the function finds a Y in the field name corresponding to that user's functional area, it returns .T.; otherwise, it returns .F.

The one weak area in this approach is that someone who knows Fox-Pro file structures could go into his own record with DEBUG and enter a Y to gain access to an area he doesn't have access to, use your program normally, then go back in and take out the Y. If you want to bullet-proof this application, write a record to a hidden file each time the function is called, reporting who's logged in and what area he's trying to enter. Then let everyone know that access attempts are logged. Remember the doomsday device in Dr. Strangelove? It doesn't deter anything if no one knows it exists.

The encryption function uses a scheme that would probably be about level 2 on a difficulty scale of 1 to 10, but I think it would befuddle the casual snooper. Alternating characters of the password either add 10 to or subtract 5 from the ASCII value of the original character, and then add 1.

The Stars routine displays the little box character where the characters users have typed so far would ordinarily appear. This provides a visual cue as to what they've entered, without letting anyone look over their shoulder and get the password.

The password file-maintenance program

Having written the two functions, all I needed was a screen to allow the system supervisor to grant or deny access to each functional area. The screen shown in Fig. 6-1 is what I had in mind.

Figure 6-1 The password system screen.

The model provided by the previously mentioned order-entry system did a lot of what I needed. It tabled a reasonable number of elements into an array, then passed control to a routine called Editor that handled the details.

In the display screen, columns are separated by vertical lines. The fly in the ointment of this approach is that Screen Builder can't help you with the vertical lines in your arrays; you have to do them yourself. It takes a while to get the hang of doing "blank" lines (you supply the vertical bars on each line) with the same spacing you get when you construct the display strings in your array using *field1* + [|] + *field2* + ... But the simplicity of the rest of the coding makes that one cosmetic task less onerous.

The one peculiarity of this application is that you don't want your program to display the actual password on the screen. Passwords are encrypted in the file, so users can't just go in and see anyone else's password and use it. They can alter their own access, of course, but a log of who's been where is a good idea in secure installations, and the knowledge that such a log exists should help the average malefactor resist the temptation.

Or you could "hash" the password with the users' Yes values when you store them, so if they change their own Yes values it wouldn't work either.

The Password Edit screen appears in Fig. 6-2, and the code in Listing 6-3.

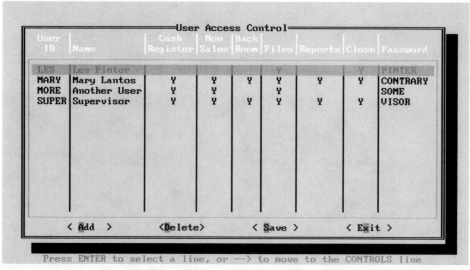

User ID	Name	Cash Register	Non Sales	Back Room	Files	Reports	Close	Password
LES	Les Pinter				Y		Y	PINTER
MARY	Mary Lantos	Y	Y	Y	Y	Y	Y	CONTRARY
MORE	Another User	Y	Y		Y			SOME
SUPER	Supervisor	Y	Y	Y	Y	Y	Y	VISOR

‹ Add ›   ‹Delete›   ‹ Save ›   ‹ Exit ›

Press ENTER to select a line, or --> to move to the CONTROLS line

Figure 6-2 The password edit screen.

Listing 6-3 The password-system screen code.

```
*
*      02/22/93          PASSWORD.SPR          15:40:13
*
```

```
#REGION 0
REGIONAL m.currarea, m.talkstat, m.compstat

IF SET("TALK") = "ON"

SET TALK OFF

m.talkstat = "ON"
ELSE

m.talkstat = "OFF"
ENDIF
m.compstat = SET("COMPATIBLE")
SET COMPATIBLE FOXPLUS

m.currarea = SELECT()
```

156   List management in screen design

6-3 Continued.

```
*
*                  ┌──────────────────────────────────────────────────┐
*                  │              MS-DOS Window definitions             │
                   └──────────────────────────────────────────────────┘


IF NOT WEXIST("password") ;
OR UPPER(WTITLE("PASSWORD")) == "PASSWORD.PJX" ;
OR UPPER(WTITLE("PASSWORD")) == "PASSWORD.SCX" ;
OR UPPER(WTITLE("PASSWORD")) == "PASSWORD.MNX" ;
OR UPPER(WTITLE("PASSWORD")) == "PASSWORD.PRG" ;
OR UPPER(WTITLE("PASSWORD")) == "PASSWORD.FRX" ;
OR UPPER(WTITLE("PASSWORD")) == "PASSWORD.QPR"

DEFINE WINDOW password ;
        FROM INT((SROW()-21)/2),INT((SCOL()-D73)/2) ;
        TO INT((SROW()-21)/2)+20,INT((SCOL() -73)/2)+72 ;
        TITLE "User Access Control" ;

        NOFLOAT NOCLOSE SHADOW NOMINIMIZE DOUBLE COLOR SCHEME 1
ENDIF


*
*                  ┌──────────────────────────────────────────────────┐
*                  │      PASSWORD/MS -DOS Setup Code   - SECTION 2     │
                   └──────────────────────────────────────────────────┘


#REGION 1
SET BLINK OFF
SET COLOR OF SCHEME 13 TO ;
 GR+/B, GR+/B, GR+/B, GR+/B, GR+/B, N/GR+*, B/B

IF NOT USED ( [PASSWORD] )
   SELECT 0
   fil = [PASSWORD]
   USE ( fil )
ENDIF

SELECT PASSWORD
SET ORDER TO UserID

m.Adding    = .F.
m.Control   = 1
m.Saved     = .T.
m.Changed   = .F.
m.Done      = .F.
m.SaveNum   = []
m.MaxLines = 100
m.ScrnSize =  14
```

6-3 Continued.

```
RELEASE   DETLINES
DIMENSION DETLINES ( MaxLines )

m.LineCount= 0

=Loader()

*
*                    ┌─────────────────────────────────────────────┐
*                    ║           PASSWORD/MS -DOS Screen Layout      ║
                     └─────────────────────────────────────────────┘


#REGION 1
IF WVISIBLE("password")

ACTIVATE WINDOW password SAME
ELSE

ACTIVATE WINDOW password NOSHOW
ENDIF
@ 2,0 GET m.Scroller PICTURE "@&N" FROM DETLINES ;
SIZE 16,71 DEFAULT 1 VALID _qdk0x15mw() COLOR SCHEME 13 ;
    MESSAGE "Press ENTER to select a line, or  - -> to move to the CONTROLS line"
@ 18,7 GET m.Control ;
PICTURE "@*HN \<Add;\<Delete;\<Save;E\<xit" ;

SIZE 1,8,8 DEFAULT 1 VALID _qdk0x15t1()
@ 1, 3 SAY "ID"
@ 1, 8 SAY "Name"
@ 0, 2 SAY "User"
@ 0,23 SAY "Cash"
@ 1,21 SAY "Register"
@ 0,31 SAY "Non"
@ 1,30 SAY "Sales"
@ 1,36 SAY "Room"
@ 1,41 SAY "Files"
@ 1,61 SAY "Password"
@ 0, 7 SAY "|"
@ 1, 7 SAY "|"
@ 0,20 SAY "|"
@ 1,20 SAY "|"
@ 0,29 SAY "|"
@ 1,29 SAY "|"
@ 0,35 SAY "|"
@ 1,35 SAY "|"
@ 0,40 SAY "|"
```

6-3 Continued.

```
@ 1,40 SAY "|"
@ 0,46 SAY "|"
@ 1,46 SAY "|"
@ 0,54 SAY "|"
@ 1,54 SAY "|"
@ 0,60 SAY "|"
@ 1,60 SAY "|"
@ 1,55 SAY "Close"
@ 1,47 SAY "Reports"

IF NOT WVISIBLE("password")

ACTIVATE WINDOW password
ENDIF

READ CYCLE

RELEASE WINDOW password
SELECT (m.currarea)

#REGION 0
IF m.talkstat = "ON"
    SET TALK ON
ENDIF
IF m.compstat = "ON"
    SET COMPATIBLE ON
ENDIF

*
*           ||                PASSWORD/MS -DOS Cleanup Code                ||
*           ||                                                             ||

#REGION 1

IF LASTKEY() = 27
    Done = .T.
ENDIF

RELEASE WINDOW PASSWORD                 && Release my own window

*** BEGINNING OF FUNCTIONS IN CLEANUP SNIPPET ***

*
*        ||      PASSWORD/MS -DOS Supporting Procedures and Functions      ||
*        ||                                                                ||
```

6-3 Continued.

```
#REGION 1
FUNCTION Editor

DEFINE WINDOW EDITWINDOW DOUBLE SHADOW FLOAT ;
    FROM 3,10 TO 16, 50 IN WINDOW PASSWORD
ACTIVATE WINDOW EDITWINDOW

m.UserID    =       SUBSTR ( DETLINES ( m.Scroller ) ,  1 ,   5 )
m.Name      =       SUBSTR ( DETLINES ( m.Scroller ) ,  7 ,  12 )
m.CashReg   =       SUBSTR ( DETLINES ( m.Scroller ) , 24 ,   1 )
m.NonSales  =       SUBSTR ( DETLINES ( m.Scroller ) , 31 ,   1 )
m.BackRoom  =       SUBSTR ( DETLINES ( m.Scroller ) , 37 ,   1 )
m.Files     =       SUBSTR ( DETLINES ( m.Scroller ) , 42 ,   1 )
m.Reports   =       SUBSTR ( DETLINES ( m.Scroller ) , 49 ,   1 )
m.Close     =       SUBSTR ( DETLINES ( m.Scroller ) , 56 ,   1 )
m.PassWord  =       SUBSTR ( DETLINES ( m.Scroller ) , 60 ,   8 )

@ 1, 2 SAY [      User ID: ] GET m.UserID   PICTURE [!!!!!!!!]
@ 2, 2 SAY [         Name: ] GET m.Name     PICTURE [!XXXXXXXXXXX]
@ 3, 2 SAY [Cash Register: ] GET m.CashReg  PICTURE [Y]
@ 4, 2 SAY [    Non Sales: ] GET m.NonSales PICTURE [Y]
@ 5, 2 SAY [    Back Room: ] GET m.BackRoom PICTURE [Y]
@ 6, 2 SAY [        Files: ] GET m.Files    PICTURE [Y]
@ 7, 2 SAY [      Reports: ] GET m.Reports  PICTURE [Y]
@ 8, 2 SAY [        Close: ] GET m.Close    PICTURE [Y]
@ 9, 2 SAY [     Password: ] GET m.PassWord PICTURE [!!!!!!!!] ;
    VALID NOT EMPTY ( m.PassWord )              ;
    ERROR [You can't leave the password field empty ]
READ

RELEASE WINDOW EDITWINDOW

IF LASTKEY() <> 27
   Changed = .T.
   Saved   = .F.
   DETLINES ( m.Scroller ) =                  ;
     m.UserID                + [|]            ;
   + m.Name                  + [|]            ;
   + SPACE(4) + m.CashReg  + SPACE(3) + [|] ;
   + SPACE(2) + m.NonSales + SPACE(2) + [|] ;
   + SPACE(2) + m.BackRoom + SPACE(1) + [|] ;
   + SPACE(2) + m.Files    + SPACE(2) + [|] ;
   + SPACE(3) + m.Reports  + SPACE(3) + [|] ;
   + SPACE(2) + m.Close    + SPACE(2) + [|] ;
   + m.PassWord
ENDIF
```

160 List management in screen design

6-3 Continued.

```
RETURN

FUNCTION Extend

m.Extended = m.Price * m.Quantity
SHOW GET m.Extended

FUNCTION BlankLine

DETLINES ( m.Scroller ) = ;
      SPACE(5)                    + [ | ]                  ;
    + SPACE(12)                   + [ | ]                  ;
    + SPACE(4) + [ ]        + SPACE(3) + [ | ] ;
    + SPACE(2) + [ ]        + SPACE(2) + [ | ] ;
    + SPACE(2) + [ ]        + SPACE(1) + [ | ] ;
    + SPACE(2) + [ ]        + SPACE(2) + [ | ] ;
    + SPACE(3) + [ ]        + SPACE(3) + [ | ] ;
    + SPACE(2) + [ ]        + SPACE(2) + [ | ] ;
    + SPACE(8)

FUNCTION Loader

DIMENSION DETLINES ( MaxLines )
SELECT PASSWORD
GO TOP
I = 1
SCAN WHILE USERID <> [ ~]
    DETLINES ( I ) = ;
      USERID                      + [ | ]                  ;
    + NAME                        + [ | ]                  ;
    + SPACE(4) +   CashReg  + SPACE(3) + [ | ] ;
    + SPACE(2) +   NonSales + SPACE(2) + [ | ] ;
    + SPACE(2) +   BackRoom + SPACE(1) + [ | ] ;
    + SPACE(2) +   Files    + SPACE(2) + [ | ] ;
    + SPACE(3) +   Reports  + SPACE(3) + [ | ] ;
    + SPACE(2) +   Close    + SPACE(2) + [ | ] ;
    + DECRYPT ( PASSWORD )
    I = I + 1
ENDSCAN
DIMENSION DETLINES ( I  - 1 )

LineCount = ALEN ( DETLINES )
=BlankLines()
SHOW GET m.Scroller
```

```
FUNCTION BlankLines

IF LineCount < ScrnSize
   Missing = ScrnSize  - LineCount
   DIMENSION DETLINES ( ScrnSize )
   FOR I = LineCount + 1 TO ScrnSize
       m.Scroller = I
       =BlankLine()
   ENDFOR
ENDIF
m.Scroller = 1

FUNCTION Saver

SELECT    PASSWORD
GO TOP

=RemovePrev()

FOR I = 1 TO ALEN ( DETLINES )
   IF LEFT ( DETLINES ( I ) , 5 ) <> SPACE(5)
      =GetABlank()
      REPLACE NEXT 1 ;
      USERID    WITH          SUBSTR ( DETLINES ( I ),  1, 5 )  , ;
      NAME      WITH          SUBSTR ( DETLINES ( I ),  7,12 )  , ;
      CashReg   WITH          SUBSTR ( DETLINES ( I ), 24, 1 )  , ;
      NonSales  WITH          SUBSTR ( DETLINES ( I ), 31, 1 )  , ;
      BackRoom  WITH          SUBSTR ( DETLINES ( I ), 37, 1 )  , ;
      Files     WITH          SUBSTR ( DETLINES ( I ), 42, 1 )  , ;
      Reports   WITH          SUBSTR ( DETLINES ( I ), 49, 1 )  , ;
      Close     WITH          SUBSTR ( DETLINES ( I ), 56, 1 )  , ;
      PASSWORD  WITH ENCRYPT ( SUBSTR ( DETLINES ( I ), 60, 8 ) )
   ENDIF
ENDFOR

Saved = .T.

FUNCTION GetABlank
SELECT PASSWORD
SEEK [ ~]
IF NOT FOUND()
   APPEND BLANK
ENDIF

FUNCTION RemovePrev
```

```
SET ORDER TO 0
GO TOP
SCAN
   SCATTER MEMVAR BLANK
   GATHER  MEMVAR
   REPLACE NEXT 1 USERID WITH [ ~]
ENDSCAN
SET ORDER TO 1
GO TOP

FUNCTION Alarm
FOR I = 1 TO 3
   SET BELL TO 800,1
   ?? CHR(7)
   SET BELL TO 1400,1
   ?? CHR(7)
ENDFOR

FUNCTION CONFIRM
* Purpose.........: Displays a confirming dialogue using the title passed
*                   to it when called; defaults to 'Yes'
PARAMETERS ctitle

currwind = WOUTPUT()

PRIVATE length,where,choice
length = LEN ( ctitle )
where  = 40  - length / 2
DEFINE POPUP CONFIRM FROM 13, where IN SCREEN ;
  COLOR N/W,N/W,N/W,N/W,N/W,W+/R
DEFINE BAR 1 OF CONFIRM PROMPT [\] + PADC ( ctitle , length )
DEFINE BAR 2 OF CONFIRM PROMPT [\ -]
DEFINE BAR 3 OF CONFIRM PROMPT      PADC ( [\<Yes] , length )
DEFINE BAR 4 OF CONFIRM PROMPT      PADC ( [\<No ] , length )
ON SELECTION POPUP CONFIRM DEACTIVATE POPUP CONFIRM

SaveConf = SET ( [CONFIRM] )
SET CONFIRM ON
ACTIVATE SCREEN

ACTIVATE POPUP CONFIRM
choice = PROMPT()
RELEASE  POPUP CONFIRM
SET CONFIRM &SaveConf
```

```
IF LEN(TRIM(currwind)) > 0
   ACTIVATE WINDOW (currwind)
ENDIF

RETURN IIF ( [Yes] $ choice , .T. , .F. )

FUNCTION ENCRYPT
PARAMETERS N

SW=0
A=1
STR=''
DO WHILE A <= LEN(N)
   IF SW  = 0
      STR = STR+CHR(ASC(SUBSTR(N,A,1))+10+A)
      SW  = 1
   ELSE
      STR = STR+CHR(ASC(SUBSTR(N,A,1))+5 -A)
      SW  = 0
   ENDIF
   A=A+1
ENDDO
RETURN STR

FUNCTION DECRYPT
PARAMETERS N

SW=0
A=1
STR=''
DO WHILE A <= LEN(N)
   IF SW  = 0
      STR = STR+CHR(ASC(SUBSTR(N,A,1)) -10 -A)
      SW  = 1
   ELSE
      STR = STR+CHR(ASC(SUBSTR(N,A,1)) -5+A)
      SW  = 0
   ENDIF
   A = A+1
ENDDO
RETURN STR

*
*    ┌──────────────────────────────────────────┐
*    │ _QDKOXL5MW              m.Scroller VALID   │
*    └──────────────────────────────────────────┘
```

```
FUNCTION _qdk0xl5mw      &&  m.Scroller VALID
#REGION 1
IF m.Scroller <> 0
   =Editor()
   _curobj = 1
ENDIF
```

```
*
*    ┌─────────────────────────────────────────────────┐
*    │  _QDK0XL5T1                    m.Control VALID    │
     └─────────────────────────────────────────────────┘
```

```
FUNCTION _qdk0xl5t1      &&  m.Control VALID
#REGION 1
DO CASE
   CASE m.Control = 1 && Add
        ArraySize = ALEN ( DETLINES )
        IF      ( ArraySize > 1 )          ;
           OR ( ( ArraySize = 1 ) ;
                   AND ( LEFT ( DETLINES ( 1 ) , 5 ) <> SPACE(5) ) )
           DIMENSION DETLINES ( ArraySize + 1 )
           m.Scroller = m.Scroller + 1
           =AINS ( DETLINES , m.Scroller )
           =BlankLine()
        ENDIF
        _curobj = 1
        KEYBOARD [{ENTER}]
   CASE m.Control = 2 && Del
        ArraySize = ALEN ( DETLINES )
        IF ArraySize  = 1
           m.Scroller = 1
           =BlankLine()
        ELSE
          =ADEL ( DETLINES , m.Scroller )
          IF m.Scroller > ALEN ( DETLINES )
             m.Scroller = m.Scroller - 1
          ENDIF
          DIMENSION DETLINES ( ArraySize -1 )
        ENDIF
        _curobj = 1
CASE m.Control = 3 && Save
     =Saver()
     LineCount = 0
     =BlankLines()
     _CurObj = 1
     KEYBOARD [{Ctrl+W}]
```

6-3 Continued.

```
   CASE m.Control = 4 && Exit
       IF Changed AND NOT Saved
          =Alarm( )
          IF CONFIRM ( [Changes not saved - Exit anyway?] )
             Done = .T.
             KEYBOARD [{Ctrl+W}]
          ENDIF
       ELSE
          Done = .T.
          KEYBOARD [{Ctrl+W}]
       ENDIF
ENDCASE
SHOW GET m.Scroller
```

Editing a line

Figure 6-3 shows what happens when you press Enter. You can't edit in place with @ GET FROM (*list*), because you have no way of knowing how many lines have scrolled past the top of the list box (see the Trick variable in the FASTPICK program later in this chapter). So you have to pop up a window, do your editing, and then refresh the selected line of the array and redisplay the list box.

I thought at first that this requirement would be immediately disliked by users, but they took to it instantly and have never complained since. If

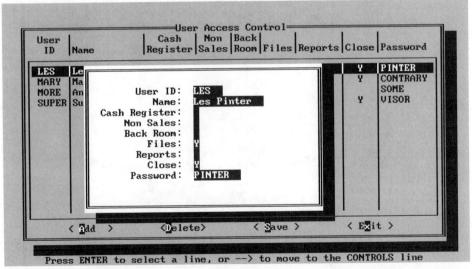

Figure 6-3 Editing a user's password entry.

I'd been afraid to try it, this software would never have been written. So don't be afraid to experiment with new design ideas. We don't want all of our software to look like the same guy wrote it, do we?

A multi-item pick list

Once I'd experienced the thrill of victory with this application, I started looking at other ways to use the feature. Alan Griver published a generic multi-item pick list in his CodeBook that was excellent. But one day I needed to pop up a list of 700 elements of which a dozen might be selected, and it took nearly 30 seconds on my '486 66 Mhz machine! So, as much as I liked @ GET...FROM (*list*), there had to be a better way.

The answer came in using arrays with my own display logic. The screen in Fig. 6-4 shows my side-by-side FASTPICK function, while Fig. 6-5 shows the associated HELP screen. It's very, very fast—two seconds or less for the same 700-element list.

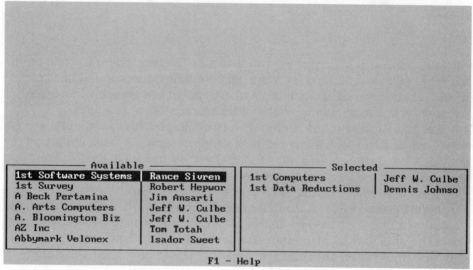

Figure 6-4 The FastPick function.

Hotkeys, arrays, and windows

The FASTPICK function needs to be handed an array of available selections, and return an array of what was selected. I decided to pass the input array using the normal approach, i.e., simply name the input array in the calling function's parameter list. But the second parameter would be a string containing the name of the array to be created. If it didn't exist upon returning, then nothing had been selected. That turned out to be easier than testing for a null array.

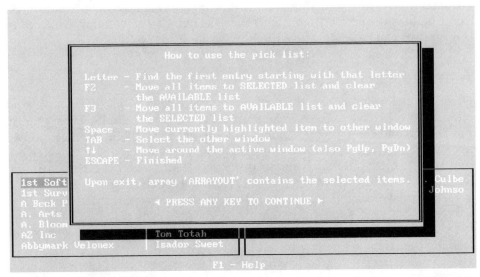

Figure 6-5 FastPick HELP.

I liked the idea of displaying two lists side-by-side, where the one on the left was available and the one on the right contained the selected lines picked from the list on the left. I don't know where I got it, but pressing the space bar to "push" a line from one list to the other seemed like a good idea.

FoxPro's windows came in handy as well. Each list needed to have a life of its own, and windows allow a kind of simple separability that simplified the coding. Also, they clean up after themselves. So the available list went into the window on the left, and the picked list into the window on the right.

I also wanted to be able to do an incremental search in either window, i.e., if you pressed R, the first element beginning with the letter R would become the first item in the window. A simple way was to hot-key each letter of the alphabet to a function that would find the first element that began with that letter and make it first in the selected display window. It sounds like a lot of code, but it's actually pretty small.

Because I had two windows that contained the same kind of lists, it seemed silly to write two sets of functions. So I described everything that was going on in each window as an element of one of two arrays, one for the left window and another for the right window. Similarly, each counter variable was dimensioned with a length of 2, so that the first element referred to the left window, and the second to the right window.

What surprised me was that what I thought would be simple was relatively difficult, while things I thought would be hard were very easy. For example, I had to do all of my own highlighting, and it takes an inordinate amount of the coding just to do that. Mouse support, on the other hand, turned out to be quite simple. The code appears in Listing 6-4.

FASTPICK program notes

This pick-list function did exactly what I wanted it to do, and did it with amazing speed. I could have used the @ GET FROM (*list*) that saved my bacon in the password application, but by pushing the software a little I increased performance over 1000 percent!

The amount of code required to do what I wanted here isn't something I'd recommend for a one-time function. I've seen multi-item pick lists coded in as little as 40 lines. On the other hand, this is a utility that I use over and over again, and that certainly spreads the development cost over a lot of real estate. Get the source code on disk (see the coupon at the back of the book), and you won't have to code it at all!

Listing 6-4 FASTPICK.PRG.

```
* Program-ID....: FastPick.PRG
* Author........: Pinter Consulting Staff
* Purpose.......: Scrolling multi-item pick list
* Parameters....:
*               : ARRAYIN      - Incoming array - REQUIRED
*               : ARRAYNAME    - Outgoing array NAME - REQUIRED
*               : WINDOWTOP    - Top line of window - DEFAULT 12
* Method........: The program displays the array (ARRAYIN).
*               : Selected items are returned in the array (ARRAYOUT).

PARAMETERS    ;
   ArrayIn    , ;
   ArrayName  , ;
   WindowTop

nParams   = PARAMETERS()
SaveAlias = ALIAS()

SET TALK OFF
SET SAFETY OFF
SET ESCAPE OFF

WinBottom = 23
@ 24, 0 SAY PADC ( [F1 - Help] , 80 )

IF nParams < 2
   =Alarm()
   WAIT WINDOW [Needs an ARRAY of data and an array NAME] TIMEOUT 2
   RETURN
ENDIF
```

```
FOR I = 1 TO ALEN(ARRAYIN)
    ARRAYIN(I) = LEFT(ARRAYIN(I)+SPACE(36),36)
ENDFOR

IF nParams   < 3
   WindowTop = 12
ENDIF

DIMENSION ARRAYOUT ( 1 )
=ACOPY(ARRAYIN,ARRAYOUT,1,1,1)  && Initialize first element of target

I          = 1
WindowNum  = 1

DIMENSION  Trick(2)
STORE 0 TO Trick
Max        = WinBottom - WindowTop - 1
Max        = IIF ( ALEN ( ARRAYIN ) > Max, Max, ALEN ( ARRAYIN ) )

DIMENSION TotRecs(2)
TotRecs(1) = ALEN ( ARRAYIN )
TotRecs(2) = 0

SET COLOR OF SCHEME 1 TO ,W+/R

NormVideo = SCHEME(1,1)
HighVideo = SCHEME(1,2)

DEFINE WINDOW LeftSide  ;
     FROM WindowTop,  0 ;
       TO WinBottom, 39 ;
       TITLE [ Available ]

DEFINE WINDOW RightSide ;
     FROM WindowTop, 40 ;
       TO WinBottom, 79 ;
       TITLE [ Selected ]

 WindowNum = 2
=FullWindow()
 WindowNum = 1
=FullWindow()

SET CURSOR OFF
```

```
ON KEY LABEL SpaceBar   DO MoveLine
ON KEY LABEL LeftMouse  DO Mouse
ON KEY LABEL Tab        DO ChangeWindow
ON KEY LABEL PgDn       DO PageDown
ON KEY LABEL PgUp       DO PageUp
ON KEY LABEL DnArrow    DO DownArrow
ON KEY LABEL UpArrow    DO UpArrow
ON KEY LABEL Home       DO Home
ON KEY LABEL End        DO End
ON KEY LABEL F1         DO ShowKeys
ON KEY LABEL F2         DO MoveLeft
ON KEY LABEL F3         DO MoveRight


FOR I = 65 TO 90
    cmd = [ON KEY LABEL ] + CHR(I) + [ DO LETTER]
    &cmd
ENDFOR


I = 1
=HiliteOn()

READ VALID Am_I_Done()

POP KEY ALL
RELEASE WINDOWS LeftSide, RightSide
SET CURSOR ON
IF NOT EMPTY ( SaveAlias )
   SELECT ( SaveAlias )

ENDIF

PUBLIC    &ArrayName ( 1 )
=ACOPY(ArrayOut,&ArrayName)

RETURN

FUNCTION Am_I_Done

IF LASTKEY() = 27
  RETURN .T.
  ELSE
  RETURN .F.
```

```
ENDIF

FUNCTION HiliteOn

IF TotRecs ( WindowNum ) > 0
   IF WindowNum = 1
      @ I-Trick(WindowNum)-1, 1 SAY ARRAYIN (I) COLOR ( HighVideo )
      ELSE
      @ I-Trick(WindowNum)-1, 1 SAY ARRAYOUT(I) COLOR ( HighVideo )
   ENDIF
ENDIF

FUNCTION HiliteOff

IF TotRecs(WindowNum) > 0
   IF WindowNum = 1
      @ I-Trick(WindowNum)-1, 1 SAY ARRAYIN (I) COLOR ( NormVideo )
      ELSE
      @ I-Trick(WindowNum)-1, 1 SAY ARRAYOUT(I) COLOR ( NormVideo )
   ENDIF
ENDIF

FUNCTION UpArrow

ON KEY LABEL UpArrow

IF I - 1 = 0
   =Alarm( )
   ON KEY LABEL UpArrow DO UpArrow
   RETURN
ENDIF
=HiliteOff( )
I = I - 1
IF I - Trick(WindowNum) = 0
   SCROLL 0, 1, Max-1, WCOLS()-2, -1
   IF WindowNum = 1
      @ 0, 1 SAY ARRAYIN ( Trick(WindowNum) ) COLOR ( NormVideo )
      ELSE
      @ 0, 1 SAY ARRAYOUT( Trick(WindowNum) ) COLOR ( NormVideo )
   ENDIF
   Trick(WindowNum) = Trick(WindowNum) - 1
ENDIF
=HiliteOn( )

ON KEY LABEL UpArrow DO UpArrow
```

6-4 Continued.

```
FUNCTION DownArrow

ON KEY LABEL DNArrow

IF I + 1 > TotRecs(WindowNum)
   =Alarm()
   ON KEY LABEL DNArrow DO DownArrow
   RETURN
ENDIF
=HiliteOff()
I = I + 1
IF (I-trick(WindowNum)) > Max)
   IF I <= TotRecs(WindowNum)
      SCROLL 0, 1, Max-1, WCOLS()-2, 1
      Trick(WindowNum) = Trick(WindowNum) + 1
    ELSE
      =Alarm()
      I = I - 1
   ENDIF
ENDIF
=HiliteOn()

ON KEY LABEL DNArrow DO DownArrow

FUNCTION PageUp

ON KEY LABEL PgUp

IF trick(WindowNum) = 0
   =Alarm()
   ON KEY LABEL PgUp DO PageUp
   RETURN
ENDIF

IF trick(WindowNum) > Max
   trick(WindowNum) = trick(WindowNum) - Max
  ELSE
   trick(WindowNum) = 0
ENDIF
=FullWindow()
I = Trick(WindowNum) + 1
=HiliteOn()

ON KEY LABEL PgUp DO PageUp
```

6-4 Continued.

```
FUNCTION PageDown

ON KEY LABEL PgDn

IF trick(WindowNum) + Max >= TotRecs(WindowNum)
   =Alarm()
   ON KEY LABEL PgDn DO PageDown
   RETURN
ENDIF
trick(WindowNum) = trick(WindowNum) + Max
=FullWindow()
I = trick(WindowNum) + 1
IF I > TotRecs(WindowNum)
   I = TotRecs(WindowNum)
ENDIF
=HiliteOn()

ON KEY LABEL PgDn DO PageDown

FUNCTION HOME

=HiliteOff()
I = IIF ( Trick(WindowNum) = 0 , 1,  Trick(WindowNum)+1 )
=HiliteOn()

FUNCTION END

=HiliteOff()
I = IIF ( Trick(WindowNum) = 0 , Max, Max) + Trick(WindowNum)
IF I > TotRecs(WindowNum)
   I = Totrecs(WindowNum)
ENDIF
=HiliteOn()

FUNCTION LETTER

Letter = UPPER ( CHR ( LASTKEY () ) )
Found  = .F.
DO CASE
   CASE WindowNum = 1
      FOR J = 1 TO TotRecs(WindowNum)
         IF LEFT(ARRAYIN(J),1) = Letter
            Found = .T.
            EXIT
         ENDIF
```

174 List management in screen design

```
        ENDFOR
    CASE WindowNum = 2
       FOR J = 1 TO TotRecs(WindowNum)
          IF LEFT(ARRAYOUT(J),1) = Letter
             Found = .T.
             EXIT
          ENDIF
       ENDFOR
ENDCASE

IF NOT Found
   =Alarm()
   RETURN
ENDIF

* -- If found item was before current top (TRICK(K)) or  after bottom of
* -- current page (trick(K)+Max), rewrite page; otherwise, change hilite

=HiliteOff()

IF J < Trick ( WindowNum ) ;
OR J > Trick ( WindowNum ) + Max
   Trick ( WindowNum ) = J - 1
   =FullWindow()
  ELSE
   I = J
   =HiliteOn()
ENDIF

FUNCTION FullWindow

DO CASE
   CASE WindowNum = 1

       ACTIVATE WINDOW LeftSide
       CLEAR
       IF TotRecs(1) = 0
          RETURN
       ENDIF
       =ASORT(ARRAYIN)
       FOR I = 1 TO Max
          IF  ( I + trick(1) ) <= TotRecs(1)
             @ I - 1 , 1 SAY ARRAYIN ( I + trick(1) ) COLOR ( NormVideo )
          ENDIF
       ENDFOR
```

```
        I = 1 + trick(1)    && highlight first entry on screen

    OTHERWISE

        ACTIVATE WINDOW RightSide
        CLEAR
        IF TotRecs(2) = 0
           RETURN
        ENDIF
        =ASORT(ARRAYOUT)
        FOR I = 1 TO Max
           IF  ( I + trick(2) ) <= TotRecs(2)
               @  I - 1 , 1 SAY ARRAYOUT ( I + trick(2) ) COLOR ( NormVideo )
           ENDIF
        ENDFOR
        I = 1 + trick(2)

ENDCASE

=HiliteOn()

RETURN

FUNCTION Alarm

PUSH KEY CLEAR

   SET BELL TO 330,1
   ?? CHR(7)
   SET BELL TO 440,1
   ?? CHR(7)
   SET BELL TO 550,1
   ?? CHR(7)
   SET BELL TO 660,1
   ?? CHR(7)

POP KEY

RETURN

FUNCTION ChangeWindow

IF   WindowNum = 1 AND TotRecs(2) = 0 ;
  OR WindowNum = 2 AND TotRecs(1) = 0
     =Alarm()
```

```
      RETURN
ENDIF

DO CASE
   CASE WindowNum = 1
      IF TotRecs(1) > 0
         @ I -1 -Trick(WindowNum) , 1 SAY ARRAYIN (I) COLOR ( NormVideo )
      ENDIF
   OTHERWISE
      IF TotRecs(2) > 0
         @ I -1 -Trick(WindowNum) , 1 SAY ARRAYOUT(I) COLOR ( NormVideo )
      ENDIF
ENDCASE

IF WindowNum = 1
   WindowNum = 2
   ACTIVATE WINDOW RightSide
  ELSE
   WindowNum = 1
   ACTIVATE WINDOW LeftSide
ENDIF

I = Trick(WindowNum)+1
DO CASE
   CASE WindowNum = 1
      IF TotRecs(1) > 0
         @ I -1 -Trick(WindowNum) , 1 SAY ARRAYIN (I) COLOR ( HighVideo )
      ENDIF
   OTHERWISE
      IF TotRecs(2) > 0
         @ I -1 -Trick(WindowNum) , 1 SAY ARRAYOUT(I) COLOR ( HighVideo )
      ENDIF
ENDCASE

FUNCTION Mouse

mRow = MROW( )
mCol = MCOL( )

IF mRow < 0 OR mCol < 0
   =Alarm( )
   RETURN
ENDIF

IF Trick(WindowNum)+mRow+1 > TotRecs(WindowNum)
```

6-4 Continued.

```
    =Alarm()
    RETURN
ENDIF

I = Trick(WindowNum) + mRow + 1
=MoveLine()

FUNCTION MoveLine

ON KEY LABEL SpaceBar                    && Turn off this function

DO CASE
   CASE WindowNum = 1
        IF TotRecs(1) = 0
           =Alarm()
           RETURN
        ENDIF
        TotRecs(2) = TotRecs(2)+1
        TotRecs(1) = TotRecs(1)-1
        DIMENSION ARRAYOUT(TotRecs(2))
        =ACOPY(ARRAYIN, ARRAYOUT, I, 1, TotRecs(2))
        =ADEL (ARRAYIN,  I, 1 )
        IF TotRecs(1) > 0                && Can't dimension it zero...
           DIMENSION ARRAYIN(TotRecs(1)) && Remember to suppress display
        ENDIF                            && if totrecs(n) = 0
        WindowNum = 2
        =FullWindow()
        =HiliteOff()
        WindowNum = 1
* If move emptied the window, reset to redisplay from the top
        IF TotRecs (1) = Trick (1)
           Trick(1) = 0
        ENDIF
* Redisplay window
        =FullWindow()
        IF TotRecs (1) = 0
           WindowNum = 2
           =FullWindow()
        ENDIF
   CASE WindowNum = 2
        IF TotRecs(2) = 0
           =Alarm()
           RETURN
        ENDIF
        TotRecs(1) = TotRecs(1)+1
```

```
        TotRecs(2) = TotRecs(2)-1
        DIMENSION ARRAYIN (TotRecs(1))
        =ACOPY(ARRAYOUT, ARRAYIN, I, 1, TotRecs(1))
        =ADEL (ARRAYOUT, I, 1 )
        IF TotRecs(2) > 0
            DIMENSION ARRAYOUT(TotRecs(2))
        ENDIF
        WindowNum = 1
        =FullWindow()
        =HiliteOff()
        WindowNum = 2
* If move emptied the window, reset to redisplay from the top
        IF TotRecs (2) = Trick (2)
            Trick(2) = 0
        ENDIF
* Redisplay window
        =FullWindow()
        IF Totrecs (2) = 0
            WindowNum = 1
            =FullWindow()
        ENDIF
ENDCASE
ON KEY LABEL SpaceBar DO MoveLine             && Turn back on

FUNCTION MoveLeft
IF TotRecs(2) = 0
   =Alarm()
   RETURN
ENDIF
ON KEY LABEL F2
Where2Start = TotRecs(1) + 1
Num2Copy    = TotRecs(2)
TotRecs(1) = TotRecs(1) + TotRecs(2)
TotRecs(2) = 0
DIMENSION ARRAYIN(TotRecs(1))
=ACOPY ( ARRAYOUT, ARRAYIN, 1, Num2Copy, Where2Start )
DIMENSION ARRAYOUT(1)
STORE 0 TO Trick && both
WindowNum = 2
=FullWindow()
=HiliteOff()
WindowNum = 1
=FullWindow()
ON KEY LABEL F2 DO MoveLeft
```

6-4 Continued.

```
FUNCTION MoveRight
IF TotRecs(1) = 0
   =Alarm()
   RETURN
ENDIF
ON KEY LABEL F3
Where2Start = TotRecs(2) + 1
Num2Copy    = TotRecs(1)
TotRecs(2) = TotRecs(1) + TotRecs(2)
TotRecs(1) = 0
DIMENSION ARRAYOUT(TotRecs(2))
=ACOPY ( ARRAYIn, ARRAYOUT, 1, Num2Copy, Where2Start )
DIMENSION ARRAYIN(1)
STORE 0 TO Trick && both
WindowNum = 1
=FullWindow()
=HiliteOff()
WindowNum = 2
=FullWindow()
ON KEY LABEL F3 DO MoveRight

FUNCTION ShowKeys
ON KEY LABEL F1

DEFINE   WINDOW KEYLIST FROM 3,10 TO 20,70 DOUBLE SHADOW
ACTIVATE WINDOW KEYLIST
*...+....1....+....2....+....3....+....4....+....5....+....6
TEXT
                How to use the pick list:

Letter - Find the first entry starting with that letter
F2      - Move all items to SELECTED list and clear
            the AVAILABLE list
F3      - Move all items to AVAILABLE list and clear
            the SELECTED list
Space  - Move currently highlighted item to other window
TAB     - Select the other window
↑↓      - Move around the active window (also PgUp, PgDn)
ESCAPE - Finished

Upon exit, array 'ARRAYOUT' contains the selected items.

                ◄ PRESS ANY KEY TO CONTINUE ►

ENDTEXT
=inkey(0)
RELEASE WINDOW KEYLIST
ON KEY LABEL F1 DO ShowKeys
```

180 List management in screen design

Summary

I hope this chapter gave you some ideas for developing your own application "look and feel." FoxPro is full of tools, but you'll undoubtedly find ways of using them that the fine folks at Microsoft and Fox never thought of. In the next chapter, we'll look at a technique for coding your own BROWSE that also yields spectacular speed. It's less of an issue in 2.5 than it was in 2.0, but for just a little code, you can write a "lean and mean" BROWSE that absolutely flies.

7
Writing your own tools

FoxPro has over 600 commands and functions, and more are sure to be added. But no language can claim to contain everything you could want; in fact, I consider many of the so-called "fourth-generation" products to be presumptuous collections of one man's opinion of what my software should look like.

In the last chapter, you saw two designs that required that you write your own replacements for some functions that FoxPro already had. In this chapter, you'll write out your own version of FoxPro's BROWSE; then you'll look at two functions I've found very useful in my own work.

Writing your own BROWSE

FoxPro's BROWSE is an amazing tool. It's hard to imagine anything more that could be added. But what if you want only a few of the 30-something features it offers? You can get better performance out of a slimmed-down, customized tool you can write in FoxPro itself.

BROWSE is a substantial chunk of the overlay file; on a network, you'll see a noticeable delay when your program calls it. Using features like the PICTURE clause can double the delay, because they call in yet additional code.

If you code only the scrolling logic and then activate one row of GETs at a time, you're asking FoxPro to do much less work. How much less? Well, I routinely get 400% faster performance out of the roll-your-own BROWSE described below. The screens look like the example in Fig. 7-1. The code is shown in Listing 7-1.

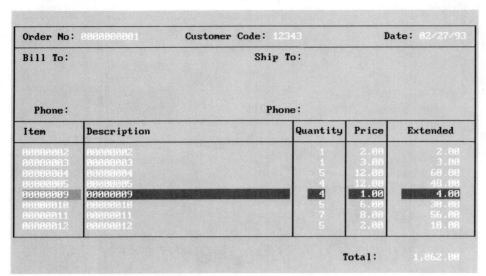

Order No: 0000000001		Customer Code: 12343		Date: 02/27/93	

Bill To: Ship To:

Phone: Phone:

Item	Description	Quantity	Price	Extended
00000002	00000002	1	2.00	2.00
00000003	00000003	1	3.00	3.00
00000004	00000004	5	12.00	60.00
00000005	00000005	4	12.00	48.00
00000009	00000009	4	1.00	4.00
00000010	00000010	5	6.00	30.00
00000011	00000011	7	8.00	56.00
00000012	00000012	5	2.00	10.00

Total: 1,062.00

Figure 7-1 The file-following browse.

Listing 7-1 The file-following browse.

```
* Program-ID.....: FOLLOWER.PRG
* Purpose........: Demonstrate file-following scrolling detail GETS

SET TALK     OFF
SET ESCAPE   OFF
SET BLINK    OFF
SET RESOURCE OFF
HIDE    MENU _MSYSMENU
DEFINE MENU _MSYSMENU
ON KEY LABEL F1  DO HelpWindow
ON KEY LABEL F10 WAIT WINDOW [No menu active] TIMEOUT 1


Line       = 1
PgUp       = 6
PgDn       = 7
ENTER      = 15
Done       = 14 && Ctrl+W
Escape     = 12
CtrlPgUp   = 34
CtrlPgDn   = 35
Alarm      = .F.

WireFrame  = .T.
WireColor  = [BG+/B]
TextColor  = [GR+/B]
DataColor  = [W+/B]
```

7-1 Continued.

```
TopLine    = 12
BottomLine = 21
MaxLines   = BottomLine - TopLine -1

GrandTotal = 0
PageTop    = 0            && Record number of first record on current page.

NewRec     = .F.
KeyChanged = .F.          && Redisplays screen if a key was edited...

USE ORDERS   IN A ORDER ORDERNUM
USE ORDERDET IN B ORDER ORDERITEM
SELECT ORDERDET

* Data columns
c1 = 2                    && Item
c2 = c1+LEN(ITEM)+1       && Description
c3 = c2+LEN(DESC)+3       && Quantity
c4 = c3+    7             && Price
c5 = c4+    7             && Extended

* Vertical bar columns
v1 = c1-1
v2 = c2-1
v3 = c3-3
v4 = c4-1
v5 = c5-1

SELECT ORDERS
Key =   ORDERS.ORDERNUM
SELECT ORDERDET
SEEK   Key                && Find first matching record in detail file
SCATTER MEMVAR            && Declare memory variables

SET COLOR OF SCHEME 1 TO ,,,,,,,,,W+/BG

=ShowPage()
=ShowGets()

ON KEY LABEL DnArrow   KEYBOARD [{PgDn}]
ON KEY LABEL UpArrow   KEYBOARD [{PgUp}]
ON KEY LABEL CTRL+A    KEYBOARD [{PgDn}] + [A]
ON KEY LABEL CTRL+DEL  KEYBOARD [{PgDn}] + [D]
ON KEY LABEL CTRL+F    KEYBOARD [{PgDn}] + [F]
ON KEY LABEL CTRL+W    KEYBOARD [{PgDn}] + [X]
ON KEY LABEL Ctrl+F10  KEYBOARD [{PgDn}] + [X]
```

```
DO WHILE .T.
   =Gets(Line)
   IF KeyChanged
      KeyChanged = .F.
      =ShowPage()
      =ShowGets()
      LOOP
   ENDIF
   LastKey = MOD(READKEY(),256)
   DO CASE
      CASE LastKey = ESCAPE
           EXIT
      CASE LastKey = Done AND EMPTY ( m.Item )
           EXIT
      CASE LastKey = PgUp
           IF NewRec
              Line = Line -1
              SCATTER MEMVAR
              NewRec = .F.
              CLEAR TYPEAHEAD
              LOOP
           ENDIF
           SaveRec = RECNO()
           SKIP -1
           IF BOF() OR OrderNum <> ORDERS.OrderNum
              =Alarm()
              GO ( SaveRec )
              LOOP
           ENDIF
           Line = Line-1
           IF Line = 0
              SCROLL TopLine+1, 1, BottomLine-1, 78, -1
              Line = 1
              =VertLines(Line)
           ENDIF
      CASE LastKey = PgDn
           IF CHRSAW()
              SET CONSOLE OFF
              LastKey = INKEY()
              SET CONSOLE ON
              DO CASE
                 CASE LastKey = ASC([A])
                      DO AddLine
                      LOOP
                 CASE LastKey = ASC([D])
```

```
                DO DeleteLine
                LOOP
           CASE LastKey = ASC([F])
                DO Finder
                LOOP
           CASE LastKey = ASC([X])
                EXIT
           ENDCASE
        ENDIF
        IF EMPTY ( m.Item )
           EXIT
        ENDIF
        SaveRec = RECNO()
        SKIP
        IF EOF() OR OrderNum <> ORDERS.OrderNum
           SKIP -1
           NewRec = .T.
        ENDIF
        Line = Line+1
        IF Line > MaxLines
           SCROLL TopLine+1, 1, BottomLine-1, 78, 1
           Line = MaxLines
           =VertLines(Line)
        ENDIF
   CASE LastKey = CtrlPgDn
        SaveRec = RECNO()
        IF Line > 1
           SKIP -Line
        ENDIF
        SKIP MaxLines
        IF EOF() OR OrderNum <> ORDERS.OrderNum
           =Alarm()
           GO ( SaveRec )
        ENDIF
        =ShowPage()
        =ShowGets()
   CASE LastKey = CtrlPgUp
        GO ( PageTop )
        SKIP -MaxLines
        IF BOF() OR OrderNum <> ORDERS.OrderNum
           SEEK ORDERS.OrderNum
        ENDIF
        NewRec = .F.
```

```
            =ShowPage( )
            =ShowGets( )
            CLEAR TYPEAHEAD
    ENDCASE
    IF NewRec
       SCATTER MEMVAR BLANK
     ELSE
       SCATTER MEMVAR
    ENDIF
ENDDO

CLEAR
CLEAR TYPEAHEAD
POP KEY ALL
SET SYSMENU TO DEFAULT

RETURN

FUNCTION ShowPage

CLEAR

@  1,0 TO BottomLine, 79        COLOR ( WireColor )

@  2, 2 SAY [Order No: ]        COLOR ( TextColor )
@  2,12 SAY ORDERS.OrderNum     COLOR ( DataColor )
@  2,30 SAY [Customer Code: ]   COLOR ( TextColor )
@  2,45 SAY ORDERS.CNO          COLOR ( DataColor )
@  2,60 SAY [    Date: ]        COLOR ( TextColor )
@  2,70 SAY DTOC(DATE( ))       COLOR ( DataColor )

=HorizLine(3)

@  4, 1 SAY [ Bill To: ]        COLOR ( TextColor )
@  4,41 SAY [ Ship To: ]        COLOR ( TextColor )

@  9, 1 SAY [   Phone: ]        COLOR ( TextColor )
@  9,41 SAY [   Phone: ]        COLOR ( TextColor )

=HorizLine(TopLine-2)
@ TopLine-1,v1+1 SAY [Item]         COLOR ( TextColor )
@ TopLine-1,v2+1 SAY [Description]  COLOR ( TextColor )
@ TopLine-1,v3+1 SAY [Quantity]     COLOR ( TextColor )
@ TopLine-1,v4+1 SAY [ Price]       COLOR ( TextColor )
@ TopLine-1,v5+4 SAY [Extended]     COLOR ( TextColor )
```

7-1 Continued.

```
=HorizLine(TopLine)

=DetLines()

FUNCTION DetLines

IF WireFrame
    @ TopLine-2   , v2 SAY [┬]                    COLOR ( WireColor )
    @ TopLine-1   , v2 SAY [│]                    COLOR ( WireColor )
    @ TopLine     , v2 SAY [┼]                    COLOR ( WireColor )
    @ BottomLine  , v2 SAY [┴]                    COLOR ( WireColor )

    @ TopLine-2   , v3 SAY [┬]                    COLOR ( WireColor )
    @ TopLine-1   , v3 SAY [│]                    COLOR ( WireColor )
    @ TopLine     , v3 SAY [┼]                    COLOR ( WireColor )
    @ BottomLine  , v3 SAY [┴]                    COLOR ( WireColor )

    @ TopLine-2   , v4 SAY [┬]                    COLOR ( WireColor )
    @ TopLine-1   , v4 SAY [│]                    COLOR ( WireColor )
    @ TopLine     , v4 SAY [┼]                    COLOR ( WireColor )
    @ BottomLine  , v4 SAY [┴]                    COLOR ( WireColor )

    @ TopLine-2   , v5 SAY [┬]                    COLOR ( WireColor )
    @ TopLine-1   , v5 SAY [│]                    COLOR ( WireColor )
    @ TopLine     , v5 SAY [┼]                    COLOR ( WireColor )
    @ BottomLine  , v5 SAY [┴]                    COLOR ( WireColor )

    @ TopLine+1   , v2 TO BottomLine-1,v2         COLOR ( WireColor )
    @ TopLine+1   , v3 TO BottomLine-1,v3         COLOR ( WireColor )
    @ TopLine+1   , v4 TO BottomLine-1,v4         COLOR ( WireColor )
    @ TopLine+1   , v5 TO BottomLine-1,v5         COLOR ( WireColor )

ENDIF

FUNCTION ShowGets
PRIVATE I
I = 1
SaveRec = RECNO()
PageTop = SaveRec
SCAN WHILE I <= MaxLines AND ORDERDET.OrderNum = ORDERS.OrderNum
    =Says(I)
    I = I + 1
ENDSCAN
GO ( SaveRec )
Line = 1
=TotalCalc()
```

```
FUNCTION Gets
PARAMETERS CurLine

GrandTotal = GrandTotal - Extended                && Back out line amount
m.OrderNum = ORDERS.OrderNum
m.LineNum  = CurLine

@ TopLine+CurLine, c1 GET m.Item VALID Finished()
@ TopLine+CurLine, c2 GET m.Desc
@ TopLine+CurLine, c3 GET m.Quantity    PICTURE [###]        VALID TotCalc()
@ TopLine+CurLine, c4 GET m.Price       PICTURE [###.##]     VALID TotCalc()
@ TopLine+CurLine, c5+2 GET m.Extended  PICTURE [###,###.##] DISABLE
READ COLOR ,W+/R
IF LASTKEY() <> 27
   =Replaces()
ENDIF
=Says(Line)
GrandTotal = GrandTotal + Extended
=ShowTotal()

IF MOD(READKEY(),256) = ENTER
   KEYBOARD [{DnArrow}]
ENDIF


FUNCTION Finished
IF EMPTY ( m.Item )
   KEYBOARD [{Ctrl+W}]
   RETURN
ENDIF
IF m.Item <> ORDERDET.Item
   KeyChanged = .T.
ENDIF


FUNCTION TotCalc
m.Extended = m.Quantity * m.Price
SHOW GET m.Extended DISABLE

FUNCTION Replaces
IF NOT EMPTY ( m.Item )
   m.OrderNum = ORDERS.OrderNum
   IF NewRec
      APPEND BLANK
   ENDIF
   GATHER MEMVAR
```

```
    NewRec = .F.
ENDIF

FUNCTION Says
PARAMETERS CurLine

IF NOT NewRec
    @ TopLine+CurLine, c1 SAY ORDERDET.Item
    @ TopLine+CurLine, c2 SAY ORDERDET.Desc
    @ TopLine+CurLine, c3 SAY STR(ORDERDET.Quantity,3  )
    @ TopLine+CurLine, c4 SAY STR(ORDERDET.Price   ,6,2)
    @ TopLine+CurLine, c5+2 SAY TRAN(ORDERDET.Extended,'@Z ###,###.##')
  ELSE
    @ TopLine+CurLine,  1 CLEAR TO TopLine+CurLine, 78
ENDIF
=VertLines(CurLine)

FUNCTION VertLines
PARAMETERS HLine
IF WireFrame
    @ TopLine+HLine, v2 SAY [|] COLOR ( WireColor )
    @ TopLine+HLine, v3 SAY [|] COLOR ( WireColor )
    @ TopLine+HLine, v4 SAY [|] COLOR ( WireColor )
    @ TopLine+HLine, v5 SAY [|] COLOR ( WireColor )
ENDIF

FUNCTION HorizLine
PARAMETERS CurLine
@ CurLine,0  TO CurLine,78 COLOR ( WireColor )
@ CurLine,0  SAY '├'       COLOR ( WireColor )
@ CurLine,79 SAY '┤'       COLOR ( WireColor )

FUNCTION Alarm
IF Alarm
 FOR I = 1 TO 3
    SET BELL TO 1000,1
    ?? CHR(7)
    SET BELL TO 1600,1
    ?? CHR(7)
 ENDFOR
ENDIF

FUNCTION Finder

PUSH KEY CLEAR
```

```
DEFINE WINDOW FINDER FROM 3,10 TO 20, 70 DOUBLE SHADOW
SET LIBRARY TO JKEY
ON KEY LABEL ENTER KEYBOARD CHR(23)
=JkeyInit([U],ORDERS.OrderNum,[Item number: ])
BROWSE WINDOW FINDER ;
  FIELDS ;
    ITEM, DESC :H=[Description] ;
  COLOR GR+/B,W+/R,B/W+*,GR+/B,GR+/B,GR+/B,W+/R ;
  KEY ORDERS.ORDERNUM, ORDERS.ORDERNUM
ON KEY  LABEL ENTER
RELEASE WINDOW FINDER
=JkeyCanc()
=ShowPage()
=ShowGets()
SCATTER MEMVAR
POP KEY


FUNCTION TotalCalc

SaveRec = RECNO()
SEEK ORDERS.ORDERNUM
SUM Extended TO GrandTotal WHILE OrderNum = ORDERS.ORDERNUM
=ShowTotal()
GO ( SaveRec )


FUNCTION ShowTotal

@ 23,57   SAY [Total: ]                              COLOR (TextColor)
@ 23,c5-1 SAY TRANSFORM ( GrandTotal, '@Z ##,###,###.##' ) COLOR (DataColor)


FUNCTION AddLine
* If there aren't enough detail lines to fill a page, jump to the first
* blank line; otherwise, display the last (MaxLines-1) records and jump
* to the last line, which will be blank.
Key = TRAN(VAL(ORDERS.OrderNum)+1, [@L #########] )
* Find the first record following this order number
SET NEAR ON
SEEK Key
SET NEAR OFF
IF EOF()
   GO BOTTOM
  ELSE
   SKIP -1
ENDIF
LastRec = RECNO()
```

```
HowMuch = MaxLines -2
SKIP -HowMuch
IF ORDERDET.OrderNum <> ORDERS.OrderNum OR BOF()   && < 'MaxLines' lines...
   SEEK ORDERS.OrderNum
   Line = 1
   SCAN REST
      SKIP
      IF ORDERDET.OrderNum <> ORDERS.OrderNum OR EOF()
         EXIT
      ENDIF
      Line = Line + 1
   ENDSCAN
 ELSE
   Line = MaxLines - 1
ENDIF
SaveLine = Line
=ShowPage()
=ShowGets()
GO ( LastRec )
Line = SaveLine +1
NewRec = .T.
SCATTER MEMVAR BLANK

FUNCTION DeleteLine
IF CONFIRM ( [ Delete this line? ] )
   SaveLine = Line
   DelRec   = RECNO()
   TopLineOffset = Line -1
   SKIP -TopLineOffset
   SaveRec  = RECNO()
   GO ( DelRec )
   SCATTER MEMVAR BLANK
   GATHER  MEMVAR
   REPLACE NEXT 1 OrderNum WITH [~], ITEM WITH [~]
   GO ( SaveRec )
   =ShowPage()
   =ShowGets()
   GO ( SaveRec )
   Line = SaveLine
   SKIP ( Line-1 )
   IF OrderNum <> ORDERS.OrderNum
      SEEK ORDERS.OrderNum
      =ShowPage()
      =ShowGets()
```

```
    ENDIF
    SCATTER MEMVAR
    KEYBOARD [{ENTER}]
ENDIF

FUNCTION Confirm
PARAMETERS ctitle

currwind = WOUTPUT()

PRIVATE length,where,choice
length = LEN ( ctitle )
where  = 40 - length / 2
DEFINE POPUP CONFIRM FROM 12, where IN SCREEN ;
  COLOR N/W,N/W,N/W,N/W,N/W,W+/R,W+/W
DEFINE BAR 1 OF CONFIRM PROMPT [\] + PADC ( ctitle   , length )
DEFINE BAR 2 OF CONFIRM PROMPT [\-]
DEFINE BAR 3 OF CONFIRM PROMPT      PADC ( [ \<Yes] , length )
DEFINE BAR 4 OF CONFIRM PROMPT      PADC ( [ \<No ] , length )
ON SELECTION POPUP CONFIRM DEACTIVATE POPUP CONFIRM

SaveConf = SET ( [CONFIRM] )
SET CONFIRM ON
ACTIVATE POPUP CONFIRM
choice = PROMPT()
RELEASE POPUP CONFIRM
SET CONFIRM &SaveConf

IF LEN(TRIM(currwind)) > 0
    ACTIVATE WINDOW (currwind)
ENDIF

RETURN IIF ( [Yes] $ choice , .T. , .F. )

FUNCTION HelpWindow

PUSH KEY CLEAR
DEFINE   WINDOW HELPWINDOW FROM 9,23 TO 20, 57 SHADOW DOUBLE
ACTIVATE WINDOW HELPWINDOW

@ 0, 0 SAY PADC('Hot Key Commands',WCOLS()-1)
@ 1, 0 TO 1, WCOLS()-1

@ 3,5 SAY 'Ctrl-A   - Add a line'
@ 4,5 SAY 'Ctrl-F   - Find a line'
```

7-1 Continued.

```
@ 5,5 SAY 'Ctrl-Del - Delete a line'
@ 6,5 SAY 'Ctrl-PgUp- Prev screen'
@ 7,5 SAY 'Ctrl-PgDn- Next screen'
@ 8,5 SAY 'F10      - Exit screen'

WAIT WINDOW
RELEASE WINDOW HELPWINDOW

POP KEY
```

How it works

This is called a "file-following" BROWSE because the current record on the screen is the current record in the file, and you force it to follow along with the screen.

There is a simpler way to handle this Browse, but deadlines have a way of sneaking up on me. The source-code disk, available with the coupon at the end of the book, contains the new, improved version of this code.

I used Joe Gotthelf's excellent JKEY modification to BROWSE in order to find a record and make it the top of the current display screen. You don't often get that much functionality that easily.

Next, the wireframe that dresses up the screen is controlled by the WireFrame variable. If .False., no wireframe is displayed. WireColor controls its color.

Finally, BROWSE adds records to the bottom of the screen when you press Ctrl–N. But as soon as you PgUp or PgDn, the screen shuffles to place your new record(s) in the order determined by the current ORDER expression. If you're controlling the screen, you can defer or completely suppress that reorganization. The version published here doesn't do it—you can call or write for the "fixed" version, or have the fun of doing it yourself. No pain, no gain . . .

Saving history data

Have your history files overflowed your hard disk yet? The bad news is that they will. The good news is that there's an easy fix that will postpone the inevitable hard-disk upgrade. The solution is to use packed data fields to cut your numeric storage by over half.

This is like those ugly wide ties that occasionally come back in style. Packed fields have been around forever. They're ugly, but they store big numbers in little fields, and that's what you need in your history files.

For a little review of what's going to happen, let's go to Math 101. A number like, say, 125 is 5 ones, 2 tens, and 1 hundred. Or, it's 5 times 10 to the 0 power plus 2 times 10 to the 1 power plus 1 times 10 to the 2 power. That's why our number system is called base 10.

The largest digit that can be represented in base 10 is 9. In general, the largest digit in a base n system is $n-1$. So if you can find a numbering system with lots of values in a single digit, you could use a larger base and fewer digits, right? Stay with me on this—we're almost there.

The IBM character set consists of ASCII characters—in effect, single "digits" with values from 0 to 255. They'll do just fine, thank you. So you can represent a 1 with CHR(1), 2 with CHR(2), all the way up to CHR(255) for 255.

But wait, there's more! Just like the 1 in 10, you can use the next digit to the left to represent the number of, not tens (10^1), but multiples of 256 (256^1). So 257 would be CHR(1) + CHR(1) concatenated into a two-character string.

So how big a number can you store in two hex digits? 256 times 256 looks promising. Actually, it's 256 squared minus 1, or 65535. (In base 10, it's 10 squared minus 1, or 99 in two decimal digits.)

But there's another wrinkle. My customers' data usually consists, not of integers, but dollars. This technique doesn't take the digits to the right of the decimal place into account. You can do so by dividing by 100, but that reduces the size of the maximum representable number by the same factor. So you'll need a larger string, and a mechanism for telling your program when to divide by 100.

As to the number of base 256 digits you'll need, $256^3 - 1$ is 16,777,215, and $256^4 - 1$ is 4,294,967,295. Four digits ought to do it. Even after dividing by 100, the four-digit hex field can hold more money than I make in a day.

The two functions shown in Listing 7-2 convert numbers into character strings and back again. The first, WriteHex, takes a number, a length, and (optionally) the letter D to indicate that the number is in dollars and cents. The second, ReadHex, takes such strings and converts them back. It doesn't need to know how long they are, thanks to the LEN( ) function, but the D gets your cents back.

How it works

If you want to store your transactions into a history file, create one four-byte character field for each numeric variable, and use the WriteHex( ) function to stuff in the data, like this:

```
REPLACE NEXT 1 Amount WITH WriteHex(ORDER.Amount,4,'D')
```

The 'D' tells WriteHex( ) to multiply ORDER.Amount by 100 before storing. Your report program will have to know that this field was a dollar amount, and use ReadHex(Amount,'D') to get the correct value back.

You can use ReadHex( ) in your own programs, in report forms, and of course in FoxFire. You can build it into the field definitions so that your users don't even know it's there.

Listing 7-2 Hexadecimal conversion functions.

```
FUNCTION WriteHex
PARAMETERS number, digits, numtype

IF numtype = [D]
   number  = number * 100
ENDIF

DO CASE
   CASE digits  = 4
      one        =            INT (   number            / 256 ^3      )
      number     = number -           one               * 256 ^3
      two        =            INT (   number            / 256 ^2      )
      number     = number -           two               * 256 ^2
      three      =            INT (   number            / 256         )
      number     = number -           three             * 256
      four       = number
      RETURN     CHR(one) + CHR(two) + CHR(three) + CHR(four)
   CASE digits  = 3
      one        =            INT ( number              / 256 ^2      )
      number     = number -           one        * 256 ^2
      two        =            INT ( number              / 256         )
      number     = number -           two        * 256
      three      = number
      RETURN     CHR(one) + CHR(two) + CHR(three)
   CASE digits  = 2
      one        =            INT ( number              / 256         )
      two        = number -           one               * 256
      RETURN     CHR(one) + CHR(two)
   OTHERWISE
      RETURN     CHR(number)
ENDCASE

FUNCTION ReadHex
PARAMETERS number, numtype
base     = 256
STORE 0 TO one,two,three,four
one       = ASC(SUBSTR(number,1,1))
IF LEN(number)>1
   two           = ASC(SUBSTR(number,2,1))
ENDIF
IF LEN(number)>2
   three         = ASC(SUBSTR(number,3,1))
ENDIF
IF LEN(number)>3
   four          = ASC(SUBSTR(number,4,1))
```

```
ENDIF
DO CASE
   CASE digits = 1
        value  = one
   CASE digits = 2
        value  = one * base + two
   CASE digits = 3
        value  = one * base^2 + two * base   + three
   CASE digits = 4
        value  = one * base^3 + two * base^2 + three * base + four
ENDCASE
IF PARAMETERS()<2
   RETURN value
   ELSE             && it must be a 'D'ollar value
   RETURN value /100
 ENDIF
```

If you run the test bed HISTORY.PRG shown in Listing 7-3, you'll see how compactly numbers can be stored using these routines. A BROWSE of the file it produces is shown in Fig. 7-2.

Listing 7-3 A testbed for the hex conversion functions.

```
* Program-ID.....: History.PRG
* Purpose........: Demonstrates history file with packed numeric fields
SET TALK    OFF
SET HEADING OFF
SET PATH TO DBFS\;SOURCE\

* Structure for database: HISTORY.DBF
* Field   Field Name  Type        Width
*    1   ORDERNUM    Character     10
*    2   DATE        Character      3
*    3   QUANTITY    Character      1
*    4   PRICE       Character      2
*    5   EXTENDED    Character      3
* ** Total **                      20
USE HISTORY EXCLUSIVE
ZAP
FOR I = 1 TO 5
   APPEND BLANK
   REPLACE TEXT 1 ;
      OrderNum  WITH '12345'                           , ;
      Date      WITH WriteHex(VAL(SYS(11,DATE()))),3)  , ;
```

```
      Quantity  WITH WriteHex(I,1)                    ; ;
      Price     WITH WriteHex(2.95*I,2,'D')           ; ;
      Extended  WITH WriteHex(2.95*I*I,3,'D')         , ;

ENDFOR
GO TOP
LIST OFF FIELDS                   ;
   OrderNum                   , ;
   SYS(10,ReadHex(Date))      , ;
   ReadHex(Quantity)          , ;
   ReadHex(Price    ,'D')     , ;
   ReadHex(Extended,'D')
```

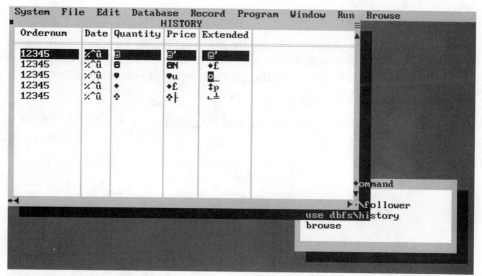

Figure 7-2 A hexadecimal history file.

Reports with a "thermometer"

Reports can take a long, long time, even if they're written using FoxFire. Users have been known to reboot the computer because they thought it was in an infinite loop.

What we have here is a failure to communicate. You can't make your users smarter, but your reports can state their progress elegantly if they're written in a certain way. It looks like a lot of work, but it avoids CHKDSK/F.

The FoxPro Report Writer is very easy to use, and integrates seamlessly with RQBE. It's the heart of FoxFire, MicroMega's blockbuster add-in report writer for applications developers. (I implemented it for a client's product the other day, and a $30,000 project that I wasn't looking forward to evaporated. It did everything I could think of and a few that I hadn't.)

But it wasn't exactly what I needed for one set of reports. These guys could take forever, with the attendant Ctrl–Alt–Delete risk. I wanted that cute little thermometer to display how far along I was, for my short-attention-span clients.

I thought that each report would be a thing unto itself, and budgeted a few hours for each one. Well, lo and behold, they're all pretty much the same old stuff. So the development time wasn't nearly as bad as I thought. And a few serendipitous spinoffs resulted as well.

The thermometer screen is shown in action in Fig. 7-3. The code in Listing 7-4 is commented where it's not obvious (the comments are enclosed between lines of asterisks). Try this, and you might never go back.

How it works

This example, which was developed by my good friend Dr. José Rodriguez-Santana, uses the same file structure used in the BROWSE program shown earlier in this chapter. The line that calculates what constitutes 100% is:

```
TotalRec = RECCOUNT()
```

If you're using a filter expression, you'd replace that with:

```
SET FILTER TO filterexpr
COUNT TO TotalRec
```

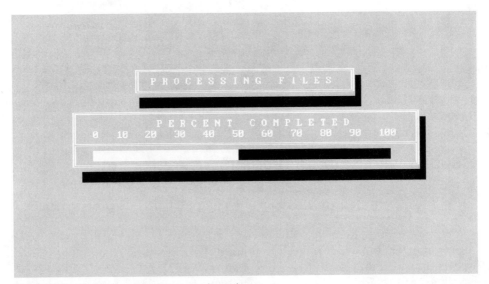

Figure 7-3 The thermometer screen in action.

Listing 7-4 A report with a thermometer.

```
* Program-ID....: REPORT.PRG
* Authors.......: José Rodríguez-Santana, M.D. and Les Pinter

* Structure for database: ORDERS.DBF
* Field  Field Name     Type          Width    Dec    Index
*    1   CNO            Character       5              Asc
*    2   DATE           Date            8
*    3   AMOUNT         Numeric         7        2
*    4   ORDERNUM       Character      10              Asc
* ** Total **                         31

SET DEFAULT TO DBFS\;SOURCE\

IF USED ( 'ORDERS' )
   SELECT      ORDERS
   ELSE
   SELECT      0
   USE         ORDERS
ENDIF
SET ORDER TO ORDERNUM


* Structure for database: ORDERDET.DBF
* Field  Field Name     Type          Width    Dec    Index
*    1   ORDERNUM       Character      10              Asc
*    2   LINENUM        Character       2
*    3   ITEM           Character      10
*    4   DESC           Character      35
*    5   QUANTITY       Numeric         3
*    6   PRICE          Numeric         6        2
*    7   EXTENDED       Numeric         8        2
* ** Total **                         75

IF USED ( 'ORDERDET' )
   SELECT ORDERDET
   ELSE
   SELECT 0
   USE    ORDERDET
ENDIF
SET ORDER TO ORDERNUM

SELECT ORDERS

OrderCount    = 0
TotalRec      = RECCOUNT()
```

7-4 Continued.

```
*    Page Totals
PQuanTot         = 0
PExtTot          = 0
* Report Totals
GQuanTot         = 0
GExtTot          = 0

LineCount        = 60
Page             =  0
FirstTime        = .T.

=Percent()

SET TEXTMERGE TO SAMPLE. NOSHOW
SET TEXTMERGE ON

SCAN

    OrderCount = OrderCount + 1
    =Bargraph(OrderCount*100/TotalRec)
    IF LineCount > 58
      IF NOT FirstTime
         =PrintFoot()
         \\<<CHR(12)>>
      ENDIF
      FirstTime  = .F.
      =PrintHead()
    ENDIF

    \Invoice : <<OrderNum>>   Date: <<Date>>   Amount: <<TRAN(Amount,'##,###.##')>>
    \

***********************************************************************
The best way to line these guys up is to put all of the spacing that follows
each field down on the next line, after the backslash and before the next
field. It makes it very easy to move them around until they line up.
***********************************************************************

    LineCount = LineCount + 2
    SELECT ORDERDET
    SEEK ORDERS.OrderNum
    SCAN WHILE OrderNum = ORDERS.OrderNum
```

```
    \<<Item>>
    \\    <<Desc>>
    \\                        <<TRANSFORM(Quantity,'###'        )>>
    \\ <<TRANSFORM(Price,    '#,###.##'  )>>
    \\ <<TRANSFORM(Extended,'###,###.##')>>
    LineCount = LineCount + 1

  ENDSCAN

  SELECT ORDERS

* Page Totals
   PQuanTot      = PQuanTot        + ORDERDET.Quantity
   PExtTot       = PExtTot         + ORDERDET.Extended
* Report Totals
   GQuanTot      = GQuanTot        + ORDERDET.Quantity
   GExtTot       = GExtTot         + ORDERDET.Extended

   LineCount = LineCount + 1

ENDSCAN

=GrandTot()

SET TEXTMERGE TO

ON KEY  LABEL  ENTER              KEYBOARD CHR(23)
DEFINE  WINDOW VIEWER    FROM 0,0 TO 24, 79 SHADOW TITLE ' REPORT '
MODIFY  COMM   SAMPLE.   NOMODIFY WINDOW VIEWER
ON KEY  LABEL  ENTER
RELEASE WINDOW VIEWER

IF CONFIRM ( ' Print Report? ' )
   SET HEADING OFF
   SET CONSOLE OFF
   TYPE VIEWER. TO PRINT                && or RUN PRINT VIEWER.
   SET CONSOLE ON
ENDIF

FUNCTION PrintHead

Page              = Page + 1
```

```
\Report Date:  <<DTOC(DATE())>>                        Page:  <<STR(Page,2)>>
\<<REPL('-',70)>>
\<<PADC('* DAILY TRANSACTION REPORT *',70)>>
\
\Item
\\    Description
\\                     Quantity
\\   Price
\\   Total
\<<REPL('-',70)>>
LineCount = 5


**************************************************************************
To get the report indented an inch from the left margin, use _PreText =
SPACE(10). _PreText will be inserted before each print line.
**************************************************************************


FUNCTION PrintFoot

DO WHILE LineCount < 62
    \
    LineCount = LineCount + 1
ENDDO
\<<REPLICATE('-',70)>>
\<<LEFT('Totals for this page:    ', 25 )>>
\\<<TRANSFORM ( PQuanTot    , '@Z ######.##' )>>
\\<<TRANSFORM ( PExtTot     , '@Z ######.##' )>>
\<<REPLICATE('-',70)>>
PQuanTot  = 0
PExtTot   = 0


FUNCTION GrandTot

IF LineCount > 50
   =PrintHead()
ENDIF

\
\<<REPLICATE('-',70)>>
\<<LEFT('T o t a l s:          ' ,25 )>>
\\<<TRANSFORM ( GQuanTot , '@Z ######.##' )>>
\\<<TRANSFORM ( GExtTot  , '@Z ######.##' )>>
\<<REPLICATE('-',70)>>
```

```
FUNCTION printerok

STORE CHR(187) TO a    && ┑
STORE CHR(201) TO b    && ╔
STORE CHR(205) TO c    && ═
STORE CHR(188) TO d    && ╝
STORE CHR(200) TO e    && ╚
DEFINE WINDOW w1 FROM 2,26 TO 9,76 DOUBLE shadow FLOAT CLOSE MINIMIZE ;
       TITLE  A + REPLICATE(B + C + C + A, 5) + B ;
       FOOTER D + REPLICATE(E + C + C + D, 5) + E ;

COLOR , , W+/B,W+/B,W+/B

DEFINE WINDOW w2 IN W1 FROM 0,1 TO 5,47 DOUBLE ;

TITLE  C + D + REPLICATE(E + C + C + D, 5) + E + C ;

FOOTER     A + REPLICATE(B + C + C + A, 5) + B ;

COLOR , , W+/B,W+/B,W+/B
inputkey = 0
ON KEY LABEL ESCAPE
SET CURSOR OFF
DO WHILE inputkey <> 27 .AND. (.NOT. PRINTSTATUS())
   ACTIVATE WINDOW w1
   ACTIVATE WINDOW w2
   @ 0, 2 say "Printer not ready..."
   @ 1, 2 say " "
   @ 2, 2 say "Ready the printer and press ←┘, or "
   @ 3, 2 say "or press ESCAPE to cancel report."
   =inkey(0)
ENDDO
ON KEY LABEL ESCAPE *
SET CURSOR ON
DEACT WIND w1
DEACT WIND w2
RETURN (inputkey <> 27)

FUNCTION BARGRAPH
PARAMETERS Pct
Pct = IIF(Pct>100, 100, Pct)
@ 13,14 SAY REPLICATE ("█", (Pct/2)+1)
```

7-4 Continued.

```
*************************************************************************
This is where the thermometer is displayed on the screen, and this is
all it takes to do it.
*************************************************************************
```

```
FUNCTION MESSBOX
PARAMETERS line, Mess, Shadow, SD, BC
    MLen            = LEN(Mess)
    Scol            = (80 - Mlen) / 2
    T               = Line - 1
    L               = Scol - 2
    B               = Line + 1
    R               = Scol + MLen + 2
    Dummy           = BOXES(T,L,B,R,Shadow,SD,BC)
    @ Line, Scol SAY Mess


FUNCTION BOXES
PARAMETERS T,L,B,R,Shadow,SD,BC
DO CASE
    Case SD     = "D"
         Kind   = "Double"
    Case SD     = "S"
         Kind   = "  "
    Case SD     = "N"
         Kind   = "None"
ENDCASE

IF Shadow
    @ T+1,L+1 FILL TO B+1,R+1 COLOR N+/N
ENDIF

@ T,L CLEAR     TO B,R
@ T,L           TO B,R &Kind


FUNCTION Percent
@ 10,12 FILL TO 15,70 COLOR N+/N
@ 09,10 TO 14,69 DOUBLE COLOR W+/B
@ 12,11 TO 12,68 DOUBLE COLOR W+/B
@ 12,10 SAY "╟"                     COLOR W+/B
@ 12,69 SAY "╢"                     COLOR W+/B
@ 10,11 SAY "      P E R C E N T    C O M P L E T E D    " COLOR W+/B
@ 11,11 SAY "  0    10    20    30    40    50 "         COLOR W+/B
@ 11,41 SAY "  60    70    80    90    100       "       COLOR W+/B
@ 13,11 SAY "       "      COLOR B/B
@ 13,65 SAY "       "      COLOR B/B
```

7-4 Continued.

```
Dummy = MESSBOX(06, " P R O C E S S I N G   F I L E S", .T., "D")

RETURN
```

The PERCENT function displays the thermometer overlay, and the line:

```
=Bargraph(OrderCount*100/TotalRec)
```

displays a solid bar in the middle of the overlay. Use this example to write your own detail-line-reporting program in a parent-child environment. I like FoxPro's report writer, but this provides a better testbed for demonstrating the thermometer example code precisely.

Lisa Slater developed a variant of this approach you can use with Report Form by including it as a detail-line element, a UDF that updates the solid bar. Alan Griver updated it and included it in his excellent book.

After opening files and counting the number of records that will be included in the report, you can use the REPLICATE( ) function to produce a horizontal bar graph of percentage completion, by "normalizing" the percentage to the display width. For example, if:

```
( RECNO() / RECCOUNT() )
```

is the percentage read, then:

```
REPL('*',(RECNO()/RECCOUNT()*60)
```

will be 60 characters long when it's finished. However, you can use RECNO( ) only if the file isn't indexed, and RECCOUNT( ) is appropriate only if you aren't using a filter and there are no recycled records in the file. So you'll have to count TotRecs yourself, and then use your own counter as you scan the file.

Also, I presume you're writing to disk during this process. Even my users can tell something's happening if the printer's chattering. So displaying to the screen without writing to the printer device at the same time is going to be important. Happily, TEXTMERGE makes most of this pretty easy.

The last routine displays a nice box in which the thermometer display grows. The resulting progress monitoring instills confidence in the user that the computer is indeed not in an infinite loop, and will eventually be finished with its report.

Notes and comments

A large part of client satisfaction is perception of control. I've long believed that some users are terrified by their computers because they represent loss of control. Give them the ability to control the software, or the *perception* that they're in control, and they won't be nearly so frustrated or intimidated.

As simple as MODIFY REPORT is, it'll probably take a whiney user to get you to try this technique. It's easier than it looks, and users love it.

Summary

You'd think that writing your own BROWSE would be a huge amount of work. It's really just a matter of taking one step at a time. I write pseudo-code that describes what I want to happen under each circumstance, and then write the code that's needed.

What happens if the user presses the down arrow on the last line of the display of an invoice? If there are no more matching detail lines in the file, do you want to automatically add a blank line? With BROWSE, you do it FoxPro's way. If it's your BROWSE, you have more flexibility.

In the next two chapters, we'll examine two types of applications that use many of the techniques developed up to now, plus a few more.

8
Special estimating applications

It's time to put some of these fine ideas into practice. I've written a book about a number of different applications (*FoxPro 2.5 Applications*, also from WindCrest), but there are always more interesting ones. This chapter and the next one deal with a couple of my favorites.

I often get pulled into projects when people who have tried to write complex applications have gotten in over their heads. The reason isn't usually that they aren't smart enough—most folks who try to teach themselves programming are extremely bright. Instead, it's often that their basic design is flawed. The harder they work, the more problems pop up. Eventually they feel that the program has taken control of them rather than the other way around.

I mention *estimating* in this context because the single thread that characterizes my estimating bailouts is design. Cost estimators have taken to spreadsheets like ducks to water because spreadsheets can visually represent the complex formulas that estimating often requires.

Unfortunately, there's no simple way to sum a hundred spreadsheets. Lotus 1-2-3 got its name from its three alleged capabilities: spreadsheet, database, and graphics. I think it should be called Lotus 1-3, however, because there isn't a database in it. So when the database requirements surface, the spreadsheet approach falls short.

The application design

For this application, we'll use an invoice-model screen header on top, detail lines in the middle, and total at the bottom. Job and customer information will be stored in a header record, and detail line information in a detail record.

In many estimating applications, detail information is quite complex. The invoice model is appropriate for retail applications because quantity, description, price, and extension pretty much says it all. But estimating frequently involves many, many factors. So while the invoice model is fine to display what the customer is buying and how much he owes, each line of detail represents many additional fields.

Detail lines

For this example, I'll use carpet installation. The application is typical of many types of contractors. There's a basic product, with two labor rates, variable mark-up, and a number of add-ons. The basic product can be from any of several manufacturers, and each manufacturer has several styles. Prices for the add-ons are stored in a CONTROL file, which management can change from time to time.

I'll use the metaphor of a spreadsheet because it's familiar to the people using the application. They used to do this with a spreadsheet, and the FoxPro screen will mimic, as much as possible, their original spreadsheet format. So we'll have an invoice screen like the one shown in Fig. 8-1, and the detail line item screen shown in Fig. 8-2.

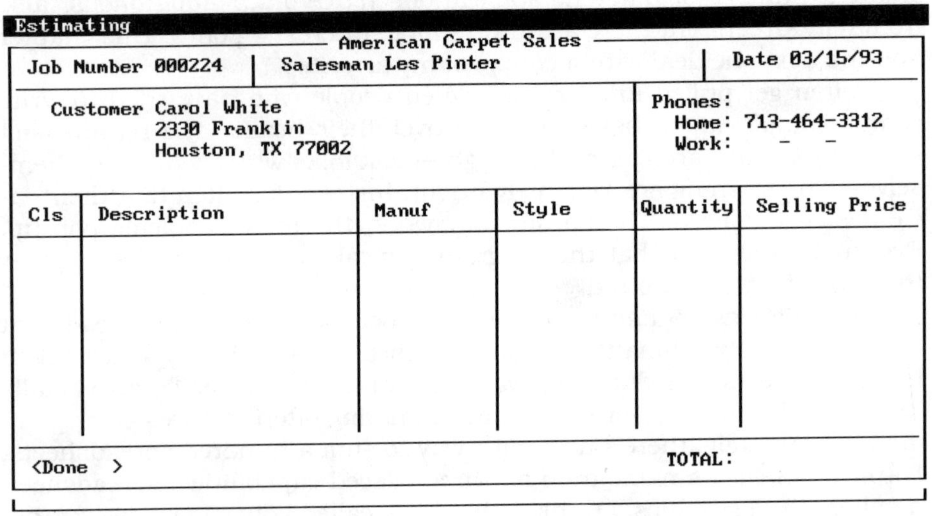

Figure 8-1 The Invoice screen.

Cursor movement

On the invoice screen, you want to simplify cursor movement. The users have assured you that two or three line items is about as big as this gets, so the line-item area doesn't need to be scrolled. That allows a luxury that you seldom get—the program will move smoothly from the top of the header to the first line item, and from the last line item to the first field in the footer.

Specifically, you want the first input line to come alive when you move

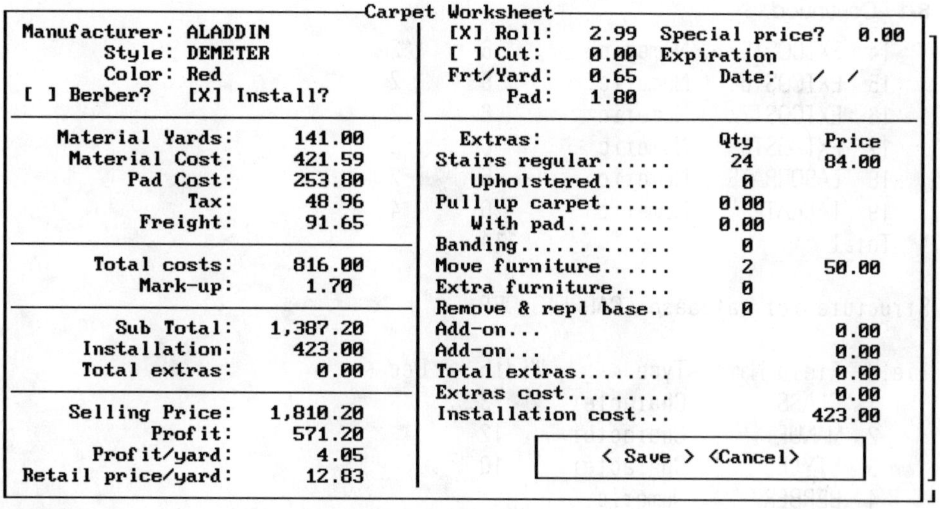

Figure 8-2 The Spreadsheet screen for line items.

down from the last field in the header area. If you press the up arrow from the top detail line, you want to return to the header. Similarly, when the user leaves the last detail line, you want a fluid transition to the first input field in the footer area.

File structures

The file structures used in this application appear in Listing 8-1. This example doesn't include file maintenance on the CARPETS and CONTROL file, but the application generated by FOXAPP would probably be quite adequate.

Listing 8-1 The file structures used in this chapter.

Structure for database: CONTROL.DBF

Field	Field Name	Type	Width	Dec	Index
1	JOBNUM	Numeric	6		
2	EXTPRICE1	Numeric	6	2	
3	EXTPRICE2	Numeric	6	2	
4	EXTPRICE3	Numeric	6	2	
5	EXTPRICE4	Numeric	6	2	
6	EXTPRICE5	Numeric	6	2	
7	EXTPRICE6	Numeric	6	2	
8	EXTPRICE7	Numeric	6	2	
9	EXTPRICE8	Numeric	6	2	
10	EXTCOST1	Numeric	6	2	
11	EXTCOST2	Numeric	6	2	
12	EXTCOST3	Numeric	6	2	
13	EXTCOST4	Numeric	6	2	

14	EXTCOST5	Numeric	6	2
15	EXTCOST6	Numeric	6	2
16	EXTCOST7	Numeric	6	2
17	EXTCOST8	Numeric	6	2
18	LABORRATE	Numeric	5	2
19	TAXRATE	Numeric	6	4
** Total **			114	

Structure for database: CARPETS.DBF

Field	Field Name	Type	Width	Dec
1	CLASS	Character	3	
2	MANUF	Character	12	
3	STYLE	Character	10	
4	BERBER	Numeric	1	
5	CODE	Character	5	
6	DESCRIP	Character	35	
7	PRICE1	Numeric	7	2
8	PRICE2	Numeric	7	2
9	COST1	Numeric	7	2
10	COST2	Numeric	7	2
11	SPECIALPRC	Numeric	7	2
12	EXPIRES	Date	8	
13	SELLPRICE	Numeric	7	2
** Total **			117	

Structure for database: ESTIMATE.DBF

Field	Field Name	Type	Width	Dec	Index
1	ESTIMATENO	Character	6		Asc
2	DATE	Date	8		Asc
3	SALESMAN	Character	25		Asc
4	CUSTNAME	Character	40		Asc
5	CUSTADD1	Character	40		
6	CUSTADD2	Character	40		
7	CUSTADD3	Character	40		
8	TOTALAMT	Numeric	8	2	
9	ACCEPTED	Character	1		
10	STARTDATE	Date	8		
** Total **			217		

Structure for database: DETAIL.DBF

Field	Field Name	Type	Width	Dec	Index
1	ESTIMATENO	Character	6		Asc
2	CLASS	Character	3		

3	DESCRIP	Character	20	
4	MANUF	Character	10	
5	STYLE	Character	10	
6	CLINE	Character	1	
7	QUANTITY	Numeric	6	2
8	SELLPRICE	Numeric	8	2
9	BERBER	Numeric	1	
10	MARKUP	Numeric	4	2
11	USEROLL	Numeric	1	
12	ROLL	Numeric	6	2
13	USECUT	Numeric	1	
14	CUT	Numeric	6	2
15	SPECIALPRC	Numeric	6	2
16	QTY1	Numeric	3	
17	QTY2	Numeric	3	
18	QTY3	Numeric	6	2
19	QTY4	Numeric	6	2
20	QTY5	Numeric	3	
21	QTY6	Numeric	3	
22	QTY7	Numeric	3	
23	QTY8	Numeric	3	
24	ADD1	Character	19	
25	EXTPRICE9	Numeric	7	2
26	ADD2	Character	19	
27	EXTPRICE10	Numeric	7	2
Total **			172	

The Screen Builder screen

The Screen Builder screen for the invoice appears in Fig. 8-3. The screen in Fig. 8-4 shows an invoice with one detail line filled in. The second, or current, detail line is completely highlighted. You can accomplish this trick with the WHEN and VALID clauses for the line items, using the @ FILL...COLOR *pair* command.

The application code

The project file application is very simple, consisting of three programs and two screens. The MAIN program is shown in Listing 8-2.

The MENU

The menu code appears in Listing 8-3. This menu is very sparse, with the calendar, calculator, and a bar to enter a new estimate. The menu includes the function DONE, which sets the global variable Done to .True. and forces termination of the READ with a CLEAR READ ALL. Note the use of SKIP FOR to prevent recursive calls to the estimating screen.

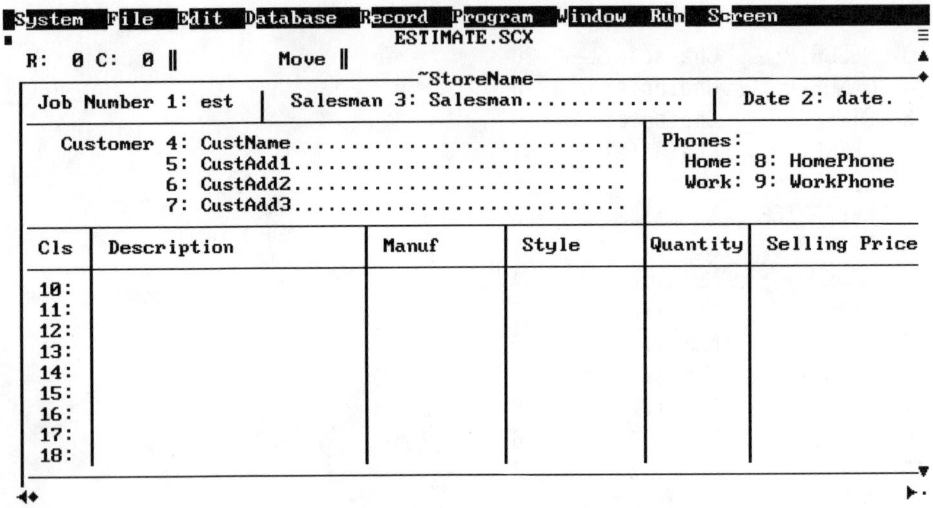

```
System File Edit Database Record Program Window Run Screen
                              ESTIMATE.SCX                              ≡
  R:  0 C:  0 ‖         Move ‖                                          ▲
┌─────────────────────────────────~StoreName~─────────────┬───────────────┐
│  Job Number 1: est  │ Salesman 3: Salesman............. │ Date 2: date. │
├─────────────────────┴──────────────────────────────┬────┴───────────────┤
│   Customer 4: CustName........................      │ Phones:            │
│            5: CustAdd1........................      │   Home: 8: HomePhone│
│            6: CustAdd2........................      │   Work: 9: WorkPhone│
│            7: CustAdd3........................      │                    │
├──────┬──────────────────┬────────────┬─────────┬────────────┬───────────┤
│ Cls  │ Description      │ Manuf      │ Style   │ Quantity   │ Selling Price│
├──────┼──────────────────┼────────────┼─────────┼────────────┼───────────┤
│ 10:  │                  │            │         │            │           │
│ 11:  │                  │            │         │            │           │
│ 12:  │                  │            │         │            │           │
│ 13:  │                  │            │         │            │           │
│ 14:  │                  │            │         │            │           │
│ 15:  │                  │            │         │            │           │
│ 16:  │                  │            │         │            │           │
│ 17:  │                  │            │         │            │           │
│ 18:  │                  │            │         │            │         ▼ │
└──────┴──────────────────┴────────────┴─────────┴────────────┴───────────┘
◄◆                                                                      ►·
```

Figure 8-3 The Screen Builder with the Invoice screen loaded.

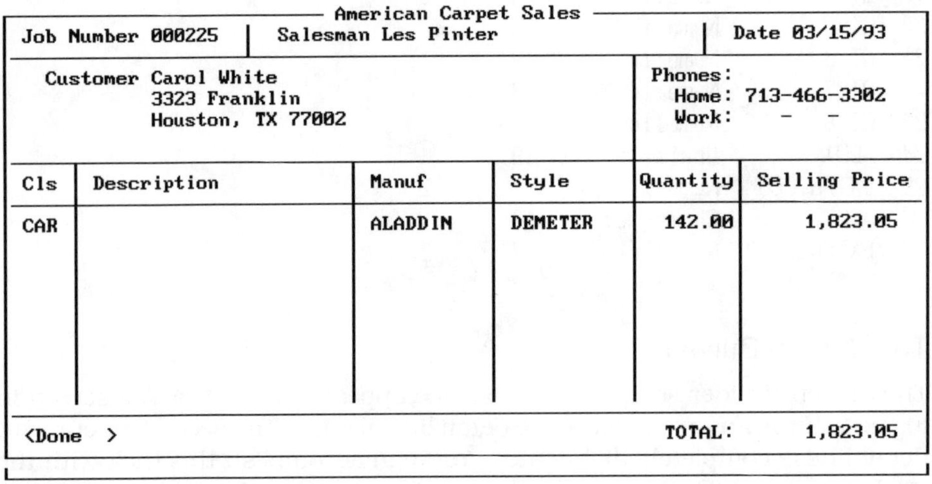

```
┌──────────────────────── American Carpet Sales ─────────────────────────┐
│  Job Number 000225  │ Salesman Les Pinter        │ Date 03/15/93        │
├─────────────────────┴────────────────────────┬───┴──────────────────────┤
│   Customer Carol White                        │ Phones:                  │
│            3323 Franklin                       │   Home: 713-466-3302     │
│            Houston, TX 77002                   │   Work:    -   -         │
├──────┬──────────────────┬────────────┬─────────┬────────────┬───────────┤
│ Cls  │ Description      │ Manuf      │ Style   │ Quantity   │ Selling Price│
├──────┼──────────────────┼────────────┼─────────┼────────────┼───────────┤
│ CAR  │                  │ ALADDIN    │ DEMETER │ 142.00     │ 1,823.05  │
│      │                  │            │         │            │           │
│      │                  │            │         │            │           │
│      │                  │            │         │            │           │
│      │                  │            │         │            │           │
├──────┴──────────────────┴────────────┴─────────┼────────────┼───────────┤
│ <Done  >                                        │ TOTAL:     │ 1,823.05  │
└─────────────────────────────────────────────────┴────────────┴───────────┘
```

Figure 8-4 The Invoice screen in action.

Listing 8-2 The MAIN program.

```
* Program-ID.....: Main.PRG
* Author.........: Pinter Consulting Staff
* Purpose........: Launches estimating system

SET TALK    OFF
SET CONFIRM ON
SET SAFETY  OFF
SET ESCAPE  OFF

SET COLOR OF SCHEME 1 to ,,,,,,,,,GR+/B
```

8-2 Continued.

```
ON ERROR DO ERRTRAP

SET PATH TO DBFS\

USE CARPETS   IN A

* Create validation array for CARPETS screen
SELECT DISTINCT MANUF FROM CARPETS INTO ARRAY MANUFACTS

SELECT CARPETS
SET ORDER TO 1

USE CONTROL   IN B
USE ESTIMATE  IN C ORDER 1
USE DETAIL    IN D ORDER 1

* Create 'PUBLIC' memvars for all field names in parent, child files
SELECT  ESTIMATE
SCATTER MEMVAR
SELECT  DETAIL
SCATTER MEMVAR

DEFINE   WINDOW BACKGROUND FROM 1,0 TO 23, 79
ACTIVATE WINDOW BACKGROUND

@ 10, 30 SAY [ ** Logo here ** ]
@ WROWS()-1, 0 SAY PADC ( [ Press F10 for Menu ** ] , WCOLS() )

StoreName    = [ American Carpet Sales ]    && used in SCREEN title

Done         = .F.         && Switch to control program termination
Estimating   = .F.         && Switch to suppress a menu option

DO MAIN.MPR
ACTIVATE MENU _MSYSMENU PAD ESTIMATE

READ VALID AM_I_DONE()

RELEASE  WINDOW BACKGROUND

CLEAR WINDOW
CLEAR

RELEASE WINDOW CALCULATOR
RELEASE WINDOW DIARY
```

8-2 Continued.

```
SET SYSMENU TO DEFAULT

RETURN               && QUIT

FUNCTION AM_I_DONE
IF NOT Done
   RETURN .F.
ENDIF
```

Listing 8-3 The MENU program.

```
*
*   ┌─────────────────────────────────────────────────────┐
*   │  03/11/93              MAIN.MPR            08:44:14   │
*   └─────────────────────────────────────────────────────┘


*   ┌─────────────────────────────────────────────────────┐
*   │                   Menu Definition                    │
*   └─────────────────────────────────────────────────────┘

SET SYSMENU TO
SET SYSMENU AUTOMATIC

DEFINE PAD ESTIMATE OF _MSYSMENU PROMPT "Estimating" COLOR SCHEME 3
ON PAD ESTIMATE OF _MSYSMENU ACTIVATE POPUP estimating

DEFINE POPUP estimating MARGIN RELATIVE SHADOW COLOR SCHEME 4
DEFINE BAR 1 OF estimating PROMPT "\<New estimate" ;
   KEY ALT+N, "ALT+N" ;
   SKIP FOR Estimating
DEFINE BAR _MST_CALCU OF estimating PROMPT "\<Calculator" ;
   KEY ALT+C, "ALT+C"
DEFINE BAR _MST_DIARY OF estimating PROMPT "\<Diary/Calendar" ;
   KEY ALT+D, "ALT+D"
DEFINE BAR 4 OF estimating PROMPT "\<Quit" ;
   KEY ALT+Q, "ALT+Q"
ON SELECTION BAR 1 OF estimating DO ESTIMATE.SPR
ON SELECTION BAR 4 OF estimating DO DONE IN MAIN.MPR

ON SELECTION MENU _MSYSMENU

*   ┌─────────────────────────────────────────────────────┐
*   │               Cleanup Code & Procedures              │
*   └─────────────────────────────────────────────────────┘
```

```
FUNCTION DONE
Done = .T.
CLEAR READ ALL
KEYBOARD CHR(23)
```

The CONFIRM program

Utility programs are a part of almost every application. While this function is standard, there are many ways to write it. The program in Listing 8-4 lets you pass a parameter that determines whether the dialog defaults to Yes or No.

Listing 8-4 The CONFIRM program.

```
* Program-ID......: Confirm.PRG
* Purpose.........: Displays a confirming dialogue using the title
*                   passed to it when called; defaults to 'Y' unless a
*                   second parameter (Y/N) is supplied.
PARAMETERS ctitle, defaultcode
currwind = WOUTPUT()
PRIVATE length,where,choice
length = LEN ( ctitle ) + 2
where  = 40 -  length  / 2
DEFINE POPUP CONFIRM FROM 13, where IN SCREEN ;
   COLOR N/W,N/W,N/W,N/W,N/W,W+/R,W+/W
DEFINE BAR 1 OF CONFIRM PROMPT [\] + PADC ( ctitle  , length )
DEFINE BAR 2 OF CONFIRM PROMPT [\-]
DEFINE BAR 3 OF CONFIRM PROMPT       PADC ( [ \<Yes] , length )
DEFINE BAR 4 OF CONFIRM PROMPT       PADC ( [ \<No ] , length )
BarNum = []
IF PARAMETERS() > 1
   DO CASE
      CASE UPPER(defaultcode) = 'Y'
         BarNum = [ BAR 3]
      OTHERWISE
         BarNum = [ BAR 4]
   ENDCASE
ENDIF
ON SELECTION POPUP CONFIRM DEACTIVATE POPUP CONFIRM
SaveConf = SET ( [CONFIRM] )
SET CONFIRM OFF
ACTIVATE SCREEN
ACTIVATE POPUP CONFIRM &BarNum
choice = PROMPT()
```

8-4 Continued.

```
RELEASE POPUP CONFIRM
SET CONFIRM &SaveConf
IF LEN(TRIM(currwind)) > 0
   ACTIVATE WINDOW (currwind)
ENDIF
RETURN IIF ( [Yes] $ choice , .T. , .F. )
```

The ESTIMATE screen

The ESTIMATE screen code appears in Listing 8-5. The next available invoice number is generated from the CONTROL file. Note that, in a multiuser system, if you don't want gaps in your numbering system you have
to do things a bit differently. I use SYS(3) to give me a temporary invoice
number, and then replace all occurrences of the temporary number with
the next available number once I know the sale wasn't canceled.

Listing 8-5 The ESTIMATE code.

```
*
*                           ESTIMATE.SPR
*


#REGION 0
REGIONAL m.currarea, m.talkstat, m.compstat

IF SET("TALK") = "ON"
   SET TALK OFF
   m.talkstat = "ON"
   ELSE
   m.talkstat = "OFF"
ENDIF
m.compstat = SET("COMPATIBLE")
SET COMPATIBLE FOXPLUS


*
*                       MS-DOS Window definitions
*


IF NOT WEXIST("estimate") ;
   OR UPPER(WTITLE("ESTIMATE")) == "ESTIMATE.PJX" ;
   OR UPPER(WTITLE("ESTIMATE")) == "ESTIMATE.SCX" ;
   OR UPPER(WTITLE("ESTIMATE")) == "ESTIMATE.MNX" ;
   OR UPPER(WTITLE("ESTIMATE")) == "ESTIMATE.PRG" ;
   OR UPPER(WTITLE("ESTIMATE")) == "ESTIMATE.FRX" ;
   OR UPPER(WTITLE("ESTIMATE")) == "ESTIMATE.QPR"
   DEFINE WINDOW estimate ;
```

```
        FROM 1, 0 ;
        TO 22,79 ;
        TITLE StoreName ;
        NOFLOAT ;
        NOCLOSE ;
        NOMINIMIZE ;
        COLOR SCHEME 1
ENDIF


*
*               ┌────────────────────────────────────────────────┐
*               │    ESTIMATE/MS-DOS Setup Code - SECTION 2        │
*               └────────────────────────────────────────────────┘


#REGION 1
* Used to tell Screen Builder that screen title is a memvar

SELECT  ESTIMATE
SCATTER MEMVAR BLANK
SELECT  CONTROL
SCATTER MEMVAR
REPLACE NEXT 1 JOBNUM WITH JOBNUM + 1
SELECT  ESTIMATE
m.ESTIMATENO = TRAN ( CONTROL.JOBNUM, '@L ######' )
m.DATE        = DATE()
SHOW GET m.ESTIMATENO
SHOW GET m.DATE


Estimating = .T.     && turn option off
Canceled   = .F.
Finished   = [ Done ]

STORE SPACE(3) TO ;
 Class1 , ;
 Class2 , ;
 Class3 , ;
 Class4 , ;
 Class5 , ;
 Class6 , ;
 Class7 , ;
 Class8 , ;
 Class9


*
*               ┌────────────────────────────────────────────────┐
*               │         ESTIMATE/MS-DOS Screen Layout           │
*               └────────────────────────────────────────────────┘
```

```
#REGION 1
IF WVISIBLE("estimate")
    ACTIVATE WINDOW estimate SAME
ELSE
    ACTIVATE WINDOW estimate NOSHOW
ENDIF
@ 0,62 SAY "Date" ;
    SIZE 1,4, 0
@ 0,23 SAY "Salesman" ;
    SIZE 1,8, 0
@ 0,1 SAY "Job Number" ;
    SIZE 1,10, 0
@ 1,0 TO 1,77
@ 2,3 SAY "Customer" ;
    SIZE 1,8, 0
@ 2,53 TO 5,53
@ 2,55 SAY "Phones:" ;
    SIZE 1,7, 0
@ 3,57 SAY "Home:" ;
    SIZE 1,5, 0
@ 4,57 SAY "Work:" ;
    SIZE 1,5, 0
@ 1,53 SAY "┬" ;
    SIZE 1,1, 0
@ 0,20 SAY "|" ;
    SIZE 1,1, 0
@ 0,59 SAY "|" ;
    SIZE 1,1, 0
@ 1,59 SAY "⊥" ;
    SIZE 1,1, 0
@ 1,20 SAY "⊥" ;
    SIZE 1,1, 0
@ 0,12 GET m.estimateno ;
    SIZE 1,6 ;
    DEFAULT " " ;
    DISABLE
@ 0,67 GET m.date ;
    SIZE 1,8 ;
    DEFAULT {  /  /  } ;
    WHEN WHENDATE() ;
    DISABLE
@ 0,32 GET m.Salesman ;
    SIZE 1,25 ;
    DEFAULT " " ;
    PICTURE "!XXXXXXXXXXXXXXXXXXXXXXXX" ;
```

```
   MESSAGE "Enter SALESMAN ^G Pressing ESCAPE cancels estimate entry"
@ 2,12 GET m.CustName ;
   SIZE 1,40 ;
   DEFAULT " " ;
   PICTURE "!XXXXXXXXXXXXXXXXXXXXXXXXXXXXXXXXXXXXXXXX"
@ 3,12 GET m.CustAdd1 ;
   SIZE 1,40 ;
   DEFAULT " " ;
   PICTURE "!XXXXXXXXXXXXXXXXXXXXXXXXXXXXXXXXXXXXXXXX"
@ 4,12 GET m.CustAdd2 ;
   SIZE 1,40 ;
   DEFAULT " " ;
   PICTURE "!XXXXXXXXXXXXXXXXXXXXXXXXXXXXXXXXXXXXXXXX"
@ 5,12 GET m.CustAdd3 ;
   SIZE 1,40 ;
   DEFAULT " " ;
   PICTURE "!XXXXXXXXXXXXXXXXXXXXXXXXXXXXXXXXXXXXXXXX"
@ 3,63 GET m.HomePhone ;
   SIZE 1,12 ;
   DEFAULT " " ;
   PICTURE "999-999-9999"
@ 4,63 GET m.WorkPhone ;
   SIZE 1,12 ;
   DEFAULT " " ;
   PICTURE "999-999-9999"
@ 6,0 TO 6,77
@ 8,0 TO 8,77
@ 7,29 TO 17,29
@ 7,5 TO 17,5
@ 7,31 SAY "Manuf" ;
   SIZE 1,5, 0
@ 7,41 TO 17,41
@ 7,43 SAY "Style" ;
   SIZE 1,5, 0
@ 7,53 TO 17,53
@ 7,54 SAY "Quantity" ;
   SIZE 1,8, 0
@ 7,62 TO 17,62
@ 7,64 SAY "Selling Price" ;
   SIZE 1,13, 0
@ 7,7 SAY "Description" ;
   SIZE 1,11, 0
@ 7,1 SAY "Cls" ;
   SIZE 1,3, 0
@ 9,1 GET m.Class1 ;
```

```
   SIZE 1,3 ;
   DEFAULT " " ;
   PICTURE "!!!" ;
   WHEN Hilite(1) ;
   VALID CLASS1()
@ 10,1 GET m.Class2 ;
   SIZE 1,3 ;
   DEFAULT " " ;
   PICTURE "!!!" ;
   WHEN ShowLines() AND Hilite(2) ;
   VALID CLASS2()
@ 11,1 GET m.Class3 ;
   SIZE 1,3 ;
   DEFAULT " " ;
   PICTURE "!!!" ;
   WHEN ShowLines() AND Hilite(3) ;
   VALID CLASS3()
@ 12,1 GET m.Class4 ;
   SIZE 1,3 ;
   DEFAULT " " ;
   PICTURE "!!!" ;
   WHEN ShowLines() AND Hilite(4) ;
   VALID CLASS4()
@ 13,1 GET m.Class5 ;
   SIZE 1,3 ;
   DEFAULT " " ;
   PICTURE "!!!" ;
   WHEN ShowLines() AND Hilite(5) ;
   VALID CLASS5()
@ 14,1 GET m.Class6 ;
   SIZE 1,3 ;
   DEFAULT " " ;
   PICTURE "!!!" ;
   WHEN ShowLines() AND Hilite(6) ;
   VALID CLASS6()
@ 15,1 GET m.Class7 ;
   SIZE 1,3 ;
   DEFAULT " " ;
   PICTURE "!!!" ;
   WHEN ShowLines() AND Hilite(7) ;
   VALID CLASS7()
@ 16,1 GET m.Class8 ;
   SIZE 1,3 ;
   DEFAULT " " ;
   PICTURE "!!!" ;
```

```
   WHEN ShowLines() AND Hilite(8) ;
   VALID CLASS8()
@ 17,1 GET m.Class9 ;
   SIZE 1,3 ;
   DEFAULT " " ;
   PICTURE "!!!" ;
   WHEN ShowLines() AND Hilite(9) ;
   VALID CLASS9()
@ 18,0 TO 18,77
@ 19,56 SAY "TOTAL:" ;
   SIZE 1,6, 0
@ 19,1 GET m.Finished ;
   PICTURE "@*HT  Done " ;
   SIZE 1,8,1 ;
   DEFAULT 1 ;
   WHEN FINWHEN() ;
   VALID FINVALID()
@ 8,5 SAY "┼" ;
   SIZE 1,1, 0
@ 8,29 SAY "┼" ;
   SIZE 1,1, 0
@ 8,41 SAY "┼" ;
   SIZE 1,1, 0
@ 8,53 SAY "┼" ;
   SIZE 1,1, 0
@ 8,62 SAY "┼" ;
   SIZE 1,1, 0
@ 6,5 SAY "┬" ;
   SIZE 1,1, 0
@ 6,29 SAY "┬" ;
   SIZE 1,1, 0
@ 6,41 SAY "┬" ;
   SIZE 1,1, 0
@ 6,62 SAY "┬" ;
   SIZE 1,1, 0
@ 6,53 SAY "┼" ;
   SIZE 1,1, 0

IF NOT WVISIBLE("estimate")
   ACTIVATE WINDOW estimate
ENDIF

*
*       MS-DOSREAD contains clauses from SCREEN estimate
*
```

```
READ CYCLE ;
    VALID READVALID() ;
    COLOR W+/R,W+/R

#REGION 0
IF m.talkstat = "ON"
    SET TALK ON
ENDIF
IF m.compstat = "ON"
    SET COMPATIBLE ON
ENDIF


*
*                    ┌─────────────────────────────────────────────┐
*                    ║            ESTIMATE/MS-DOS Cleanup Code       ║
*                    └─────────────────────────────────────────────┘


#REGION 1
RELEASE WINDOW ESTIMATE
* Clear last message off desktop
ACTIVATE SCREEN
CLEAR
ACTIVATE WINDOW BACKGROUND

IF Canceled
    =Alarm()
    WAIT WINDOW [ ** Canceled ** ] TIMEOUT 1
    Estimating = .F.     && turn option back on
    RETURN
ENDIF
SELECT DETAIL
SEEK m.EstimateNo
IF NOT FOUND()
    =Alarm()
    WAIT WINDOW [ ** Canceled ** ] TIMEOUT 1
    Estimating = .F.     && turn option back on
    RETURN
ENDIF
SELECT ESTIMATE
SEEK m.Estimateno
IF NOT FOUND()
    INSERT INTO ESTIMATE FROM MEMVAR
    ELSE
    GATHER MEMVAR
ENDIF
Estimating = .F.     && turn option back on
```

```
*
*         ┌──────────────────────────────────────────────────────────┐
*         │  ESTIMATE/MS-DOS Supporting Procedures and Functions      │
          └──────────────────────────────────────────────────────────┘


#REGION 1
FUNCTION Hilite
PARAMETERS Line
Var = VARREAD()
=ShowALine()
@      9,0 FILL TO WROWS()-1,77          COLOR GR+/B
@ Line+8,1 FILL TO Line+8,   WCOLS()-1 COLOR W+/R

FUNCTION ShowLines
GrandTotal = 0
FOR Line = 1 TO 9
   =ShowALine()
   GrandTotal = GrandTotal + DETAIL.SellPrice
ENDFOR
@ 19, 67 SAY GrandTotal PICTURE '@Z ##,###.##'

FUNCTION SHOWaLine
SELECT DETAIL
HLine = STR(Line,1)
SEEK m.Estimateno + m.HLine
@ 8+Line, 7 SAY Descrip
@ 8+Line,31 SAY Manuf
@ 8+Line,43 SAY Style
@ 8+Line,56 SAY TRAN(Quantity , '@Z    ###.##' )
@ 8+Line,67 SAY TRAN(SellPrice, '@Z ##,###.##' )

FUNCTION PRODUCT
PARAMETERS Line
m.SaveEst = m.Estimateno
CLine = STR(Line,1)
Var = [m.Class] + m.CLine
IF NOT &Var $ [CAR/CAB/]
   DEFINE POPUP CLASSES FROM 5,5 SHADOW MARGIN ;
      COLOR N/W, N/W, N/W, N/W, N/W, W+/R, W+/W
   DEFINE BAR 1 OF CLASSES PROMPT [\Products]
   DEFINE BAR 2 OF CLASSES PROMPT [\-       ]
   DEFINE BAR 3 OF CLASSES PROMPT [CARPETS  ]
   DEFINE BAR 4 OF CLASSES PROMPT [\CABINETS ]
   DEFINE BAR 5 OF CLASSES PROMPT [\SHELVING ]
   ON SELECTION POPUP CLASSES DEACTIVATE POPUP CLASSES
   ACTIVATE POPUP CLASSES
```

```
      &Var    = PROMPT()
      RELEASE  POPUP CLASSES
      IF EMPTY ( &Var )
         &Var = SPACE(3)
         ELSE
         &Var = LEFT ( &Var, 3 )
      ENDIF
ENDIF
SELECT DETAIL
m.Class = &Var
SEEK m.Estimateno + m.CLine
IF FOUND()
   Adding = .F.
   SCATTER MEMVAR
   ELSE
   Adding = .T.
   SCATTER MEMVAR BLANK
   CLine = STR(Line,1)  && because it's a field name and we just erased it.
   m.Class = &var
ENDIF
m.Estimateno = m.SaveEst
DO CASE
   CASE m.Class = [CAR]
        DO CARPET.SPR
*  CASE m.Class = [CAB]    && other product classes would go here...
*        DO CABINETS.SPR
   OTHERWISE
        WAIT WINDOW [ No such product class ] TIMEOUT 1
        RETURN .F.
ENDCASE
SELECT DETAIL
IF Adding
   IF NOT EMPTY ( m.Manuf )    && Don't save if they left it blank
      INSERT INTO DETAIL FROM MEMVAR
   ENDIF
   ELSE
   GATHER MEMVAR
   IF EMPTY ( m.Style )        && Blank the record if STYLE is blank
      SCATTER TO   X BLANK
      GATHER   FROM X
   ENDIF
ENDIF
=ShowALine()
=Hilite(Line)
```

8-5 Continued.

```
Adding = .F.
* RETURN .F.

FUNCTION WHENDATE       &&  m.date WHEN
#REGION 1
IF EMPTY ( m.date )
   m.Date = DATE()
ENDIF

FUNCTION CLASS1      &&  m.Class1 VALID
#REGION 1
@ 9,0 FILL TO 17,WCOLS()-1 COLOR GR+/B
IF LASTKEY() = 13
   =PRODUCT(1)
ENDIF

FUNCTION CLASS2      &&  m.Class2 VALID
#REGION 1
@ 9,0 FILL TO 17,WCOLS()-1 COLOR GR+/B
IF LASTKEY() = 13
   =PRODUCT(2)
ENDIF

FUNCTION CLASS3      &&  m.Class3 VALID
#REGION 1
@ 9,0 FILL TO 17,WCOLS()-1 COLOR GR+/B
IF LASTKEY() = 13
   =PRODUCT(3)
ENDIF

FUNCTION CLASS4      &&  m.Class4 VALID
#REGION 1
IF LASTKEY() = 13
   =PRODUCT(4)
ENDIF

FUNCTION CLASS5      &&  m.Class5 VALID
#REGION 1
IF LASTKEY() = 13
   =PRODUCT(5)
ENDIF

FUNCTION CLASS6      &&  m.Class6 VALID
#REGION 1
IF LASTKEY() = 13
```

```
   =PRODUCT(6)
ENDIF


FUNCTION CLASS7      &&  m.Class7 VALID
#REGION 1
IF LASTKEY() = 13
   =PRODUCT(7)
ENDIF


FUNCTION CLASS8      &&  m.Class8 VALID
#REGION 1
IF LASTKEY() = 13
   =PRODUCT(8)
ENDIF


FUNCTION CLASS9      &&  m.Class9 VALID
#REGION 1
IF LASTKEY() = 13
   =PRODUCT(9)
ENDIF


FUNCTION FINWHEN     &&  m.Finished WHEN
#REGION 1
@ 9,0 FILL TO WROWS()-1,77         COLOR GR+/B


FUNCTION FINVALID    &&  m.Finished VALID
#REGION 1
CLEAR READ LEVEL 2


FUNCTION READVALID  && Read Level Valid
*
* Valid Code from screen: ESTIMATE
*
#REGION 1
IF   EMPTY ( m.Salesman  ) ;
 AND EMPTY ( m.Class1    ) ;
 AND LASTKEY() = 27
   Done = .T.
ENDIF
IF NOT Done
   RETURN .F.
ENDIF
```

The spreadsheet screen

The code for the carpet spreadsheet appears in Listing 8-6. This is where the estimator's rules have to be turned into code. So you have your most interesting interpersonal communications right here.

Listing 8-6 The SPREADSHEET code.

```
*
*                    ┌─────────────────────────────────────────────┐
*                    │                CARPET.SPR                   │
*                    └─────────────────────────────────────────────┘

#REGION 0
REGIONAL m.currarea, m.talkstat, m.compstat

IF SET("TALK") = "ON"
   SET TALK OFF
   m.talkstat = "ON"
ELSE
   m.talkstat = "OFF"
ENDIF
m.compstat = SET("COMPATIBLE")
SET COMPATIBLE FOXPLUS


*
*                    ┌─────────────────────────────────────────────┐
*                    │            MS-DOS Window definitions         │
*                    └─────────────────────────────────────────────┘

IF NOT WEXIST("carpet") ;
   OR UPPER(WTITLE("CARPET")) == "CARPET.PJX" ;
   OR UPPER(WTITLE("CARPET")) == "CARPET.SCX" ;
   OR UPPER(WTITLE("CARPET")) == "CARPET.MNX" ;
   OR UPPER(WTITLE("CARPET")) == "CARPET.PRG" ;
   OR UPPER(WTITLE("CARPET")) == "CARPET.FRX" ;
   OR UPPER(WTITLE("CARPET")) == "CARPET.QPR"
   DEFINE WINDOW carpet ;
      FROM INT((SROW()-24)/2),INT((SCOL()-79)/2) ;
      TO INT((SROW()-24)/2)+23,INT((SCOL()-79)/2)+78 ;
      TITLE "Carpet Worksheet" ;
      FLOAT ;
      NOCLOSE ;
      SHADOW ;
      NOMINIMIZE ;
      COLOR SCHEME 1
ENDIF
```

8-6 Continued.

```
*
*              ╔═══════════════════════════════════════════════╗
*              ║        CARPET/MS-DOS Setup Code - SECTION 2    ║
*              ╚═══════════════════════════════════════════════╝


#REGION 1
* Initialize screen variables:

m.Class       = [CAR]
m.Manuf       = SPACE(12)
m.Style       = SPACE(10)
m.Type        = SPACE(10)
m.Color       = SPACE(10)
m.Quantity    = 0
m.Roll        = 0
m.Cut         = 0
m.UseRoll     = 0
m.UseCut      = 1
m.Price2Use   = 0
m.Freight     = 0.65
m.Pad         = 1.80
m.TaxRate     = 0.0725
m.LaborRate   = 3.50
m.Add1        = SPACE(20)
m.Add2        = SPACE(20)
m.Qty1        = 0
m.Qty2        = 0
m.Qty3        = 0
m.Qty4        = 0
m.Qty5        = 0
m.Qty6        = 0
m.Qty7        = 0
m.Qty8        = 0
m.ExtPrice9   = 0
m.ExtPrice10  = 0
m.Markup      = 0
m.MatCost     = 0
m.PadCost     = 0
m.PadAndMat   = 0
m.CalFreight  = 0
m.TotCosts    = 0
m.SubTotal    = 0
m.Install     = 1          && on-screen switch 0 = no, 1 = yes
m.Installed   = 0
m.TotExtras   = 0
m.TotExtCost  = 0
```

8-6 Continued.

```
m.ExtraTot    = 0
m.SellPrice   = 0
m.Profit      = 0
m.Profitperyd = 0
m.RetPrcPrYD  = 0

IF NOT Adding

   SELECT DETAIL
   SCATTER MEMVAR
   SEEK m.Estimateno + m.CLine

   m.Berber    = CARPETS.Berber
   m.Roll      = CARPETS.Cost1
   m.Cut       = CARPETS.Cost2
   m.SpecialPrc = IIF ( DATE() < CARPETS.Expires, CARPETS.SpecialPrc, 0 )
   m.Expires   = CARPETS.Expires

   IF m.SpecialPrc > 0
      m.Price2Use   = m.SpecialPrc
      m.UseRoll     = 0
      m.UseCut      = 0
      SHOW GET m.UseRoll
      SHOW GET m.UseCut
      ELSE
      IF m.UseCut    = 1
         m.Price2Use = m.Cut
         ELSE
         m.Price2Use = m.Roll
      ENDIF
   ENDIF

   IF m.Markup = 0
      m.Markup = ;
         IIF ( m.Price2Use <= 6.99,          1.7, ;
         IIF ( m.Price2Use >= 7.00 AND m.Price2Use <= 8.99, 1.6, ;
         IIF ( m.Price2Use >= 9.00,          1.5, 0 ) ) )
   ENDIF

   SHOW GET m.Berber
   SHOW GET m.Roll
   SHOW GET m.Cut
   SHOW GET m.SpecialPrc
   SHOW GET m.Expires
```

```
    SHOW GET m.Markup

    =TotCalc()
    =ExtCalc()

ENDIF

* Override hard-coded defaults with those in file, if any...
SaveAlias = ALIAS()
SELECT CONTROL
SCATTER MEMVAR
IF NOT EMPTY ( SaveAlias )
    SELECT    ( SaveAlias )
ENDIF
HIDE MENU _MSYSMENU


*
*              ┌─────────────────────────────────────────────┐
*              │          CARPET/MS-DOS Screen Layout          │
*              └─────────────────────────────────────────────┘
*


#REGION 1
IF WVISIBLE("carpet")
    ACTIVATE WINDOW carpet SAME
ELSE
    ACTIVATE WINDOW carpet NOSHOW
ENDIF
@ 0,1 SAY "Manufacturer:" ;
    SIZE 1,13, 0
@ 1,8 SAY "Style:" ;
    SIZE 1,6, 0
@ 5,38 SAY "Extras:" ;
    SIZE 1,7, 0
@ 2,8 SAY "Color:" ;
    SIZE 1,6, 0
@ 2,37 SAY "Frt/Yard:" ;
    SIZE 1,9, 0
@ 3,42 SAY "Pad:" ;
    SIZE 1,4, 0
@ 2,60 SAY "Date:" ;
    SIZE 1,5, 0
@ 5,4 SAY "Material Yards:" ;
    SIZE 1,15, 0
@ 6,5 SAY "Material Cost:" ;
    SIZE 1,14, 0
```

```
@ 7,10 SAY "Pad Cost:" ;
   SIZE 1,9, 0
@ 11,7 SAY "Total costs:" ;
   SIZE 1,12, 0
@ 14,9 SAY "Sub Total:" ;
   SIZE 1,10, 0
@ 18,5 SAY "Selling Price:" ;
   SIZE 1,14, 0
@ 19,12 SAY "Profit:" ;
   SIZE 1,7, 0
@ 20,7 SAY "Profit/yard:" ;
   SIZE 1,12, 0
@ 21,1 SAY "Retail price/yard:" ;
   SIZE 1,18, 0
@ 16,6 SAY "Total extras:" ;
   SIZE 1,13, 0
@ 9,11 SAY "Freight:" ;
   SIZE 1,8, 0
@ 1,55 SAY "Expiration" ;
   SIZE 1,10, 0
@ 0,55 SAY "Special price?" ;
   SIZE 1,14, 0
@ 4,0 TO 4,76
@ 0,34 TO 21,34
@ 6,36 SAY "Stairs regular......" ;
   SIZE 1,20, 0
@ 7,39 SAY "Upholstered......" ;
   SIZE 1,17, 0
@ 5,60 SAY "Qty" ;
   SIZE 1,3, 0
@ 5,69 SAY "Price" ;
   SIZE 1,5, 0
@ 8,36 SAY "Pull up carpet......" ;
   SIZE 1,20, 0
@ 9,39 SAY "With pad........." ;
   SIZE 1,17, 0
@ 10,36 SAY "Banding............." ;
   SIZE 1,20, 0
@ 11,36 SAY "Move furniture......" ;
   SIZE 1,20, 0
@ 12,36 SAY "Extra furniture....." ;
   SIZE 1,20, 0
@ 13,36 SAY "Remove & repl base.." ;
   SIZE 1,20, 0
@ 16,36 SAY "Total extras........" ;
```

8-6 Continued.

```
   SIZE 1,20, 0
@ 14,36 SAY "Add-on..." ;
   SIZE 1,9, 0
@ 15,36 SAY "Add-on..." ;
   SIZE 1,9, 0
@ 17,36 SAY "Extras cost........." ;
   SIZE 1,20, 0
@ 18,36 SAY "Installation cost..." ;
   SIZE 1,20, 0
@ 6,21 GET m.MatCost ;
   SIZE 1,9 ;
   DEFAULT " " ;
   PICTURE "##,###.##" ;
   DISABLE
@ 7,21 GET m.PadCost ;
   SIZE 1,9 ;
   DEFAULT " " ;
   PICTURE "##,###.##" ;
   DISABLE
@ 8,21 GET m.PadAndMat ;
   SIZE 1,9 ;
   DEFAULT " " ;
   PICTURE "##,###.##" ;
   DISABLE
@ 9,21 GET m.CalFreight ;
   SIZE 1,9 ;
   DEFAULT " " ;
   PICTURE "##,###.##" ;
   DISABLE
@ 10,0 TO 10,33
@ 13,0 TO 13,33
@ 17,0 TO 17,33
@ 11,21 GET m.TotCosts ;
   SIZE 1,9 ;
   DEFAULT " " ;
   PICTURE "##,###.##" ;
   DISABLE
@ 14,21 GET m.SubTotal ;
   SIZE 1,9 ;
   DEFAULT " " ;
   PICTURE "##,###.##" ;
   DISABLE
@ 15,21 GET m.Installed ;
   SIZE 1,9 ;
   DEFAULT " " ;
```

8-6 Continued.

```
      PICTURE "##,###.##" ;
      DISABLE
   @ 16,21 GET m.ExtraTot ;
      SIZE 1,9 ;
      DEFAULT " " ;
      PICTURE "##,###.##" ;
      DISABLE
   @ 18,21 GET m.SellPrice ;
      SIZE 1,9 ;
      DEFAULT " " ;
      PICTURE "##,###.##" ;
      DISABLE
   @ 19,21 GET m.Profit ;
      SIZE 1,9 ;
      DEFAULT " " ;
      PICTURE "##,###.##" ;
      DISABLE
   @ 20,21 GET m.Profitperyd ;
      SIZE 1,9 ;
      DEFAULT " " ;
      PICTURE "##,###.##" ;
      DISABLE
   @ 21,21 GET m.RetPrcPrYD ;
      SIZE 1,9 ;
      DEFAULT " " ;
      PICTURE "##,###.##" ;
      DISABLE
   @ 16,65 GET m.TotExtras ;
      SIZE 1,9 ;
      DEFAULT " " ;
      PICTURE "##,###.##" ;
      DISABLE
   @ 0,70 GET m.SpecialPrc ;
      SIZE 1,6 ;
      DEFAULT 0 ;
      PICTURE "###.##" ;
      DISABLE
   @ 2,66 GET m.Expires ;
      SIZE 1,10 ;
      DEFAULT " " ;
      PICTURE "@D" ;
      DISABLE
   @ 17,65 GET m.TotExtCost ;
      SIZE 1,9 ;
      DEFAULT " " ;
```

8-6 Continued.

```
      PICTURE "##,###.##" ;
      DISABLE
@ 8,15 SAY "Tax:" ;
      SIZE 1,4, 0
@ 12,11 SAY "Mark-up:" ;
      SIZE 1,8, 0
@ 15,6 SAY "Installation:" ;
      SIZE 1,13, 0
@ 18,65 GET m.InstallCost ;
      SIZE 1,9 ;
      DEFAULT " " ;
      PICTURE "##,###.##" ;
      DISABLE
@ 6,68 GET m.cExtPrice1 ;
      SIZE 1,6 ;
      DEFAULT " " ;
      PICTURE "@Z ###.##" ;
      DISABLE
@ 7,68 GET m.cExtPrice2 ;
      SIZE 1,6 ;
      DEFAULT " " ;
      PICTURE "@Z ###.##" ;
      DISABLE
@ 8,68 GET m.cExtPrice3 ;
      SIZE 1,6 ;
      DEFAULT " " ;
      PICTURE "@Z ###.##" ;
      DISABLE
@ 9,68 GET m.cExtPrice4 ;
      SIZE 1,6 ;
      DEFAULT " " ;
      PICTURE "@Z ###.##" ;
      DISABLE
@ 10,68 GET m.cExtPrice5 ;
      SIZE 1,6 ;
      DEFAULT " " ;
      PICTURE "@Z ###.##" ;
      DISABLE
@ 11,68 GET m.cExtPrice6 ;
      SIZE 1,6 ;
      DEFAULT " " ;
      PICTURE "@Z ###.##" ;
      DISABLE
@ 12,68 GET m.cExtPrice7 ;
      SIZE 1,6 ;
```

```
     DEFAULT " " ;
     PICTURE "@Z ###.##" ;
     DISABLE
@ 13,68 GET m.cExtPrice8 ;
     SIZE 1,6 ;
     DEFAULT " " ;
     DISABLE
@ 19,44 TO 21,72
@ 0,15 GET m.Manuf ;
     SIZE 1,12 ;
     DEFAULT " " ;
     PICTURE "!!!!!!!!!!!!!" ;
     VALID _qe10k1g1h()
@ 1,15 GET m.Style ;
     SIZE 1,10 ;
     DEFAULT " " ;
     PICTURE "!!!!!!!!!!!" ;
     VALID _qe10k1g58()
@ 2,15 GET m.Color ;
     SIZE 1,18 ;
     DEFAULT " " ;
     PICTURE "!XXXXXXXXXXXXXXXXX"
@ 3,1 GET m.Berber ;
     PICTURE "@*C Berber?" ;
     SIZE 1,11 ;
     DEFAULT 0 ;
     VALID _qe10k1gm8()
@ 3,15 GET m.Install ;
     PICTURE "@*C Install?" ;
     SIZE 1,12 ;
     DEFAULT 0 ;
     VALID TotCalc()
@ 5,23 GET m.Quantity ;
     SIZE 1,7 ;
     DEFAULT 0 ;
     PICTURE "####.##" ;
     VALID _qe10k1gqd()
@ 12,25 GET m.Markup ;
     SIZE 1,4 ;
     DEFAULT " " ;
     PICTURE "#.##" ;
     VALID TotCalc()
@ 0,37 GET m.UseRoll ;
     PICTURE "@*C Roll:" ;
     SIZE 1,9 ;
```

```
    DEFAULT 0 ;
    VALID _qe10k1gtu()
@ 0,47 GET m.Roll ;
    SIZE 1,6 ;
    DEFAULT 0 ;
    PICTURE "###.##" ;
    VALID UseWhich() AND TotCalc()
@ 1,37 GET m.UseCut ;
    PICTURE "@*C  Cut:" ;
    SIZE 1,9 ;
    DEFAULT 1 ;
    VALID _qe10k1gzc()
@ 1,47 GET m.Cut ;
    SIZE 1,6 ;
    DEFAULT 0 ;
    PICTURE "###.##" ;
    VALID UseWhich() AND TotCalc()
@ 2,47 GET m.Freight ;
    SIZE 1,6 ;
    DEFAULT 0 ;
    PICTURE "###.##" ;
    VALID _qe10k1h5t()
@ 3,47 GET m.Pad ;
    SIZE 1,6 ;
    DEFAULT 0 ;
    PICTURE "###.##" ;
    VALID _qe10k1h8y()
@ 6,60 GET m.Qty1 ;
    SIZE 1,3 ;
    DEFAULT " " ;
    PICTURE "###" ;
    VALID _qe10k1hc3()
@ 7,60 GET m.Qty2 ;
    SIZE 1,3 ;
    DEFAULT " " ;
    PICTURE "###" ;
    VALID _qe10k1hfd()
@ 8,58 GET m.Qty3 ;
    SIZE 1,6 ;
    DEFAULT " " ;
    PICTURE "###.##" ;
    VALID _qe10k1him()
@ 9,58 GET m.Qty4 ;
    SIZE 1,6 ;
    DEFAULT " " ;
```

```
    PICTURE "###.##" ;
    VALID _qe10k1hlx()
@ 10,60 GET m.Qty5 ;
    SIZE 1,3 ;
    DEFAULT " " ;
    PICTURE "###" ;
    VALID _qe10k1hp6()
@ 11,60 GET m.Qty6 ;
    SIZE 1,3 ;
    DEFAULT " " ;
    PICTURE "###" ;
    VALID _qe10k1hsh()
@ 12,60 GET m.Qty7 ;
    SIZE 1,3 ;
    DEFAULT " " ;
    PICTURE "###" ;
    VALID _qe10k1hwp()
@ 13,60 GET m.Qty8 ;
    SIZE 1,3 ;
    DEFAULT " " ;
    PICTURE "###" ;
    VALID _qe10k1hzz()
@ 14,46 GET m.Add1 ;
    SIZE 1,19 ;
    DEFAULT " " ;
    PICTURE "!XXXXXXXXXXXXXXXXXX"
@ 14,66 GET m.ExtPrice9 ;
    SIZE 1,8 ;
    DEFAULT " " ;
    PICTURE "#,###.##" ;
    VALID ExtCalc()
@ 15,46 GET m.Add2 ;
    SIZE 1,19 ;
    DEFAULT " " ;
    PICTURE "!XXXXXXXXXXXXXXXXXX"
@ 15,66 GET m.ExtPrice10 ;
    SIZE 1,8 ;
    DEFAULT " " ;
    PICTURE "#,###.##" ;
    VALID ExtCalc()
@ 20,50 GET m.Action ;
    PICTURE "@*HT \<Save;\<Cancel" ;
    SIZE 1,8,1 ;
    DEFAULT 1 ;
    VALID _qe10k1i5q()
```

```
IF NOT WVISIBLE("carpet")
   ACTIVATE WINDOW carpet
ENDIF

READ CYCLE ;
   WHEN _qe10k1i96()

RELEASE WINDOW carpet

#REGION 0
IF m.talkstat = "ON"
   SET TALK ON
ENDIF
IF m.compstat = "ON"
   SET COMPATIBLE ON
ENDIF

*
*         CARPET/MS-DOS Supporting Procedures and Functions
*

#REGION 1
FUNCTION UseWhich

IF m.UseCut = 0 AND m.UseRoll = 0
   =Alarm()
   WAIT WINDOW [ ** You must choose a price ** ] TIMEOUT 1
   IF VARREAD() = [ROLL]
      m.UseRoll = 1
      SHOW GET m.UseRoll
      ELSE
      m.UseCut  = 1
      SHOW GET m.UseCut
   ENDIF
ENDIF

DO CASE
   CASE m.UseRoll = 1
      m.Price2Use = m.Roll
   CASE m.UseCut  = 1
      m.Price2Use = m.Cut
ENDCASE

FUNCTION TotCalc
```

8-6 Continued.

```
BerberAdd = 1.00

m.MatCost          = m.Quantity * m.Price2Use
SHOW GET             m.MatCost   DISABLE
m.PadCost          = m.Quantity * m.Pad
SHOW GET             m.PadCost   DISABLE
m.PadAndMat        = m.TaxRate   * ( m.MatCost + m.PadCost )
SHOW GET             m.PadAndMat DISABLE
m.CalFreight       = m.Quantity * m.Freight
SHOW GET             m.CalFreight DISABLE
m.TotCosts         = m.MatCost + m.PadCost + m.PadAndMat + m.CalFreight
SHOW GET             m.TotCosts   DISABLE

m.SubTotal         = m.TotCosts * m.Markup
SHOW GET             m.SubTotal

m.Labor            = IIF ( m.Berber = 0, m.LaborRate, m.LaborRate +
BerberAdd )
m.Installed        = IIF ( m.Install = 0,0, m.Labor * m.Quantity )
SHOW GET             m.Installed
m.InstallCost      = m.Installed
SHOW GET             m.InstallCost

m.SellPrice        = m.SubTotal + m.Installed + m.ExtraTot
SHOW GET             m.SellPrice

m.Profit           = m.SellPrice ;
                   - ( m.TotCosts + m.TotExtCost + m.Installcost )
SHOW GET             m.Profit

m.ProfitPerYd      = m.Profit / m.Quantity
SHOW GET             m.ProfitPerYd

m.RetPrcPrYD       = m.SellPrice / m.Quantity
SHOW GET             m.RetPrcPrYd

FUNCTION ExtCalc

TotExtras ;
 = Qty1 * ExtPrice1 ;
 + Qty2 * ExtPrice2 ;
 + Qty3 * ExtPrice3 ;
 + Qty4 * ExtPrice4 ;
 + Qty5 * ExtPrice5 ;
```

```
+ Qty6 * ExtPrice6 ;
+ Qty7 * ExtPrice7 ;
+ Qty8 * ExtPrice8 ;
+         ExtPrice9 ;
+         ExtPrice10

TotExtCost ;
= Qty1 * ExtCost1 ;
+ Qty2 * ExtCost2 ;
+ Qty3 * ExtCost3 ;
+ Qty4 * ExtCost4 ;
+ Qty5 * ExtCost5 ;
+ Qty6 * ExtCost6 ;
+ Qty7 * ExtCost7 ;
+ Qty8 * ExtCost8 ;
+ .80  * ExtPrice9;
+ .80  * ExtPrice10

m.ExtraTot = TotExtras

SHOW GET m.TotExtras
SHOW GET m.TotExtCost
SHOW GET m.ExtraTot

=TotCalc()

FUNCTION CARPMANU
EXTERNAL ARRAY MANUFACTS
IF ASCAN ( MANUFACTS, m.Manuf ) > 0
    RETURN
ENDIF
DEFINE   WINDOW MANUFACTS FROM 1,30 TO 21, 45 IN SCREEN SHADOW
ACTIVATE WINDOW MANUFACTS
@ 0,0 GET m.ManufNum FROM MANUFACTS PICTURE '@&' DEFAULT 1
SET CONFIRM ON
READ COLOR ,W+/R
SET CONFIRM OFF
RELEASE WINDOW MANUFACTS
m.Manuf = IIF ( m.ManufNum = 0 , SPACE(12), MANUFACTS ( m.ManufNum ) )
SELECT DETAIL

FUNCTION _qe10k1g1h      && m.Manuf VALID
#REGION 1
SaveMfg = Manuf
=CarpManu()
```

8-6 Continued.

```
FUNCTION _qe10k1g58      && m.Style VALID
#REGION 1
SELECT CARPETS
SEEK 'CAR' + m.Manuf + m.Style

IF NOT FOUND()
   WAIT WINDOW [ Building table of styles for ] + m.Manuf NOWAIT
   * Build popup of styles for this manufacturer
   SEEK 'CAR' + m.Manuf
   DEFINE POPUP STYLES FROM 2,15 SHADOW MARGIN ;
     COLOR N/W, N/W, N/W, N/W, N/W, N/W, W+/R, W+/W
   I = 1
   SCAN WHILE MANUF = m.MANUF
      DEFINE BAR I OF STYLES PROMPT CARPETS.STYLE
      I = I + 1
   ENDSCAN
   ON SELECTION POPUP STYLES DEACTIVATE POPUP STYLES
   ACTIVATE POPUP STYLES
   mPrompt = PROMPT()
   RELEASE POPUP STYLES
   IF EMPTY ( mPrompt )
      m.Style = SPACE(10)
      ELSE
      m.Style = mPrompt
   ENDIF
   * If they didn't pick a style, they don't get carpet..
   IF EMPTY ( mPrompt )
      WAIT WINDOW [ ** Cancelling ** ] TIMEOUT 1
      CLEAR READ
      SELECT DETAIL
      RETURN
   ENDIF
ENDIF

* Find the carpet and update all related screen variables
SEEK [CAR] + m.Manuf + m.Style

m.Berber     = CARPETS.Berber
m.Roll       = CarpetS.Cost1
m.Cut        = CARPETS.Cost2
m.SpecialPrc = IIF ( DATE() < CARPETS.Expires, CARPETS.SpecialPrc, 0 )
m.Expires    = CARPETS.Expires

IF m.SpecialPrc > 0
   m.Price2Use = m.SpecialPrc
```

```
   m.UseRoll   = 0
   m.UseCut    = 0
   SHOW GET m.UseRoll
   SHOW GET m.UseCut
   ELSE
   IF m.UseCut = 1
      m.Price2Use = m.Cut
      ELSE
      m.Price2Use = m.Roll
   ENDIF
ENDIF


IF m.Markup = 0
   m.Markup = ;
      IIF ( m.Price2Use <= 6.99,            1.7, ;
      IIF ( m.Price2Use >= 7.00 AND m.Price2Use <= 8.99, 1.6, ;
      IIF ( m.Price2Use >= 9.00,            1.5, 0 ) ) )
ENDIF


SHOW GET m.Berber
SHOW GET m.Roll
SHOW GET m.Cut
SHOW GET m.SpecialPrc
SHOW GET m.Expires
SHOW GET m.Markup


=TotCalc()


SELECT DETAIL


FUNCTION _qe10k1gm8      && m.Berber VALID
#REGION 1
IF m.Berber = 1
   SELECT CARPETS
   REPLACE NEXT 1 BERBER WITH 1
ENDIF
=TotCalc()


FUNCTION _qe10k1gqd      && m.Quantity VALID
#REGION 1
=TotCalc()


FUNCTION _qe10k1gtu      && m.UseRoll VALID
#REGION 1
IF m.UseRoll = 1
```

```
     m.UseCut   = 0
     SHOW GET m.UseCut
     m.Price2Use = m.Roll
ENDIF

IF m.UseCut = 0 AND m.UseRoll = 0
   IF m.SpecialPrc = 0
      =Alarm()
      WAIT WINDOW [ ** You must choose a price ** ] TIMEOUT 1
      m.UseRoll = 1
   ENDIF
ENDIF
=TotCalc()


FUNCTION _qe10k1gzc      &&  m.UseCut VALID
#REGION 1
IF m.UseCut   = 1
   m.UseRoll = 0
   SHOW GET m.UseRoll
   m.Price2Use = m.Cut
ENDIF
IF m.UseCut = 0 AND m.UseRoll = 0
   IF m.SpecialPrc = 0
      =Alarm()
      WAIT WINDOW [ ** You must choose a price ** ] TIMEOUT 1
      m.UseCut = 1
   ENDIF
ENDIF

=TotCalc()


FUNCTION _qe10k1h5t      &&  m.Freight VALID
#REGION 1
m.CalFreight = m.Freight * m.Quantity
SHOW GET m.CalFreight
=TotCalc()


FUNCTION _qe10k1h8y      &&  m.Pad VALID
#REGION 1
m.PadCost = m.Pad * m.Quantity
SHOW GET m.PadCost
=TotCalc()


FUNCTION _qe10k1hc3      &&  m.Qty1 VALID
#REGION 1
```

```
m.cExtPrice1 = m.Qty1 * m.ExtPrice1
SHOW GET m.cExtPrice1
=ExtCalc()

FUNCTION _qe10k1hfd     && m.Qty2 VALID
#REGION 1
m.cExtPrice2 = m.Qty2 * m.ExtPrice2
SHOW GET m.cExtPrice2
=ExtCalc()

FUNCTION _qe10k1him     && m.Qty3 VALID
#REGION 1
m.cExtPrice3 = m.Qty3 * m.ExtPrice3
SHOW GET m.cExtPrice3
=ExtCalc()

FUNCTION _qe10k1hlx     && m.Qty4 VALID
#REGION 1
m.cExtPrice4 = m.Qty4 * m.ExtPrice4
SHOW GET m.cExtPrice4
=ExtCalc()

FUNCTION _qe10k1hp6     && m.Qty5 VALID
#REGION 1
m.cExtPrice5 = m.Qty5 * m.ExtPrice5
SHOW GET m.cExtPrice5
=ExtCalc()

FUNCTION _qe10k1hsh     && m.Qty6 VALID
#REGION 1
m.cExtPrice6 = m.Qty6 * m.ExtPrice6
SHOW GET m.cExtPrice6
=ExtCalc()

FUNCTION _qe10k1hwp     && m.Qty7 VALID
#REGION 1
m.cExtPrice7 = m.Qty7 * m.ExtPrice7
SHOW GET m.cExtPrice7
=ExtCalc()

FUNCTION _qe10k1hzz     && m.Qty8 VALID
#REGION 1
m.cExtPrice8 = m.Qty8 * m.ExtPrice8
SHOW GET m.cExtPrice8
=ExtCalc()
```

8-6 Continued.

```
FUNCTION _qe10k1i5q        && m.Action VALID
#REGION 1
DO CASE
   CASE m.Action  =  1
      Canceled    = .F.
   CASE m.Action  =  2
      Canceled    = .T.
ENDCASE

FUNCTION _qe10k1i96        && Read Level When
*
* WHEN Code from screen: CARPET
*
#REGION 1
* Show current values in case they've re-entered an existing line
m.cExtPrice1 = m.Qty1 * m.ExtPrice1
m.cExtPrice2 = m.Qty1 * m.ExtPrice2
m.cExtPrice3 = m.Qty1 * m.ExtPrice3
m.cExtPrice4 = m.Qty1 * m.ExtPrice4
m.cExtPrice5 = m.Qty1 * m.ExtPrice5
m.cExtPrice6 = m.Qty1 * m.ExtPrice6
m.cExtPrice7 = m.Qty1 * m.ExtPrice7
m.cExtPrice8 = m.Qty1 * m.ExtPrice8
SHOW GET m.cExtPrice1
SHOW GET m.cExtPrice2
SHOW GET m.cExtPrice3
SHOW GET m.cExtPrice4
SHOW GET m.cExtPrice5
SHOW GET m.cExtPrice6
SHOW GET m.cExtPrice7
SHOW GET m.cExtPrice8
```

I always get customers who want me to program their software and at the same time answer all their questions. It's not so much that they don't know what they want me to do; typically, these folks can do massively complex calculations in their heads. It's just that sometimes there are things about the way they do business that they'd rather not tell anyone.

I have a subscriber who works in the deep south. In the process of writing a receivable system for a country store, he found out that his esteemed clients were committing theft with every transaction. When the store's credit customers—mostly poor and mostly black—bought groceries on account, the bill was doubled. The customers couldn't add, so they never knew. But the bill was routinely adjusted upward . And I'm not talking about 50 years ago; this was reported to me in February of 1993.

I had an even more chilling personal experience. My customers, two securities salesmen, were explaining to me how they wanted their clients to see the investment potential of their Magnetic Resonance Imaging deal. They were playing fast and loose with the discounting and appreciation formulas you learn in graduate-school economics, and I just couldn't understand their math. The more I pressed them for details, the more agitated they became. Finally I understood it. They wanted a program to lie to their investors. I left and didn't come back. One of them ended up committing suicide and the other is in jail. True story.

In the contractor estimating game, things aren't nearly as nefarious, although some clients are hesitant to let me see the markups upon markups that go into their calculations. Material represented as being sold at retail are routinely bought at wholesale and marked up, so that the customer isn't getting nearly the bargain he thinks he is.

Happily, in this case, my clients were entirely above board. But there was considerable disagreement about how things should be done. It turned out that each salesman used a slightly different technique. It took several days and the intervention of the owner to come to an agreement. The resulting formulas are embedded in the code in Listing 8-6.

How it works

This is a very long program, but what it does is quite simple. There's a global recalculation program called TOTCALC. Every field that could have an effect on any other variable includes a reference to TOTCALC in its VALID clause. In TOTCALC, all calculated variables are redisplayed at the end of the function.

Calculated variables are DISABLED GETs. This feature of FoxPro is essential to spreadsheet-style presentations. It means that a simple `SHOW GET m SubTotal DISABLE` redisplays the value of m.SubTotal without having to remember where it was on the screen.

If you do calculations within a valid clause that has issued another READ and you want to show all GETs, you have to `SHOW GETS LEVEL ( RDLEVEL()-1 )` because SHOW GETs shows only the GETs at the current read level.

Summary

You can do spreadsheets in FoxPro with none of the shortcomings of traditional spreadsheet programs. The amount of coding looks daunting, but it's generally not as much as you'd think. You'll have to write your own RECALC function, and your clients might have a hard time thinking like a computer. But the end result will be a precise tool that does exactly what the user needs.

In the next chapter, you'll turn your attention to a tool for programmers. Data conversion is a frequent requirement in my business, and provides an interesting framework for a short course in software design.

9
Special data-conversion applications

Data conversion is a topic that comes up a lot in my work. I've been fortunate to help develop several products that are stealing customers from the competition, and you can bet those guys don't make it easy to leave the flock. Even if such products provide a function to export data, the resulting data is unlikely to be in the format your programs require. The program developed in this chapter makes it easy to convert data from a variety of sources.

The basic approach

Each time I convert a new set of files, I have to go through the same steps: snoop around the files to find out what's where, determine whether the records end with linefeed/carriage returns, pray for fixed-length records, create a work file to hold the intermediate results, and write recodes to change their values to my values.

For several years, I've wanted to make this process table-driven so I could use the same software over and over again. Well, here it is. It didn't take that long to write, but there were a lot of choices to make, and that takes emotional energy. Hopefully, the basic design is extensible enough to take care of all of the things I know I left out.

The table-driven design was an easy decision. Each field in the output file consists of something from the input file—a field, part of a field, or a converted value from a field. *Converted* can mean anything from DTOC to *if it's an A, code a 1*. That's where macro expansion comes in handy.

I don't use REPLACE to put the data into the output file. Instead, I start each conversion cycle with the commands:

```
SELECT OUTPUT
SCATTER MEMVAR MEMO BLANK
```

This gives me a complete set of memvars corresponding to the fields in the output file. Next, I use the input file (which might be an intermediate work file loaded from a text file) to create values for as many memvars as can be extracted from the input file. In some cases, values need to be truncated, concatenated, or transformed with a lookup table. When I've gotten all I can from the input file, I just:

```
SELECT OUTPUT
APPEND BLANK
GATHER MEMVAR MEMO
```

All of the memvars created during the conversion of the input record are then stuffed into the output file's fields.

The conversion table

```
Structure for database: CONVERT.DBF
Field  Name           Type        Width
   1   SRC_IN         Character       8
   2   FLD_IN         Character      10
   3   STA_IN         Numeric         3
   4   END_IN         Numeric         3
   5   FUNC_IN        Character      50
   6   FLD_OUT        Character      10
** Total **                         85
```

The conversion table consists of a source, which contains either the alias INPUT or the letter M, and the input field name FLD_IN. In the simplest case, conversion consists simply of moving data from the source name to the FLD_OUT output field.

Because extracting a substring of an input field and stuffing it into an output field is a common requirement, it's handled in a special way. STA_IN and END_IN provide starting and ending positions for substring operations. If the conversion routine finds:

```
FLD_IN = "CUSTCODE", STA_IN = 3, END_IN = 6 and FLD_OUT = "CUST"
```

it would put `SUBSTR(CUSTCODE,3,4)` into CUST. If you code INPUT as the source of your data, the program knows that the data comes from your input file. Fixed-length and delimited data files are "preprocessed" into an intermediate work file that the user defines, and which has the alias TRANSFER. When processing formulas, the conversion program refers to both TRANSFER and INPUT with the alias INPUT. There's no conflict because you're always using either one or the other, but never both.

I used BROWSE to manage the conversion table. Using the CHANGE command in the BROWSE system menu pull-down, users can toggle between the browse view and the edit view—and BROWSE/EDIT is kind enough to use my headings in both modes.

Complex conversion formulas

Generally, a simple name change or substring extraction will do what I need. But just in case, I've included a field that can contain any valid Fox-Pro expression. It can refer to a field name in the source file or to a memory variable. But it can also include complex expressions containing fields and memory variables. If I need to do something complex, like refer to a one-time function placed in the CONVERT directory for just one job, I can stuff:

```
MYFUNCT(a,b,2.5)
```

into the FUNCTION field and my program will expand it into a valid expression.

Types of input files

As anyone who's done much data conversion knows, there are really two kinds of conversions: those that are in some standard form (.DBF, .SDF, or DELIMITED), and those that aren't. For better or worse, I wanted to write a single program to deal with both cases.

The TYPE field defines six types of files: The first four are standard, and the next two are nonstandard. Standard files can be DBFs, fixed-length files, or comma-delimited files. Fixed-length files that can be viewed with a text editor are called *carriage-return delimited*, while those that have nothing separating one record from another are called *fixed-length nondelimited files*.

CONVERT would prefer to read a .DBF and write a .DBF. If the file is standard but not a DBF, you have to define a TRANSFER file (a .DBF) and move the data into it. This is pretty easy for fixed-length CR-delimited files or comma-delimited files, because FoxPro has the command APPEND FROM `filename` SDF/DELIM. If the file has no record separators but you know the record length, you can use low-level file I/O (LLIO) to create a CR-delimited file, then APPEND FROM SDF. Users have an opportunity to view their transfer file to verify that it has everything in the right fields before conversion takes place.

If the file can't be preprocessed into a TRANSFER file, you'll have to return one record at a time using your own functions. I've found that even the most complex files can be reduced to two routines: finding the first record and finding the next record. In many cases, these two routines are the same, in which case you just plug the same function name into both fields. With nonstandard output, about the best you can do is look at the first few records with DEBUG and SET STEP ON, and determine that the READFIRST and READNEXT routines are creating the right memvars for the conversion rules table.

Simple vs. complex conversions

If you're given a .DBF, the usual conversions involve field names, length differences, data-type differences, and recoding of values. For example,

PHONE in the source file might be called TELEPHONE in the target file. It might also be 14 characters instead of 12. NAME in the target file might be the concatenation of several fields in the source file; a typical conversion is:

```
Name = ALLTRIM(FNAME)+[ ] + MI + [ ] + LNAME
```

Dates might be in either a character format or a European format in the source. And, for example, GENDER (M/F) could be a numeric variable with a value of 1 for female and 2 for male in the source file.

Creating new memvars in UDFs

If you have field names in the input file, these conversions are pretty easy. If your input consists of one long character string, however, the conversion table is used to create all memory variables. Remember to use PUBLIC if the variable is created in your own UDFs; otherwise, they'll be invisible to the CONVERTR program. For example, in the "next record" program, you might use something like this:

```
FUNCTION GETNEXT
IF TYPE('m.Name') = [U]
    PUBLIC Name
ENDIF
m.Name = SUBSTR ( data , 1 , 25 )
```

Subsequently, the table can refer to m.Name as if it were a field in the source file. The IF TYPE (*memvar*) = [U] condition (which asks whether the variable has already been declared PUBLIC) is necessary because you can't make a memvar PUBLIC that's already PUBLIC. The memvar data, assigned in the MAIN program, is the only global memvar defined for use by nonstandard functions.

I've separated reports as a distinct type because, with a small amount of work, you can write a program to build the table entries to extract report data—even where there are multiple detail lines. I shouldn't have all the fun . . .

The project file

The project file for CONVERT.APP appears in Fig. 9-1. The STARTUP program initializes a few variables, defines the menu, calls the screen program, closes up and shuts down. The screen is shown in Fig. 9-2. In this application, all of the work is done in the VALID clauses.

FoxPro's FPATH.PLB library

When you ask users to type in filenames, you never know what you're going to get. They might leave off extensions or forget the exact spelling of the file they want to convert. In addition, you might need a path for some file, but no path for those that you require to be in the current directory. For

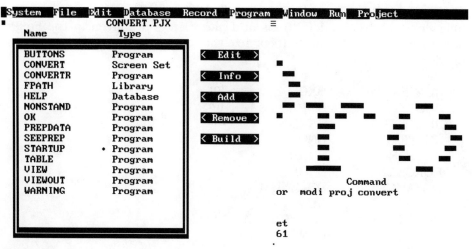

System File Edit Database Record Program Window Run Project

CONVERT.PJX

Name	Type
BUTTONS	Program
CONVERT	Screen Set
CONVERTR	Program
FPATH	Library
HELP	Database
NONSTAND	Program
OK	Program
PREPDATA	Program
SEEPREP	Program
STARTUP	• Program
TABLE	Program
VIEW	Program
VIEWOUT	Program
WARNING	Program

< Edit >
< Info >
< Add >
< Remove >
< Build >

Command
or modi proj convert

et
61

Figure 9-1 The Project File screen.

```
┌──────────Data Conversion System──────────┐
│      Conversion rules file name:  TABLE2  │
│                                           │
│  Input file type: ┌──────────────────────┤
│                   │          DBF          │
│  Name:            └──────────────────────┤
│  C:\PINTER4\CHAP09\DBFS\INVOICES          │
│                                           │
│       ◄Fixed length or delimited files►   │
│  Preprocessor file:                       │
│  (If nondelimited:) Record length:    0   │
│                                           │
│          ◄Nonstandard input files►        │
│         Name of the program to:           │
│            Read first record:             │
│            Read next record:              │
│                                           │
│       Output file name: NEWINV            │
│                                           │
│  < Edit Rules   >   <  Start Over  >      │
│  < View Input   >   <Process to End>      │
│  <  Prep Data   >   <Browse Output >      │
│  <See Prep Data>    <    Help      >      │
│  < Set Mode     >   <    Exit      >      │
└───────────────────────────────────────────┘
```

Figure 9-2 The Convert screen.

the FILE command, which is used to determine whether a file already exists, you need the extension, but for SELECT statements you don't.

I've had to write functions to do all of these things and still come up with some new wrinkle. With FoxPro 2.5, you can add such functions easily if you program in C. Such functions are compiled into library files with the extension .PLB. Using the command SET LIBRARY TO *libraryname*, you effectively add the functions in your library to FoxPro's own set of commands.

Partly by way of example, FoxPro comes with a library file called FPATH.PLB, which contains a number of useful functions. If you SET LI

BRARY TO FPATH, then LIST STATUS TO PRINT, you'll see the names in the following list. Precise definitions and parameters are given in the FoxPro documentation. If you don't recognize them from their names, you probably don't need them.

JUSTFNAME	BXOR
JUSTSTEM	BOR
JUSTEXT	BAND
JUSTPATH	BNOT
JUSTDRIVE	BSHR
FORCEEXT	BSHL
DEFAULTEXT	DBL2NUM
ADDBS	NUM2DLB
VALIDPATH	FLOAT2NUM
CLEANPATH	LONG2NUM
REDUCE	INT2NUM
STRFILTER	FPATHTEST
EUROSORT	NEXTWORD
WORDS	FCTNPARM
WORDNUM	

In this application, I've used a number of these functions to clean up filenames. So when you see a function reference like JUSTSTEM or JUSTFNAME, that's where they came from.

The source code

While the STARTUP program serves as the MAIN program, almost all of the work is controlled by the screen program CONVERT.SPR.

I've used controls at the bottom of the screen, rather than a menu, to control processing. The most important feature of control in this application is the use of the BUTTONS program to determine which push buttons are enabled at any time. Each of the field valid clauses ends with a call to BUTTONS, which refreshes the ENABLE/DISABLE status of each one of the controls, as well as that of several optional input fields. This technique avoids having to begin each of the other functions by verifying whether the function can proceed. If the necessary inputs haven't been supplied, you can't select that function.

This is in keeping with the FoxPro menu-design philosophy. Rather than beep at users if they try to convert the input file without having supplied an output filename, just don't let them choose the function until all prerequisites have been met. This type of software is less intimidating to users.

The MAIN program

The STARTUP program, shown in Listing 9-1, has been designated as the MAIN program using the SET MAIN menu bar in the PROJECT menu

Listing 9-1 The MAIN program.

```
* Program-ID....: STARTUP.PRG
* Purpose.......: MAIN program for CONVERT app

SET TALK          OFF
SET EXCLUSIVE     ON
SET SAFETY        OFF
SET LIBRARY TO FPATH
CLOSE DATABASES
CLEAR
SET HELP TO HELP


m.FileType   = 1
m.FindFirst  = SPACE(8)
m.FindNext   = SPACE(8)
m.Data       = []
UpArrow      = 5
EscapeKey    = 27


DIMENSION Types ( 6 )
TYPES (  1 ) = [DBF]
TYPES (  2 ) = [Fixed length/CR delim]
TYPES (  3 ) = [Comma delimited]
TYPES (  4 ) = [Fixed length/no delim]
TYPES (  5 ) = [Nonstandard]
TYPES (  6 ) = [Report file]


SET COLOR OF SCHEME 2 TO ,N/W,,,,W+/R

DO CONVERT.SPR       && Includes READ VALID clause invocation

CLOSE DATA

RETURN
```

popup. STARTUP doesn't have to do much, but it sets the essential settings, attaches the FPATH library, assigns the HELP file, sets a few global variables and defaults, and calls the screen program. Because there's only one screen, a "foundation READ" to bind multiple screens together isn't necessary.

The CONVERT screen program

The CONVERT screen manages the entire conversion process. Each field has a VALID clause, and that's where the real work is done. In the case of field names, the program either verifies that the file exists, or creates it if needed. The controls are push buttons—GETs with the function code *. I forced them to have the same width by adding trailing spaces to get identical lengths, then erasing the spaces. The result is centered in the original width. Figure 9-3 shows the screen's Layout dialog, and Listing 9-2 is the CONVERT screen program.

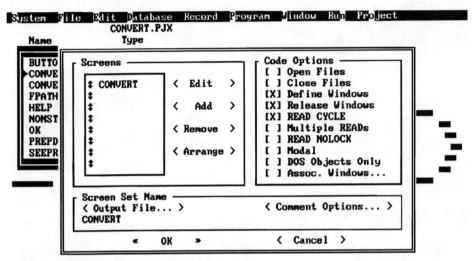

Figure 9-3 The Convert screen Layout dialog.

Listing 9-2 The CONVERT screen program.

```
*
*                         CONVERT.SPR
*


#REGION 0
REGIONAL m.currarea, m.talkstat, m.compstat

IF SET("TALK") = "ON"
   SET TALK OFF
   m.talkstat = "ON"
ELSE
   m.talkstat = "OFF"
ENDIF
m.compstat = SET("COMPATIBLE")
SET COMPATIBLE FOXPLUS


*
*                   MS-DOS Window definitions
*
```

```
IF NOT WEXIST("_qe50k9r3n")
   DEFINE WINDOW _qe50k9r3n ;
      FROM 0, 0 ;
      TO 24,43 ;
      TITLE "Data Conversion System" ;
      NOFLOAT ;
      NOCLOSE ;
      SHADOW ;
      NOMINIMIZE ;
      COLOR SCHEME 1
ENDIF

*
*
*                     CONVERT/MS-DOS Setup Code - SECTION 2
*
*


#REGION 1
m.Done       = .F.
m.Mode       = [N]   && Defaults to NonStop mode
m.FromTop    = .T.

EXTERNAL ARRAY TYPES
* Shown here for documentation; initialized in main program
* DIMENSION Types ( 6 )
* TYPES ( 1 ) = [DBF]
* TYPES ( 2 ) = [Fixed length/CR delim]
* TYPES ( 3 ) = [Comma delimited]
* TYPES ( 4 ) = [Fixed length/no delim]
* TYPES ( 5 ) = [Nonstandard]
* TYPES ( 6 ) = [Report file]

SET COLOR OF SCHEME 1 TO ,,,,, W+/R
SET COLOR OF SCHEME 2 TO ,GR+/B,,,, W+/R


*
*
*                     CONVERT/MS-DOS Screen Layout
*
*


#REGION 1
IF WVISIBLE("_qe50k9r3n")
   ACTIVATE WINDOW _qe50k9r3n SAME
```

```
   ELSE
   ACTIVATE WINDOW _qe50k9r3n NOSHOW
ENDIF
@ 16,11 SAY "Output file name:" ;
   SIZE 1,17, 0
@ 13,10 SAY "Read first record:" ;
   SIZE 1,18, 0
@ 14,11 SAY "Read next record:" ;
   SIZE 1,17, 0
@ 12,8 SAY "Name of the program to:" ;
   SIZE 1,23, 0
@ 8,2 SAY "Preprocessor file:" ;
   SIZE 1,18, 0
@ 7,4 SAY "Fixed length or delimited files" ;
   SIZE 1,25, 0
@ 3,0 SAY "Input file type:" ;
   SIZE 1,16, 0
@ 4,0 SAY "Name:" ;
   SIZE 1,5, 0
@ 0,3 SAY "Conversion rules file name:" ;
   SIZE 1,27, 0
@ 6,0 TO 6,41
@ 10,0 TO 10,41
@ 15,0 TO 15,41
@ 17,0 TO 17,41
@ 1,0 TO 1,41
@ 9,2 SAY "(If nondelimited:) Record length:" ;
   SIZE 1,33, 0
@ 0,32 GET m.TableName ;
   SIZE 1,8 ;
   DEFAULT " " ;
   PICTURE "!!!!!!!!!" ;
   VALID TABLENAME()
@ 2,17 GET m.FileType ;
   PICTURE "@^" ;
   FROM TYPES ;
   SIZE 3,24 ;
   DEFAULT 1 ;
   VALID FILETYPE() ;
   DISABLE ;
   MESSAGE "Type of file to convert" ;
   COLOR SCHEME 1, 2
@ 5,1 GET m.FileName ;
   SIZE 1,40 ;
   DEFAULT " " :
```

```
        PICTURE "!!!!!!!!!!!!!!!!!!!!!!!!!!!!!!!!!!!!!!!!!" ;
        VALID FILENAME() ;
        MESSAGE "Name of the file to convert" ;
        DISABLE
    @ 8,33 GET m.TransFile ;
        SIZE 1,8 ;
        DEFAULT " " ;
        PICTURE "!!!!!!!!!" ;
        VALID TRANSFILE() ;
        MESSAGE "Name of the file to hold preprocessed data" ;
        DISABLE
    @ 9,37 GET RecLen ;
        SIZE 1,4 ;
        DEFAULT 0 ;
        PICTURE "9999" ;
        DISABLE
    @ 13,29 GET m.ReadFirst ;
        SIZE 1,8 ;
        DEFAULT " " ;
        PICTURE "!!!!!!!!!" ;
        VALID READFIRST() ;
        MESSAGE ;
        "Name of program to find the first record in a nonstandard file" ;
        DISABLE
    @ 14,29 GET m.ReadNext ;
        SIZE 1,8 ;
        DEFAULT " " ;
        PICTURE "!!!!!!!!!" ;
        VALID READNEXT() ;
        MESSAGE ;
        "Program to execute to get the next record (nonstandard input files)" ;
        DISABLE
    @ 16,29 GET m.Outfile ;
        SIZE 1,8 ;
        DEFAULT " " ;
        PICTURE "!!!!!!!!!" ;
        VALID OUTFILE() ;
        MESSAGE ;
        "The name of the FoxPro output file to hold the converted data" ;
        DISABLE
    @ 18,4 GET m.EditRules ;
        PICTURE "@*HN \<Edit Rules" ;
        SIZE 1,15,1 ;
        DEFAULT 1 ;
```

```
    VALID Table() ;
    DISABLE
@ 19,4 GET m.ViewInput ;
    PICTURE "@*HN \<View Input" ;
    SIZE 1,15,1 ;
    DEFAULT 1 ;
    VALID View() ;
    DISABLE
@ 20,4 GET m.PrepData ;
    PICTURE "@*HN \<Prep Data" ;
    SIZE 1,15,1 ;
    DEFAULT 1 ;
    VALID DOPREP() ;
    DISABLE
@ 21,4 GET m.SeePrep ;
    PICTURE "@*HN \<See Prep Data" ;
    SIZE 1,15,1 ;
    DEFAULT 1 ;
    VALID SeePrep() ;
    DISABLE
@ 22,4 GET m.SetMode ;
    PICTURE "@*HN Set \<Mode" ;
    SIZE 1,15,1 ;
    DEFAULT 1 ;
    VALID SETMODE() ;
    MESSAGE ;
    "Step through field by field, record by record, or non-stop"
@ 18,22 GET m.StartOver ;
    PICTURE "@*HN \<Start Over" ;
    SIZE 1,16,1 ;
    DEFAULT 1 ;
    VALID STARTOVER() ;
    DISABLE
@ 19,22 GET m.Resume ;
    PICTURE "@*HN \<Process to End" ;
    SIZE 1,16,1 ;
    DEFAULT 1 ;
    VALID RESUMER() ;
    DISABLE
@ 20,22 GET m.BrowseOut ;
    PICTURE "@*HN \<Browse Output " ;
    SIZE 1,16,1 ;
    DEFAULT 1 ;
    VALID BROWSEOUT() ;
    DISABLE
```

```
@ 21,22 GET m.Help ;
   PICTURE "@*HN \<Help" ;
   SIZE 1,16,1 ;
   DEFAULT 1 ;
   VALID DOHELP()
@ 22,22 GET m.Exit ;
   PICTURE "@*HN E\<xit" ;
   SIZE 1,16,1 ;
   DEFAULT 1 ;
   VALID EXITER()

IF NOT WVISIBLE("_qe50k9r3n")
   ACTIVATE WINDOW _qe50k9r3n
ENDIF


*
*
*              MS-DOSREAD contains clauses from SCREEN convert
*
*


READ CYCLE VALID M.DONE COLOR ,W+/R
RELEASE WINDOW _qe50k9r3n

#REGION 0
IF m.talkstat = "ON"
   SET TALK ON
ENDIF
IF m.compstat = "ON"
   SET COMPATIBLE ON
ENDIF
*
*
*      TABLENAME              m.TableName VALID
*
*      Function Origin:
*
*      From Platform:     MS-DOS
*      From Screen:       CONVERT,      Record Number:    18
*      Variable:          m.TableName
*      Called By:         VALID Clause
*      Snippet Number:    1
*
*
```

```
FUNCTION TABLENAME      && m.TableName VALID
#REGION 1
* If they typed in the '.DBF' extension, remove it

IF LASTKEY() = EscapeKey
   RETURN
ENDIF


m.TableName = JustStem ( JustFName ( m.TableName ) )

IF EMPTY ( m.TableName )
   =Warning ( "You must supply a conversion table name " )
   RETURN
ENDIF

IF NOT FILE ( ForceExt ( m.TableName, "DBF" ) )
   SELECT A
   CREATE TABLE ( m.TableName ) ( ;
       SRC_IN   C (  8 ) , ;
       FLD_IN   C ( 10 ) , ;
       STA_IN   N (  3 ) , ;
       END_IN   N (  3 ) , ;
       FUNC_IN  C ( 20 ) , ;
       FLD_OUT  C ( 10 )   )
ENDIF

IF NOT USED ( 'TABLE' )
   USE ( m.TableName ) IN A EXCLUSIVE ALIAS TABLE
   ELSE
   SELECT TABLE
ENDIF

IF RECCOUNT() > 0
   =Warning ( "Table not empty - use View Table to examine contents" )
ENDIF

=Buttons()
```

9-2 Continued.

```
*
*
*       FILETYPE            m.FileType VALID
*
*       Function Origin:
*
*       From Platform:     MS-DOS
*       From Screen:       CONVERT,     Record Number:   19
*       Variable:          m.FileType
*       Called By:         VALID Clause
*       Snippet Number:    2
*
*
```

FUNCTION FILETYPE   && m.FileType VALID
#REGION 1
=Buttons()

```
*
*
*       FILENAME           m.FileName VALID
*
*       Function Origin:
*
*       From Platform:     MS-DOS
*       From Screen:       CONVERT,     Record Number:   20
*       Variable:          m.FileName
*       Called By:         VALID Clause
*       Snippet Number:    3
*
*
```

FUNCTION FILENAME   && m.FileName VALID
#REGION 1
m.FileName = ALLTRIM (m.FileName)

```
IF EMPTY ( m.FileName )

   IF LASTKEY() <> UpArrow
      =Warning ( "Your data must be SOMEWHERE..." )
   ENDIF

   m.FileName = SPACE(31)

ELSE

   IF NOT FILE ( m.FileName )
      m.FileName = GETFILE ( "", "Where is the input data file" )
      IF EMPTY ( m.FileName )
         IF LASTKEY() <> UpArrow
            =Warning ( "Your data must be SOMEWHERE..." )
         ENDIF
         m.FileName = SPACE(31)
         ELSE
         m.FileName = LEFT ( m.FileName + SPACE(31), 31 )
      ENDIF
   ENDIF
ENDIF



=Buttons()

*
*
*      TRANSFILE              m.TransFile VALID
*
*      Function Origin:
*
*      From Platform:        MS-DOS
*      From Screen:          CONVERT,     Record Number:   21
*      Variable:             m.TransFile
*      Called By:            VALID Clause
*      Snippet Number:       4
*
*
*

FUNCTION TRANSFILE      && m.TransFile VALID
#REGION 1

m.TransFile = JustStem ( JustFName ( m.TransFile ) )
```

```
m.TransFile = ALLTRIM  ( m.TransFile )
m.TransFile = LEFT     ( m.TransFile + SPACE(8), 8 )
IF EMPTY ( m.TransFile )
   =Warning ( "You'll need a file to hold preprocessed data in" )
   m.TransFile = SPACE(8)
   SHOW GET m.TransFile DISABLE
   =Buttons()
   RETURN
ENDIF


IF NOT FILE ( ForceExt ( m.TransFile, "DBF" ) )
   IF OK ( [ Transfer file doesn't exist - create? ] )
      SELECT C
      CREATE ( m.TransFile )
      USE    ( m.TransFile ) IN C ALIAS TRANSFER
      ELSE
      =Warning ( "You'll need a file to hold preprocessed data in" )
      m.TransFile = SPACE(8)
      SHOW GET m.TransFile
      =Buttons()
      RETURN
   ENDIF
 ELSE
   IF OK ( [ Modify transfer file structure? ] )
      IF NOT USED ( 'TRANSFER' )
         USE ( m.TransFile ) IN C ALIAS TRANSFER
      ENDIF
      SELECT TRANSFER
      MODIFY STRUCTURE
   ENDIF
ENDIF

=Buttons()
```

```
*
*
*          READFIRST              m.ReadFirst VALID
*
*          Function Origin:
*
*          From Platform:        MS-DOS
*          From Screen:          CONVERT,     Record Number:    23
*          Variable:             m.ReadFirst
*          Called By:            VALID Clause
*          Snippet Number:       5
*
*
```

```
FUNCTION READFIRST      &&  m.ReadFirst VALID
#REGION 1
IF NOT EMPTY ( m.ReadFirst )
   IF OK ( ' Edit the program? ' )
      MODI COMM ( m.ReadFirst )
   ENDIF
ENDIF
```

```
*
*
*          READNEXT              m.ReadNext VALID
*
*          Function Origin:
*
*          From Platform:        MS-DOS
*          From Screen:          CONVERT,     Record Number:    24
*          Variable:             m.ReadNext
*          Called By:            VALID Clause
*          Snippet Number:       6
*
*
```

```
FUNCTION READNEXT      &&  m.ReadNext VALID
#REGION 1
IF NOT EMPTY ( m.ReadNext )
   IF OK ( ' Edit the program? ' )
      MODI COMM ( m.ReadNext )
   ENDIF
ENDIF
```

```
*
*
*
*     OUTFILE              m.Outfile VALID
*
*     Function Origin:
*
*     From Platform:       MS-DOS
*     From Screen:         CONVERT,      Record Number:   25
*     Variable:            m.Outfile
*     Called By:           VALID Clause
*     Snippet Number:      7
*
*
*
```

```
FUNCTION OUTFILE      && m.Outfile VALID

#REGION 1
* If they entered an extension, remove it

m.OutFile = JustStem ( JustFName ( m.OutFile ) )
m.OutFile = ALLTRIM ( m.OutFile )
m.OutFile = LEFT     ( m.OutFile + SPACE(8), 8 )

IF EMPTY ( m.OutFile )
   IF LASTKEY() <> UpArrow
      =Warning ( "You'll need a file to store your converted data in" )
   ENDIF
   m.OutFile = SPACE(8)

   ELSE

   IF NOT FILE ( ForceExt ( m.OutFile, "DBF" ) )
      IF OK ( [ Output file doesn't exist - create? ] )
         SELECT D
         CREATE ( m.OutFile )
         USE    ( m.OutFile ) EXCLUSIVE IN D ALIAS OUTPUT
         ELSE
         =Warning ( "You'll need a file to store your converted data in" )
         m.OutFile = SPACE(8)
      ENDIF
```

```
    ELSE
      IF OK ( [ Modify output file structure? ] )
          IF NOT USED ( 'OUTPUT' )
             USE ( m.OutFile ) EXCLUSIVE IN D ALIAS OUTPUT
          ENDIF
          SELECT OUTPUT
          MODIFY STRUCTURE
      ENDIF
    ENDIF

ENDIF

=Buttons( )
```

```
*
*
*     DOPREP              m.PrepData VALID
*
*     Function Origin:
*
*     From Platform:      MS-DOS
*     From Screen:        CONVERT,      Record Number:    28
*     Variable:           m.PrepData
*     Called By:          VALID Clause
*     Snippet Number:     8
*
*
```

```
FUNCTION DOPREP        &&  m.PrepData VALID
#REGION 1
IF [Nonstandard] $ TYPES(m.FileType)
   =NonStand( )
   ELSE
   =PrepData( )
ENDIF
```

```
*
*
*
*          ┌────────────────────────────────────────────────────────┐
*          │                                                        │
*          │  SETMODE              m.SetMode VALID                  │
*          │                                                        │
*          │  Function Origin:                                      │
*          │                                                        │
*          │  From Platform:       MS-DOS                           │
*          │  From Screen:         CONVERT,     Record Number:   30 │
*          │  Variable:            m.SetMode                        │
*          │  Called By:           VALID Clause                     │
*          │  Snippet Number:      9                                │
*          │                                                        │
*          │                                                        │
*          └────────────────────────────────────────────────────────┘
```

```
FUNCTION SETMODE                     &&  m.SetMode VALID
#REGION 1
DEFINE POPUP SETMODE FROM 10,30 IN SCREEN ;
   COLOR N/W, N/W, N/W, N/W, N/W, W+/R, W+/W
DEFINE BAR 1 OF SETMODE PROMPT PADC ( [\Processing mode]    , 20 )
DEFINE BAR 2 OF SETMODE PROMPT [\-]
DEFINE BAR 3 OF SETMODE PROMPT PADC ( [\<Trace ON] , 20 )
DEFINE BAR 4 OF SETMODE PROMPT PADC ( [\<Non-stop] , 20 )
ON SELECTION POPUP SETMODE DEACTIVATE POPUP SETMODE
ACTIVATE POPUP SETMODE
mPrompt = PROMPT()
RELEASE POPUP SETMODE
m.Mode  = IIF ( [Trace] $ mPrompt, [Trace ] , ;
                                   [     ]   )
SHOW GET m.Mode
IF EMPTY ( m.Mode )
   SHOW GET m.NextStep DISABLE    && can't select next step in nonstop mode
ENDIF
```

```
*
*
*          ┌────────────────────────────────────────────────────────┐
*          │                                                        │
*          │  STARTOVER            m.StartOver VALID                │
*          │                                                        │
*          │  Function Origin:                                      │
*          │                                                        │
*          │  From Platform:       MS-DOS                           │
*          │  From Screen:         CONVERT,     Record Number:   31 │
*          │  Variable:            m.StartOver                      │
*          │  Called By:           VALID Clause                     │
*          │  Snippet Number:      10                               │
*          │                                                        │
*          └────────────────────────────────────────────────────────┘
```

```
FUNCTION STARTOVER      &&  m.StartOver VALID
#REGION 1
m.FromTop = .T.
=Convertr()
```

```
*
*
*
*        RESUMER              m.Resume VALID
*
*        Function Origin:
*
*        From Platform:     MS-DOS
*        From Screen:       CONVERT,    Record Number:    32
*        Variable:          m.Resume
*        Called By:         VALID Clause
*        Snippet Number:    11
*
*
*
```

```
FUNCTION RESUMER       &&  m.Resume VALID
#REGION 1
m.FromTop = .F.
=Convertr()
```

```
*
*
*        BROWSEOUT            m.BrowseOut VALID
*
*        Function Origin:
*
*        From Platform:     MS-DOS
*        From Screen:       CONVERT,    Record Number:    33
*        Variable:          m.BrowseOut
*        Called By:         VALID Clause
*        Snippet Number:    12
*
*
*
```

```
FUNCTION BROWSEOUT     &&  m.BrowseOut VALID
#REGION 1
SELECT OUTPUT
IF RECCOUNT() = 0
   =Warning ( " No data in output file " )
   RETURN
ENDIF
```

9-2 Continued.

```
DEFINE  WINDOW BROWSER FROM 1,0 TO 23, 79 ;
   TITLE [ View output file ] ;
   COLOR SCHEME 10
BROWSE  WINDOW BROWSER WIDTH 10
RELEASE WINDOW BROWSER
```

```
*
*
*     ┌─────────────────────────────────────────────────┐
*     │                                                   │
*     │  DOHELP            m.Help VALID                   │
*     │                                                   │
*     │  Function Origin:                                 │
*     │                                                   │
*     │  From Platform:      MS-DOS                       │
*     │  From Screen:        CONVERT,    Record Number:  34│
*     │  Variable:           m.Help                       │
*     │  Called By:          VALID Clause                 │
*     │  Snippet Number:     13                           │
*     │                                                   │
*     └─────────────────────────────────────────────────┘
```

```
FUNCTION DOHELP      && m.Help VALID
#REGION 1
HELP
```

```
*
*
*     ┌─────────────────────────────────────────────────┐
*     │                                                   │
*     │  EXITER            m.Exit VALID                   │
*     │                                                   │
*     │  Function Origin:                                 │
*     │                                                   │
*     │  From Platform:      MS-DOS                       │
*     │  From Screen:        CONVERT,    Record Number:  35│
*     │  Variable:           m.Exit                       │
*     │  Called By:          VALID Clause                 │
*     │  Snippet Number:     14                           │
*     │                                                   │
*     └─────────────────────────────────────────────────┘
```

```
FUNCTION EXITER      && m.Exit VALID
#REGION 1
Am_I_Done = .T.
CLEAR READ ALL
```

The BUTTONS program

Each time an input field is exited, FoxPro calls its VALID clause. Your valid clause does whatever it needs to do, but ends with a call to BUTTONS. This function looks at all fields entered so far, and decides which controls can be enabled. The program is shown in Listing 9-3.

Listing 9-3 The BUTTONS program.

```
FUNCTION BUTTONS
* Purpose.......: Enable/Disable controls

EXTERNAL ARRAY TYPES

DO CASE

    CASE EMPTY ( m.TableName ) ;
      OR EMPTY ( m.FileName  ) ;
      OR EMPTY ( m.FileType  ) ;
      OR EMPTY ( m.OutFile   )

          SHOW GETS LEVEL 1      DISABLE
          SHOW GET m.SetMode     ENABLE
          SHOW GET m.Exit        ENABLE
          SHOW GET m.TableName   ENABLE
          SHOW GET m.FileName    ENABLE
          SHOW GET m.FileType    ENABLE
          SHOW GET m.OutFile     ENABLE

          OTHERWISE

          SHOW GETS LEVEL 1      ENABLE

ENDCASE

SHOW GET m.Help ENABLE       && always...

IF NOT EMPTY ( m.FileName )
   SHOW GET m.ViewInput ENABLE
ENDIF

IF [Nonstandard] $ TYPES(m.FileType)
   SHOW GET m.ReadFirst ENABLE
   SHOW GET m.ReadNext  ENABLE
   ELSE
   SHOW GET m.ReadFirst DISABLE
   SHOW GET m.ReadNext  DISABLE
ENDIF
```

```
IF (  [Fixed length] $ TYPES(m.FileType)   ;
   OR [delimited]    $ TYPES(m.FileType) ) ;
   AND NOT EMPTY ( m.FileName )
   SHOW GET m.TransFile ENABLE
   IF NOT EMPTY ( m.OutFile )
      SHOW GET m.PrepData  ENABLE
   ENDIF
   IF [no delim] $ TYPES(m.FileType)
      SHOW GET m.RecLen     ENABLE
   ENDIF
   IF USED ( 'TRANSFER' )
      IF RECCOUNT ( 'TRANSFER' ) > 0
         SHOW GET m.SeePrep    ENABLE
      ENDIF
   ENDIF
ENDIF
```

The CONVERTR program

The CONVERTR program (see Listing 9-4) is the heart of the application, although it was a very small part of the total programming. The pseudo-code for the function is simple:

- Prepare the output file.
- Build an array of conversion rules from TABLE.DBF.
- Determine where input will come from.
- For each available input record: create blank memvars for all output fields, process each line in the conversion rules table, select the output file, APPEND BLANK, and GATHER MEMVAR.
- If the used requests "step through" mode, use SET STEP ON and the DEBUG window.

Users can watch the first conversion of the few records, then process the rest of the file without starting again from the beginning. That's what the Process Rest option is for.

Listing 9-4 The CONVERTR program.

```
* Program-ID....: Convertr.PRG
* Purpose.......: Data Conversion Engine

EXTERNAL ARRAY TYPES

IF NOT USED ( 'OUTPUT' )
   USE ( m.OutFile ) EXCLUSIVE IN D ALIAS OUTPUT
ENDIF
```

```
SELECT OUTPUT
SET SAFETY OFF
ZAP

m.Source = IIF ( NOT EMPTY ( m.TransFile ) , [TRANSFER] , [INPUT] )

IF m.Source  = [TRANSFER]
   IF NOT USED ( [TRANSFER] )
      =PrepData()
   ENDIF
   SELECT TRANSFER
   GO TOP
ENDIF

IF  [nonstandard] $ TYPES ( m.FileType ) ;
 OR [Report]      $ TYPES ( m.FileType )
   m.FileNumber  = FOPEN ( m.FileName )
   IF NOT EMPTY ( m.FindFirst )
      DO      ( m.FindFirst )
   ENDIF
   ELSE
   SELECT ( m.Source )
ENDIF

IF FromTop
   GO TOP
ENDIF

* ******************** *
* Start data conversion...
* ******************** *

SELECT TABLE
COPY TO ARRAY ConvertFlds FOR NOT EMPTY ( FLD_OUT )

NumFields  = ALEN(ConvertFlds) / FCOUNT()  && Number of lines in CONVERT
Done       = .F.

IF NOT (     [nonstandard] $ TYPES ( m.FileType ) ;
        OR [Report]        $ TYPES ( m.FileType )   )
   SELECT ( m.Source )
ENDIF
RecordCount = 0

DO WHILE .T.

   SELECT OUTPUT
   APPEND BLANK
   SCATTER MEMVAR BLANK
```

```
   IF NOT (      [nonstandard] $ TYPES ( m.FileType ) ;
            OR [Report]       $ TYPES ( m.FileType )   )
      SELECT ( m.Source )
   ENDIF

   =GetRecord()

   IF Done
      EXIT
   ENDIF

   RecordCount = RecordCount + 1
   WAIT WINDOW [Record #] + STR(RecordCount,5) NOWAIT

   =MoveFields()

   IF m.Mode <> "N" AND ( NOT WVISIBLE('DEBUG') )
      DEFINE WINDOW   DEBUGGER FROM 12,0 TO 24, 50
      ACTIVATE WINDOW DEBUGGER
      SET DEBUG ON
      ACTIVATE WINDOW Debug IN WINDOW DEBUGGER
      SET STEP ON
   ENDIF

   SELECT OUTPUT
   GATHER MEMVAR

ENDDO

WAIT CLEAR

IF  [Nonstandard] $ TYPES ( m.FileType ) ;
 OR [Report]       $ TYPES ( m.FileType )
   =FCLOSE ( m.FileNumber )
ENDIF

WAIT WINDOW [ Done ] TIMEOUT 1

RETURN

FUNCTION GetRecord

IF EMPTY ( m.ReadNext ) && Not a nonstandard input file...
   SELECT ( m.Source )
   IF NOT EOF()
      SKIP
   ENDIF
   IF EOF ( m.Source )
```

```
        Done = .T.
    ENDIF
    RETURN
ENDIF


DO ( m.ReadNext )          && Find the 'next' nonstandard record

IF FEOF ( m.FileNumber )
    Done = .T.
ENDIF
FUNCTION MoveFields
PRIVATE I
FOR I = 1 TO NumFields
    IF EMPTY     ( ConvertFlds ( I, 6 ) )  && no output field
        LOOP
    ENDIF
    IF   ( ConvertFlds ( I, 1 ) ) = [INPUT] AND NOT EMPTY ( m.TransFile )
            ConvertFlds ( I, 1 )   = [TRANSFER]
    ENDIF
    IF EMPTY     ( ConvertFlds ( I, 1 ) )
        FromFld   = ConvertFlds ( I, 2 )
        ELSE
        FromFld   = ALLTRIM(ConvertFlds ( I, 1 ))+'.'+ConvertFlds ( I, 2 )
    ENDIF
    Start       = ConvertFlds ( I, 3 )
    End         = ConvertFlds ( I, 4 )
    Macro       = ConvertFlds ( I, 5 )
    ToField     = ConvertFlds ( I, 6 )
    IF EMPTY ( Macro )
        IF NOT EMPTY ( Start )
            &ToField = SUBSTR ( &FromFld , Start , End-Start+1 )
            ELSE
            &ToField = &FromFld
        ENDIF
        ELSE
        &ToField = &Macro
    ENDIF
ENDFOR
```

The TABLE program

The Conversion Rules table is built using the TABLE program, shown in
Listing 9-5. I used BROWSE to manage this process, and it's quite adequate.

Each line in the table becomes one line of processing in the CON-
VERTR program. Because each line of processing creates or modifies one
memvar, you can "stack" complex calculations into several lines, passing
intermediate results from one line to the next. Be sure not to inadvertently
use a memvar name that's also a name in the output file.

Listing 9-5 The TABLE Program.

```
* Program-ID....: TABLE
* Purpose.......: Maintain conversion table

IF NOT USED ( [TABLE] )
   SELECT 3
   USE ( m.TableName ) ALIAS TABLE
ENDIF
SELECT TABLE

IF OK ( [ Wipe file clear? ] )
   ZAP
ENDIF

IF RECCOUNT() = 0
   WAIT WINDOW [ Use Ctrl+N to add records ] NOWAIT
ENDIF

DEFINE    WINDOW BROWSER FROM 1,0 TO 24, 79 DOUBLE ;
TITLE  [ Use ALT+B, Change to view entire record; Ctrl+F10 when done ]

ON KEY LABEL CTRL+F10 KEYBOARD CHR(23)
ACTIVATE  WINDOW BROWSER

BROWSE IN WINDOW BROWSER ;
 FIELDS ;
  SRC_IN:8      :H=[Source]     :P=[!!!!!!!!!]    :V=Source() :F , ;
  FLD_IN:10     :H=[FromField]  :P=[!!!!!!!!!!!]  :V=Fld()    :F , ;
  STA_IN        :H=[From]       :P=[999]                      , ;
  END_IN        :H=[To]         :P=[999]                      , ;
  FUNC_IN:10    :H=[Func]       :P=[@S20]                     , ;
  FLD_OUT:10    :H=[To Field]   :P=[!!!!!!!!!!!]  :V=Fld()    :F ;
 NOCLEAR SAVE

ON KEY LABEL CTRL+F10
PACK
GO TOP

RELEASE    WINDOW BROWSER

RETURN

FUNCTION SOURCE

IF EMPTY ( SRC_IN )
   WAIT    ;
     WINDOW  ;
     [ ** Source ALIAS or "M" should be specified ** ] ;
     TIMEOUT 1
```

```
ENDIF

IF TRIM ( SRC_IN ) $ [M/INPUT/OUTPUT/]
    RETURN
ENDIF

DEFINE POPUP SOURCES FROM 1,30
DEFINE BAR 1 OF SOURCES PROMPT [\] + PADC( [ Sources ] , 20 )
DEFINE BAR 2 OF SOURCES PROMPT [\-]
DEFINE BAR 3 OF SOURCES PROMPT [M]
DEFINE BAR 4 OF SOURCES PROMPT [INPUT]
DEFINE BAR 5 OF SOURCES PROMPT [OUTPUT]
ON SELECTION POPUP SOURCES DEACTIVATE POPUP SOURCES
ACTIVATE POPUP SOURCES
mPrompt = PROMPT()
RELEASE POPUP SOURCES
IF NOT EMPTY ( mPrompt )
    REPLACE NEXT 1 SRC_IN WITH mPrompt
ENDIF

FUNCTION FLD
DO CASE
    CASE [_IN]  $ UPPER ( VARREAD() )
        IF EMPTY ( FLD_IN )
            WAIT WINDOW ;
                [ ** Field name needed for input identification ** ] ;
                TIMEOUT 1
        ENDIF
ENDCASE
```

The NONSTAND program

The NONSTAND program (see Listing 9-6) is a programmer's utility with which you can preview the results of complex conversions using the READFIRST and READNEXT programs.

Listing 9-6 The NONSTAND program.

```
* Program-ID....: NonStand.PRG
* Purpose.......: Preview nonstandard files using user-supplied programs
*                 ( m.ReadFirst ) and ( m.ReadNext )

PRIVATE I

IF EMPTY ( m.ReadFirst )
    =Warning ( [ You have defined no 'Read first record' function ] )
    RETURN
ENDIF
```

```
IF EMPTY ( m.ReadNext )
   =Warning ( [ You have defined no 'Read next record' function ] )
   RETURN
ENDIF

m.FileNumber = FOPEN ( m.FileName )
IF m.FileNumber = -1
   WAIT WINDOW [ ** ERROR ** opening nonstandard input file ] TIMEOUT 2
   RETURN
ENDIF

SET STEP ON

DO ( m.ReadFirst )
FOR I = 1 TO 10
   DO ( m.ReadNext )
ENDFOR

SET STEP OFF

=FCLOSE ( m.FileNumber )
```

The PREPDATA program

The PREPDATA program (see Listing 9-7) builds the TRANSFER file that the conversion table requires in the case of fixed-length or comma-delimited input files. The CONVERTR program needs field names for its formulas.

Listing 9-7 The PREPDATA program.

```
* Program-ID...: PrepData
* Purpose......: Builds the transfer file if the input file type is
*              : 2, 3 or 4. Loads data and previews it.

EXTERNAL ARRAY TYPES

* TYPES ( 1 ) = [DBF]
* TYPES ( 2 ) = [Fixed-length/CR delim]
* TYPES ( 3 ) = [Comma-delimited]
* TYPES ( 4 ) = [Fixed-length/no delim]
* TYPES ( 5 ) = [Nonstandard]
* TYPES ( 6 ) = [Report file]

DEFINE WINDOW PROGRESS FROM 1,60 TO 3,79 TITLE [Preprocessing data]

DO CASE
```

```
CASE [CR delim] $ TYPES ( m.FileType )

    SELECT C
    USE ( m.TransFile ) EXCLUSIVE ALIAS TRANSFER
    ZAP
    ACTIVATE WINDOW PROGRESS
    SET TALK ON WINDOW PROGRESS
    APPEND FROM ( m.FileName ) SDF
    SET TALK OFF

CASE [Comma-delimited] $ TYPES ( m.FileType )

    SELECT C
    USE ( m.TransFile ) EXCLUSIVE ALIAS TRANSFER
    ZAP
    ACTIVATE WINDOW PROGRESS
    SET TALK ON WINDOW PROGRESS
    APPEND FROM ( m.FileName ) DELIMITED
    SET TALK OFF

CASE [no delim] $ TYPES ( m.FileType )

    IF EMPTY ( m.RecLen )
       =Warning ;
    ( "Record length is needed for nondelimited fixed-length records" )
       RETURN
    ENDIF

    SET TEXTMERGE TO TEXTFILE
    SET TEXTMERGE ON NOSHOW
    fh=FOPEN ( m.FileName )
    IF fh < 0
       =Warning ;
    ( "Can't open nondelimited fixed-length file " + m.FileName )
       RETURN
    ENDIF

    RecCount = 0
    DO WHILE NOT FEOF ( fh )
        a = FREAD ( fh, RecLen )
        RecCount = RecCount + 1
        WAIT WINDOW [ Reading record # ] + STR(RecCount,5) NOWAIT

        \<<a>>
    ENDDO
    =FCLOSE ( fh )
```

```
        SET TEXTMERGE TO
        WAIT CLEAR

        SELECT C
        USE ( m.TransFile ) EXCLUSIVE ALIAS TRANSFER
        ZAP

        APPEND FROM TextFile SDF

   ENDCASE

   RELEASE WINDOW PROGRESS
   WAIT WINDOW [ Done ] TIMEOUT 1
```

The SEEPREP program

The SEEPREP program (see Listing 9-8) lets users view the TRANSFER file created by PREPDATA. This is important, because the subsequent conversions won't work unless the TRANSFER file is correct.

Listing 9-8 The SEEPREP program.

```
FUNCTION SeePrep

IF EMPTY ( m.Transfile )
   RETURN
ENDIF

SELECT TRANSFER
IF EMPTY ( RECCOUNT() )
   =Warning ( " No data preprocessed yet " )
   RETURN
ENDIF

DEFINE  WINDOW BROWSER FROM 1,0 TO 23, 79 ;
   TITLE [ View preprocessor file ] ;
   COLOR SCHEME 10
BROWSE  WINDOW BROWSER WIDTH 10
RELEASE WINDOW BROWSER
```

The VIEW program

The VIEW program, shown in Listing 9-9, is used to directly view the original input file. Input files can be of several types, so this program uses the appropriate viewer based on the file type. If the file can't be viewed using either BROWSE or a text editor, I've used Vern Buerg's LIST program with the /Hex option set. LIST contains a number of internal functions, including search (the forward slash) and a ruler (the R option). Press the question mark for instructions, and hit Escape to exit the file viewer.

Listing 9-9 The VIEW program.

```
FUNCTION View

* Purpose........: Look at the input file

EXTERNAL ARRAY TYPES

DO CASE
    CASE [no delim]          $ TYPES ( m.FileType ) ;
      OR [Nonstandard]       $ TYPES ( m.FileType )
          cmd = 'RUN LIST ' + m.fileName + ' /H'
          &cmd
    CASE [CR delim]          $ TYPES ( m.FileType ) ;
      OR [Comma delimited]   $ TYPES ( m.FileType ) ;
      OR [Report]            $ TYPES ( m.FileType )
          cmd = 'RUN LIST ' + m.fileName
          &cmd
    CASE [DBF]               $ TYPES ( m.FileType )
        IF NOT USED ( 'INPUT' )
           USE ( m.FileName ) IN B ALIAS INPUT
           ELSE
           SELECT INPUT
        ENDIF
        DEFINE  WINDOW BROWSER FROM 1,0 TO 23, 79 ;
           TITLE [ View input file ] ;
           COLOR SCHEME 10
        BROWSE  WINDOW BROWSER WIDTH 10
        RELEASE WINDOW BROWSER
ENDCASE
```

The VIEWOUT program

The VIEWOUT program is used to look at the result of the data conversion. It uses BROWSE, so the user can use Alt–B and select the Change option from the Browse menu to change to one-field-per-line mode. The program is as follows:

```
FUNCTION ViewOut
SELECT OUTPUT
DEFINE  WINDOW BROWSER FROM 1,0 TO 23, 79 ;
    TITLE [ View output file ] ;
```

```
COLOR SCHEME 10
BROWSE  WINDOW BROWSER WIDTH 10
RELEASE WINDOW BROWSER
```

The WARNING program

The WARNING program (see Listing 9-10) is a generic dialog box loosely written in the style recommended by Common User Access (CUA) standards.

Listing 9-10 The WARNING program.

```
FUNCTION Warning
* Purpose........: Displays a dialog box, sounds an alarm, displays an
*                  error message  and waits for a keypress.

PARAMETER msg

msg = LEFT ( msg + SPACE(200) , 200 )

DEFINE WINDOW ERRMSG FROM 8,10 TO 18, 70 DOUBLE COLOR SCHEME 7
ACTIVA WINDOW ERRMSG

@ 3,2 TO 5,6 DOUBLE
@ 4,4 SAY "!"

SET BELL TO 700,1
?? CHR(7)
SET BELL TO 800,1
?? CHR(7)
SET BELL TO 900,1
?? CHR(7)

SET MEMOWIDTH TO 40
@ 2, 15 SAY PADC ( MLINE(msg,1) , 40 )
@ 3, 15 SAY PADC ( MLINE(msg,2) , 40 )
@ 4, 15 SAY PADC ( MLINE(msg,3) , 40 )
@ 5, 15 SAY PADC ( MLINE(msg,4) , 40 )
@ 6, 15 SAY PADC ( MLINE(msg,5) , 40 )

@ WROWS()-1, 1 SAY PADC('Press ◄┘ to continue',WCOLS()-1 )
SET CURSOR OFF
=INKEY(0)
SET CURSOR ON

RELEASE WINDOW ERRMSG

RETURN
```

The OK program

The OK program (see Listing 9-11) is a confirming dialog to control processing. The code structure that typically uses it is:

```
IF OK ( "prompt" )
    =ProgramAction()
ENDIF
```

Listing 9-11 The OK program.

```
FUNCTION OK
* Program-ID....: OK
* Purpose.......: Confirmation utility

PARAMETERS Wtitle
Width = LEN ( WTITLE )
Half  = Width / 2
DEFINE WINDOW OK FROM 12,40-Half-3 TO 14, 40+Half+2 ;
    DOUBLE SHADOW ;
    COLOR N/W, N/W, N/W, N/W, N/W, W+/R, W+/R, N/W, N/W;
    TITLE Wtitle
ACTIVATE WINDOW OK
@ 0, WCOLS()/2-6 GET m.Choice PICTURE '@*HT \<No;\<Yes ' DEFAULT 1
READ CYCLE COLOR ,W+/R
RELEASE WINDOW OK
RETURN IIF ( m.Choice = 1 , .F. , .T. )
```

The HELP file

The conversion program has its own HELP file, with the structure:

```
Topic      Character    10
Info       Memo         10
```

User-supplied help works just like FoxPro's HELP system, and it's easy to add. A sample HELP screen appears in Fig. 9-4.

The program requires the names of an input file as well as an output file. The conversion rules table is used by function CONVERTR to build a set of memvars that correspond to fields in the output file. At the end of processing the conversion table for each record, APPEND BLANK and GATHER MEMVAR.

Inputs to the CONVERTR function are generally fields in the INPUT file. However, if the input file consists of fixed-length records (either carriage-return delimited or nondelimited) or comma-delimited data, there are no field names—you have to provide a transfer file.

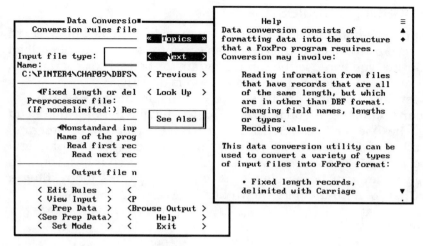

```
┌──Data Conversio■──────────────────┐  ┌─────────────────────────────────────┐
│  Conversion rules file            │  │         Help                      ≡ │
│ ─────────────────────  ┌─────────┐│  │ Data conversion consists of       ▲ │
│                        │« Topics »││  │ formatting data into the structure ◆ │
│ Input file type: ┌───┐ ├─────────┤│  │ that a FoxPro program requires.     │
│ Name:            │   │ │‹ Next  ›││  │ Conversion may involve:             │
│ C:\PINTER4\CHAP09\DBFS\ ‹ Previous ›│  │                                     │
│                                   │  │    Reading information from files   │
│   ◄Fixed length or del ‹ Look Up ›│  │    that have records that are all   │
│  Preprocessor file:               │  │    of the same length, but which    │
│  (If nondelimited:) Rec┌─────────┐│  │    are in other than DBF format.    │
│                        │ See Also ││  │    Changing field names, lengths    │
│     ◄Nonstandard inp   └─────────┘│  │    or types.                        │
│   Name of the prog                │  │    Recoding values.                 │
│      Read first rec               │  │                                     │
│      Read next rec                │  │ This data conversion utility can be │
│                                   │  │ used to convert a variety of types  │
│     Output file n                 │  │ of input files into FoxPro format:  │
│                                   │  │                                     │
│   ‹ Edit Rules  ›   ‹             │  │    • Fixed length records,          │
│   ‹ View Input  ›   ‹P            │  │      delimited with Carriage      ▼ │
│   ‹ Prep Data   ›   ‹Browse Output ›│  │                                   . │
│   ‹See Prep Data›   ‹   Help     ›│  └─────────────────────────────────────┘
│   ‹ Set Mode    ›   ‹   Exit     ›│
└───────────────────────────────────┘
```

Figure 9-4 A sample Help screen.

Using transfer files

FoxPro can read a fixed-length record straight into a .DBF record, provided that both are laid out exactly the same way, using the APPEND FROM *file name* SDF command. For example, if LOADER.DBF has a file structure that looks like this:

```
Fld Name    Type        Len    Dec
 1  NAME    Character    10
 2  AMT     Numeric       5     2
```

and the data in SAMPLE.DAT looks like this:

```
Rec   ....+....1....+....2    <== Character position ruler
 1   Davies     15.00
 2   Smith       5.25
 3   Johnson    12.50
```

the command APPEND FROM SAMPLE DAT SDF will read the data directly into the file. If you load fixed-length carriage-return delimited records into a transfer file like this, the formulas loaded into the rules table can refer to the fields in the transfer file.

Similarly, FoxPro can APPEND FROM *filename* DELIMITED right into a .DBF that has the same number and type of data fields, even though some of the data consists only of double quotes. Using the file structure from the previous example, data that looks like this:

```
"Davies",15.00
"Smith",5.25
"Johnson",12.50
```

can be loaded using the command APPEND FROM SAMPLE DAT DELIMITED.

Nonstandard input files

If the input file is nonstandard, you have to provide your own first-record and next-record routines. If the file doesn't require some kind of oddball header routine, you can use the same program for both. The program lets you edit the source code for these two programs directly.

The View Input option permits several options, including Hex and Use Nonstandard Routines. If you're looking at the file for the first time, you can use a hex viewer like LIST.EXE (Vern Buerg's shareware program) which can be used to determine both how many header bytes to skip and the record length. Once you know these, you can write your own routines accordingly. They can be as simple as my two routines for reading a Quicken Chart of Accounts file, shown here:

```
FUNCTION FirstQDT   && Reads the first record in a Quicken file
data = FREAD ( m.FileNumber , 677 )
FUNCTION NextQDT  && Reads all subsequent records in a Quicken file
data = FREAD ( m.FileNumber , 128 )
```

Using reports as input

Report files are sometimes the only source of data you can get. Because the program doesn't care what you did in the nonstandard next-record routine, you can read three lines of detail and create one set of memvars, and the CONVERTR routine will cheerfully use the memvars to build the output file.

I was once working with a program that didn't allow any kind of data export. The vendors knew darned well that people would leave their program in droves as soon as something better came along, and their hefty maintenance fees made it clear that they wanted as much of your money as possible before you dumped them. By using the PRN2FILE.COM utility (included on the source-code disk available through the coupon at the back of this book), I was able to capture reports of all of the information I needed. Then I wrote my own routines to unstring the detail lines.

Conclusion

I've got a special place in my heart for data conversion. As a result, I'm already getting "programmer's remorse" over all the features I could have included in this application. I've included a few hex and zoned-decimal decoding routines, but I've already thought of some more that would probably come in handy. Hopefully, you'll find the structure useful and can add on your own enhancements.

10
Miscellaneous topics

Although there are a number of models available for the most common types of software, there are many things you can do with FoxPro that are just a little different. This chapter contains a half dozen such examples. Some, like the spreadsheet function, can be used with few modifications in a variety of applications. Others, like the labeling program, are specific tools for specific jobs. Even if you don't need these functions, you might find the designs or the coding techniques useful.

A FoxPro spreadsheet using INKEY( )

Seems like I spend an inordinate amount of time getting my screens to do exactly what users ask for. FoxPro has so many terrific built-in tools and commands, you'd think you could slap things together in a flash and be done with it. But it's seldom the case.

I try to talk clients into doing things the easy and inexpensive way. Software changes so often that you don't want to spend more money and time than necessary on code that will soon be rewritten. But you'd be surprised how often clients don't care what it costs, as long as it acts just the way they want it to. Fortunately, FoxPro is once again well suited to the task.

A customer wanted to use a spreadsheet from within his database application. I showed him how FoxPro for Windows could call Excel. "That's great," he said, "but that's not how I want it to work." End of discussion.

The client's requirements were pretty simple. The tables to be edited were small, requiring no scrolling either vertically or horizontally, and columns needed to be continuously subtotaled. But input values had to go up in the left-hand corner, just like 1-2-3, and the arrow keys had to act exactly like they do in 1-2-3. (The arrow keys terminate input and move the cell pointer, not just in 1-2-3, but in Excel and every other spreadsheet product.)

One difference between FoxPro and spreadsheet programs really seems to irritate users. When you type a value into a 1-2-3 spreadsheet, the input appears at the upper left of the screen as you type, and goes into the cell only when you press Enter or one of the cursor-movement keys. You've undoubtedly noticed that an xBASE READ does something entirely different. If you enter 12 into a field that already contains 34, it looks like this: 12   34. If you press an arrow key instead of enter, you'll end up with 1234 in the field—not exactly what you had in mind. If you're used to Excel or Lotus, this habit can be hard to break.

PICTURE clauses

There are several ways to write your own spreadsheet in FoxPro. In fact, my newsletter has published two such articles, and they both suffered from the same READ problems alluded to in the previous section. But there's another way, and the INKEY( ) function is what makes it work. In particular, INKEY(0) waits for a keystroke and returns the numeric value of the key that was pressed. That means you can monitor each and every keystroke. You can make numeric columns be restricted to numeric input, and cursor-movement keys processed using your own rules, not FoxPro's. However, there are a few complications. For one, you have to write your own PICTURE-clause processing.

Well, other than that, Mrs. Lincoln, how did you like the play? I agree that trying to duplicate all the features of PICTURE clauses would be nearly impossible. But if all you want is text and numbers, it's pretty easy.

Going back to the source

I had to go back to Lotus and Excel to see how these features work. Sure enough, input values don't go into the current cell until you terminate the cell's input. As you type, the entry appears in the upper left-hand corner of the screen. When you press Enter or any of the arrow keys, the current cell is updated and the cell pointer moves. Also, numeric input doesn't get formatted until it's redisplayed in the current cell.

Lotus and Excel probably don't use internal arrays to store their information; in C you use pointers to arrays of pointers to arrays of pointers to . . . sorry, I got carried away. But you don't have pointers, so you'll just use arrays. Actually, arrays in FoxPro are more flexible than in C. You can have a two-dimensional array with numbers in some columns and text in others. That makes the job much, much easier.

For reasons known only to the high priests of xBASE, READKEY( ) and INKEY( ) return different values. If you use READ for spreadsheet cell input, you get a lot for your money. PICTURE formats aren't even the principal benefit; The _CUROBJ pointer is a simple mechanism for managing movement from one cell to the next, based on the last value of READKEY( ). No READ, no _CUROBJ.

Now that you know there's a tradeoff, what's the gain and what's the loss?

The design specification

Let's build a simple case that requires no scrolling. The basic principles can be demonstrated with a simple case, and extensions are rather easy. You can store the data in a .DBF, using the field names as column headings. Any .DBF can be used, provided only character and numeric fields are used. Cursor movement and cell updating will operate as they do in 1-2-3.

To demonstrate on-screen formula calculations, cell entries will be continuously subtotaled at the bottom of the screen. We won't try to implement formulas in cells just yet, although it can indeed be done. Finally, I'll demonstrate (but not fully implement) the addition of a command menu like the one that pressing the slash key (/) invokes in 1-2-3. The sample screen appears in Fig. 10-1.

	DIVISION	JANUARY	FEBRUARY	MARCH	APRIL	MAY	JUNE
						? - Help	
1	Chemicals	1.00	2.00	3.00	2.00	100.00	1.00
2	Feed	1.00	2.00	3.00	2.00	0.00	1.00
3	Equipment	1.00	2.00	3.00	2.00	0.00	1.00
4	Permits	1.00	2.00	3.00	2.00	0.00	1.00
5	Supplies	1.00	2.00	3.00	2.00	0.00	1.00
6	Salaries	1.00	2.00	3.00	2.00	0.00	1.00
7	Benefits	0.00	0.00	0.00	2.00	0.00	1.00
8	Auto	0.00	0.00	0.00	2.00	0.00	1.00
9	Air travel	0.00	0.00	0.00	2.00	0.00	1.00
10	Entertainmnt	0.00	0.00	0.00	2.00	0.00	1.00
11	Fuel	0.00	0.00	0.00	2.00	0.00	1.00
12	Outside Svcs	0.00	0.00	0.00	2.00	0.00	1.00
13	Post Product	0.00	0.00	0.00	2.00	0.00	1.00
14	Accounting	0.00	0.00	0.00	2.00	0.00	1.00
15	Contract svc	0.00	0.00	0.00	2.00	0.00	1.00
16	Postage	0.00	0.00	0.00	2.00	0.00	1.00
17	Shipping	0.00	0.00	0.00	2.00	0.00	1.00
18	String	0.00	0.00	0.00	2.00	0.00	1.00
19	Glue	0.00	0.00	0.00	2.00	0.00	1.00
20	Bindings	0.00	0.00	0.00	2.00	99.00	1.00
		6.00	12.00	18.00	40.00	199.00	20.00

Figure 10-1 The Spreadsheet screen.

How it works

The LOCFILE( ) function returns the name of a file, or the null string if Escape was pressed. This is a simple mechanism for letting users work with files anywhere on the disk, provided they know what a directory structure is. The LOCFILE( ) dialog appears in Fig. 10-2.

CLEAR MACROS removes the definitions of the function keys that FoxPro starts with. You can use CONFIG.FP to deactivate their default as-

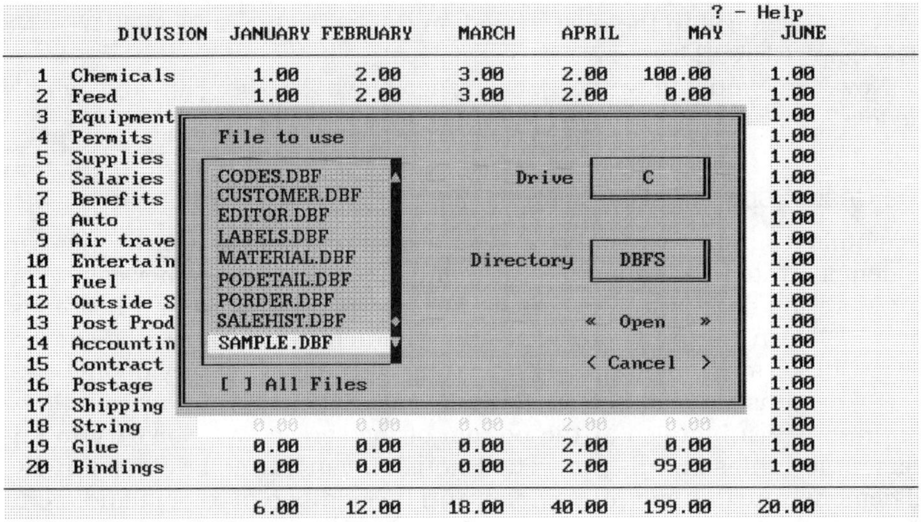

```
              DIVISION   JANUARY FEBRUARY    MARCH    APRIL     MAY     JUNE

   1   Chemicals      1.00     2.00     3.00     2.00   100.00     1.00
   2   Feed           1.00     2.00     3.00     2.00     0.00     1.00
   3   Equipment ┌─────────────────────────────────────────────┐  1.00
   4   Permits   │  File to use                                 │  1.00
   5   Supplies  │                                              │  1.00
   6   Salaries  │  ┌CODES.DBF─────▲    Drive   ┌───────────┐   │  1.00
   7   Benefits  │  │CUSTOMER.DBF   │            │     C     │   │  1.00
   8   Auto      │  │EDITOR.DBF     │            └───────────┘   │  1.00
   9   Air trave │  │LABELS.DBF     │                            │  1.00
  10   Entertain │  │MATERIAL.DBF   │  Directory ┌───────────┐   │  1.00
  11   Fuel      │  │PODETAIL.DBF   │            │   DBFS     │   │  1.00
  12   Outside S │  │PORDER.DBF     │            └───────────┘   │  1.00
  13   Post Prod │  │SALEHIST.DBF   ▼       «  Open  »           │  1.00
  14   Accountin │  │SAMPLE.DBF     ▼                            │  1.00
  15   Contract  │  └───────────────┘    <  Cancel  >           │  1.00
  16   Postage   │  [ ] All Files                               │  1.00
  17   Shipping  └─────────────────────────────────────────────┘  1.00
  18   String         0.00     0.00     0.00     2.00     0.00     1.00
  19   Glue           0.00     0.00     0.00     2.00     0.00     1.00
  20   Bindings       0.00     0.00     0.00     2.00    99.00     1.00

                      6.00    12.00    18.00    40.00   199.00    20.00
```

Figure 10-2 The LOCFILE() dialog.

signments, too, but CONFIG.FP is easy to erase, and it's the last thing you'll check for when your client calls in a bug report.

Next define the INKEY() values of the keys you want to test for, and initialize global variables that will in some cases be assigned correct values in some subsequent function call. I went a little crazy with the PUBLIC command earlier in my career, defining variables in subroutines where they were first assigned a value. Now, I'd rather name everything that's global right up front, and then calculate their values in functions. The code's easier to read because you know what to look for.

The three strings—Numerics, Alphas, and Symbols—contain the only values the user can enter into cells. This lets you process everything else as an OTHERWISE in the DO CASE that handles keystrokes. Notice that the blank has to be included.

The four arrays—ColType, Width, StartCol, and Mask—have one element for each column in the screen display. ColTypes are character and numeric, Width is the width of the column, StartCol is the starting location of each column on the screen, and Mask is a PICTURE clause for numeric columns only. Because of the way macro substitution works, Mask(j) contains the word PICTURE if the variable for its column is numeric.

LoadPage() reads data into the data array from the selected file; LoadStats() initializes the aforementioned type, width, and picture arrays; ShowPage() displays the data array; and ReCalc() recalculates and displays column totals.

The Colr variable is initially null, but is reassigned the white-on-red color pair (W+/R) before entering the main loop. This is done so the same element display routine can be used to do the initial screen display, which doesn't color each individual cell, and the subsequent post-keystroke cell display, which does. The spreadsheet program is shown in Listing 10-1.

Listing 10-1 The SPREADSHEET program.

```
FUNCTION SPREADSH

* Purpose.....: Manages an on-screen spreadsheet

SET TALK OFF
SET ESCAPE OFF
SET CURSOR OFF

FileName = GETFILE ( "DBF", "File to use" )
IF EMPTY ( FileName )
    RETURN
ENDIF

USE &Filename EXCLUSIVE
CLEAR

CLEAR MACROS

ESC            =  27
BackSpace      = 127
Slash          =  47
Question       =  63
Up             =   5
Down           =  24
Left           =  19
Right          =   4
LastKey        =   0
MaxRows        = 128
MaxLines       =  20
Row            =   1
Col            =   1
ScrRows        =   1
ScrCols        =   1
MaxCols        =   1
Colr           =  []

Numerics       = [-0123456789.]
Alphas         = [ABCDEFGHIJKLMNOPQRSTUVWXYZabcdefghijklmnopqrstuvwxyz]
Symbols        = [$#*&(),"'] + [ ] && be sure to include the blank (CHR(32))

DIMENSION ColType (       ScrCols )
DIMENSION Width   (       ScrCols )
DIMENSION StartCol(       ScrCols )
DIMENSION Mask    (       ScrCols )

=LoadPage()               && Read array elements
```

```
=LoadStats()              && Initialize type, width, picture
=ShowPage()               && Display data
=ReCalc()                 && Calculate and display column totals


Row     =   1
Col     =   1
Colr    = [COLOR W+/R]
DO WHILE .T.

   =ShowCell()
   =GetCell()   && Get the cell value
 * =Debugger()  && Remove asterisk to follow the program's flow
   =ShowCell()  && Display the cell value
   @ 0,0 FILL TO 24, 79 COLOR W+/B    && Hide the previous highlights
   =ReCalc()

   DO CASE
      CASE LastKey      = Question      && Help key
            DO SSHELP
      CASE LastKey      = ESC           && Done
            EXIT
      CASE LastKey      = Down
         IF Row    < MaxRows
                   Row  = Row + 1
                   ELSE
                   =Alarm()
         ENDIF
      CASE LastKey       = Up
         IF Row    > 1
                   Row  = Row - 1
                   ELSE
                   =Alarm()
         ENDIF
      CASE LastKey       = Left
         IF Col    > 1
                   Col  = Col - 1
                   ELSE
                   =Alarm()
         ENDIF
      CASE LastKey       = Right
         IF Col    < MaxCols
                   Col  = Col + 1
                   ELSE
                   =Alarm()
         ENDIF
```

```
*       CASE LastKey       = Slash          && Remove asterisk to test
* This assumes you've redefined the system menu.
*           ACTIVATE MENU _MSYSMENU         && Remove asterisk to test
    ENDCASE
ENDDO

IF CONFIRM ( ' Save spreadsheet? ' )
    ZAP
    APPEND FROM ARRAY Data
ENDIF

RESTORE MACROS

RETURN  && END OF SPREADSHEET MAIN ROUTINE
```

The GetCell( ) function in Listing 10-2 reads the input value for the current cell using INKEY(0). The cell's input is terminated by any key other than those defined in the Alphas, Numerics, and Symbols strings for character type, or Numerics for numeric type.

Listing 10-2 The GetCell() function.

```
FUNCTION GetCell

Cell = []
@ 0, 0 CLEAR TO 0, 60
@ 0, 0 SAY Cell
SET CURSOR ON
DO WHILE .T.
    Key = INKEY(0)
    DO CASE
        CASE Key  < 0
            LOOP
        CASE Key  = BackSpace
            IF LEN(Cell) > 0
                Cell = LEFT ( Cell , LEN ( Cell ) -1 )
            ENDIF
        CASE ColType ( Col ) = [N] ;
            AND CHR ( Key ) $ Numerics
                Cell = Cell + CHR ( Key )
        CASE ColType ( Col ) = [C] ;
            AND CHR ( Key ) $ Numerics + Alphas + Symbols
                Cell = Cell + CHR ( Key )
                IF LEN ( Cell ) > Width ( Col )
                    Cell = LEFT ( Cell , Width ( Col ) )
```

```
                ENDIF
        OTHERWISE
              LastKey = Key
              EXIT
    ENDCASE
    @ 0, 0 CLEAR TO 0, 60
    @ 0, 0 SAY Cell
ENDDO
IF NOT EMPTY ( Cell )
    IF   ColType        ( Col ) = [C]
        Wide = Width ( Col )
        IF Cell == ["] Cell == [']
            Cell = SPACE(Wide)
        ENDIF
          Data ( Row, Col ) =  LEFT ( Cell + SPACE ( Wide ), Wide )
      ELSE
          Data ( Row, Col ) =  VAL  ( Cell )
    ENDIF
ENDIF
@ 0, 0 CLEAR TO 0, 60
SET CURSOR OFF
```

Listing 10-3 contains ShowCell( ), LoadPage( ), and ShowStats( ) functions. ShowCell( ) redisplays the value of the cell if the contents changed. Numeric fields use the PICTURE clause for the column. The macro expansion of &Colr is what displays the cell in a different color.

Listing 10-3 The ShowCell( ), LoadPage( ), and ShowStats( ) functions.

```
FUNCTION ShowCell

Fld  = Data ( Row, Col )
Fmat = Mask (       Col )
@ Row+2, StartCol( Col ) SAY Fld &Fmat &Colr


FUNCTION LoadPage

IF NOT EMPTY ( DBF() )
    MaxRows = RECCOUNT()
    MaxCols = FCOUNT()
    RELEASE DATA
    PUBLIC  DATA ( MaxRows , MaxCols )
    COPY TO ARRAY Data
    MaxRows  = IIF ( RECCOUNT() > 20, 20 , RECCOUNT() )
    MaxLines = MaxRows
    IF RECCOUNT() > 20
```

10-3 Continued.

```
        =Warning("Only the first 20 records loaded; only 20 will be saved.")
    ENDIF
    ELSE
    WAIT WINDOW [ No file open ] TIMEOUT 2
    CANCEL
ENDIF

FUNCTION LoadStats

=AFIELDS ( Struc )
MaxCols = ALEN ( Struc ) / 4
DIMENSION ;
  ColType  ( MaxCols ) , ;
  StartCol ( MaxCols ) , ;
  Width    ( MaxCols ) , ;
  Mask     ( MaxCols )

STORE 0 TO StartCol

ColTotal = 0

FOR Col = 1 TO ALEN ( Struc ) /  4
   ColType ( Col ) = Struc ( Col , 2 )
   Width   ( Col ) = Struc ( Col , 3 )

* Don't try to edit more than will fit on the screen
   ColTotal = ColTotal + Width ( Col )
   IF ColTotal + Width ( Col ) > 76
      MaxCols = Col - 1
      =Warning ( [ Only used first ] + STR ( MaxCols, 1 ) + [ fields ] )
      EXIT
   ENDIF

   IF Col = 1
      StartCol( Col ) = 6
    ELSE      StartCol( Col ) = StartCol ( Col - 1 ) + Width ( Col - 1 )
   ENDIF
   Mask      ( Col ) = []
   IF ColType( Col ) = [N]
      Decimals       = Struc ( Col , 4 )
      IF Decimals    = 0
         Mask ( Col )= [PICTURE ]   + ["] ;
          + REPL ( [#] , Width( Col )-Decimals -1 )      && Important!
       ELSE
         Mask ( Col )= [PICTURE ]   + ["] ;
```

```
            + REPL ( [#] , Width( Col )-Decimals -2 )       && Important!
        Mask ( Col )= Mask ( Col ) + [.] ;
            + REPL ( '#', Decimals)
      ENDIF
      Mask ( Col ) = Mask ( Col ) + ["]
   ENDIF
   @ 1, StartCol ( Col ) SAY PADL ( FIELD ( Col ),Width ( Col ) )
ENDFOR
@ 2, 0 SAY REPL([−],80)
@23, 0 SAY REPL([−],80)
```

LoadPage( ) builds an array consisting of up to 20 records from the current .DBF. Because this example doesn't support vertical scrolling, excess records aren't loaded and will disappear if SAVE is selected.

LoadStats( ) is where the program decides how many columns will fit on the page and what data type each column is. If a column is numeric, a format picture is saved in the mask array.

ShowPage( ), shown in Listing 10-4, is called before any cell editing has been done and displays the two-dimensional array containing the spreadsheet's data, ending with the help-key prompt. It can use the function ShowCell( ) because the Colr variable hasn't been assigned a value yet. Recalc( ) sums all the numeric columns and redisplays them on the last line of the screen. The Confirm( ) function at the end of the listing is useful for dialogs like the one that saves or discards the spreadsheets, shown in Fig. 10-3.

Listing 10-4 Remaining spreadsheet functions.

```
FUNCTION ShowPage

FOR Row = 1 TO MaxLines
   @ Row+2, 1 SAY STR(Row,3) + [ ]
   FOR Col = 1 TO MaxCols
       =ShowCell()
   ENDFOR
ENDFOR
@ 0, 61 SAY " ? - Help "

FUNCTION Recalc

PRIVATE Row, Col

IF TYPE   ( 'TOTALS(      1)' ) = [U]
```

```
    DIMENSION TOTALS(MaxCols)
ENDIF

STORE 0 TO Totals

FOR         Row    = 1 TO MaxRows
    FOR     Col    = 1 TO MaxCols
    IF ColType(Col) = [N]
      TOTALS  (Col) = TOTALS (Col) + DATA ( Row, Col )
    ENDIF
    ENDFOR
ENDFOR

FOR Col  = 1 TO MaxCols
    IF ColType(Col) = [N]
       Fmat = MASK    ( Col )
        @ 24, StartCol ( Col ) SAY TOTALS ( Col ) &Fmat
    ENDIF
ENDFOR

FUNCTION Alarm

SET BELL TO 700,1
?? CHR(7)
SET BELL TO 800,1
?? CHR(7)
SET BELL TO 900,1
?? CHR(7)

FUNCTION  Debugger

KeyName = ;
    IIF ( LastKey = 27 , 'ESC' , ;
    IIF ( LastKey =  5 , '↑' , ;
    IIF ( LastKey = 24 , '↓' , ;
    IIF ( LastKey = 19 , '←' , ;
    IIF ( LastKey =  4 , '→' , ;
    IIF ( LastKey = 13 , '↵' , STR(LastKey,3) )))))) 
WAIT WINDOW [ Last key pressed was ] + KeyName TIMEOUT 1

FUNCTION Warning

PARAMETER msg
msg = LEFT ( msg + SPACE(200) , 200 )
```

```
DEFINE WINDOW WARNING FROM 8,10 TO 18, 70 DOUBLE COLOR SCHEME 7
ACTIVA WINDOW WARNING

@ 3,2 TO 5,6 DOUBLE
@ 4,4 SAY "!"

=Alarm()

SET MEMOWIDTH TO 40
@ 2, 15 SAY PADC ( MLINE(msg,1) , 40 )
@ 3, 15 SAY PADC ( MLINE(msg,2) , 40 )
@ 4, 15 SAY PADC ( MLINE(msg,3) , 40 )
@ 5, 15 SAY PADC ( MLINE(msg,4) , 40 )
@ 6, 15 SAY PADC ( MLINE(msg,5) , 40 )

@ WROWS()-1, 1 SAY PADC('Press ⏎ to continue',WCOLS()-1 )
SET CURSOR OFF
=INKEY(0)
SET CURSOR ON

RELEASE WINDOW WARNING

RETURN

FUNCTION Confirm
* Purpose.........: Displays a confirming dialogue using the title passed
*                   to it when called; defaults to 'Yes'
PARAMETERS ctitle

PRIVATE choice
length = LEN ( ctitle )

DEFINE WINDOW CONFIRM FROM 10,10 TO 16, 70 DOUBLE COLOR SCHEME 5
ACTIVA WINDOW CONFIRM

@ 1, 0 SAY PADC ( cTitle, WCOLS()-1 )
@ WROWS()-2, 18 GET choice PICTURE "@*H \<Yes;No" SIZE 1,10 DEFAULT 1
READ
RELEASE WINDOW CONFIRM

RETURN IIF ( choice = 1 , .T. , .F. )

FUNCTION SSHELP
```

10-4 Continued.

```
ACTIVA WINDOW SSHELP
@ 1, 0 SAY PADC('Special keys',WCOLS())
@ 3,10 SAY " /  - activates command menu"
@ 4,10 SAY "       (if menu is defined.) "
@ 6,10 SAY "ESC - exit"
@ 7,10 SAY "       (prompts to save or discard changes)"

WAIT WINDOW

RELEASE WINDOW SSHELP
```

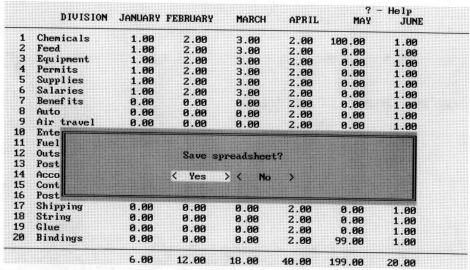

Figure 10-3 The confirming dialog that exits the spreadsheet.

Concluding remarks

This spreadsheet acts like you'd expect it to act. It's easy to add extensions, such as vertical and horizontal scrolling, a slash-activated menu, and formulas in cells.

Printing labels

I've worked on a number of applications that needed to print labels. FoxPro's LABEL FORM command does a fabulous job of printing one label for each record in the file. Unfortunately, that's not always the way data needs to be printed.

The case that clarified this for me involved shipping labels for SBT's sales-order system. As you'd expect, each line item in a sales order consists of the part number and the quantity to ship to the customer. The shipping department gets the order and proceeds to print the labels. But LABEL FORM prints one label per record, not order_qty labels for each record.

To further complicate the issue, items to be shipped can often be packaged differently. For example, if the customer wants 10 lamps, you might want to pack three each in three boxes, and the final lamp in a fourth box. That's four labels—not a number that would be easily inferred from the number 10.

This demonstration program lets the user pick from the list of all available purchase orders only the ones that are to be shipped today, and then provides a simple mechanism for converting a single record for a quantity of 10 into four records with the correct quantity on each record. The LABELS file is the final result. It has one record for each label to be printed, with fields containing the customer ID, P/O#, part number, and how many are inside the box. Figure 10-4 shows the original data, and Fig. 10-5 the file used to print the labels, one label per record.

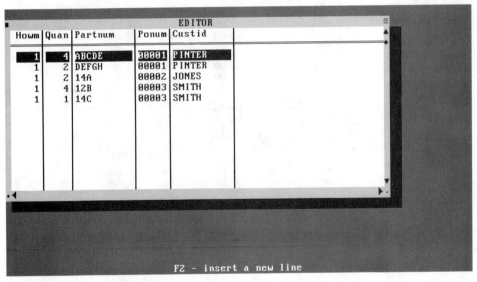

Figure 10-4 The source file for the LABELS program.

The LABELS program appears in Listing 10-5. I substituted my own file structures and test data rather than use SBT's. I think Bob Davies would prefer that you buy his SBT file structures from him.

The program continues in Listing 10-6. The FASTPICK function used to pick the items to be printed is from my June, 1992 newsletter. You can also use Alan Griver's routine, or the DEFINE POPUP MULTISELECT command in FoxPro. The two tables are work files: EDITOR is where you determine how many labels (HowMany) each part number will need and LABELS is the file from which the labels are printed. It contains one record for each label. Quantity is the count of how many pieces are inside each box.

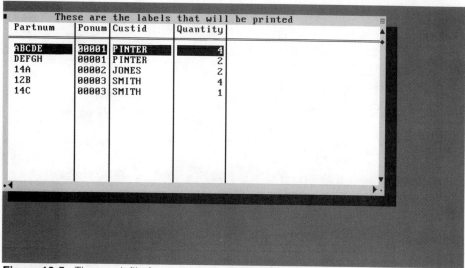

Figure 10-5 The result file from which labels are actually printed.

Listing 10-5 Label management with the LABELS program.

```
* Program-ID......: LABELS.PRG
* Purpose.........: Permits a user to turn detail records into
*                   one record per label
*
* Files:
*
*    PORDER.DBF:
*       PONUM      Character  5
*       PODATE     Date       8
*       CUSTID     Character 10
*
* Test data:
*
*       PONUM CUSTID     DATE
* -----------------------------
*       00001 PINTER     02/15/93
*       00002 JONES      01/01/93
*       00003 SMITH      03/01/93
* -----------------------------
*
*    PODETAIL.DBF:
*       PONUM      Character  5
*       PARTNUM    Character 10
*       QUANTITY   Numeric    3
*
* Test data:
*
```

Continued.

```
*      PONUM PARTNUM    QUANTITY
* ----------------------------
*     00001 ABCDE          4
*     00001 DEFGH          2
*     00002 14A            2
*     00003 12B            4
*     00003 14C            1
* ----------------------------


USE PORDER   IN A ORDER PONUM
USE PODETAIL IN B ORDER PONUM

* First, give user a list of purchase orders to select from:
* Display format should be " PONUM | Customer ID    "
SELECT PORDER
COPY TO ARRAY LISTER FIELDS PORDER.PONUM, PORDER.CUSTID
DIMENSION PICKER ( ALEN(LISTER)/2 )
FOR I = 1 TO ALEN(LISTER)/2
    PICKER(I) = LISTER(I,1)+[ | ] + LISTER(I,2)
ENDFOR
```

Listing 10-6 LABELS.PRG, continued.

```
DO FASTPICK WITH PICKER, "PICKED", 1

SELECT PORDER
SET FILTER TO ASCAN ( PICKED, PORDER.PONUM )   > 0

* Only look at records that were picked

SELECT PODETAIL
SET FILTER TO ASCAN ( PICKED, PODETAIL.PONUM ) > 0

SELECT C
CREATE TABLE EDITOR ( ;
   HOWMANY              N( 4) , ;
   PARTNUM              C(10) , ;
   PONUM                C( 5) , ;
   CUSTID               C(10) , ;
   QUANTITY             N( 4)   )
USE EDITOR EXCLUSIVE
ZAP
APPEND FROM PODETAIL

* Put in customer Id and set
* label quantity initially to 1 each
```

```
SET RELATION TO PONUM INTO PORDER
REPLACE ALL ;
  HOWMANY WITH 1 , ;
  CUSTID  WITH PORDER.CUSTID

SELECT D
CREATE TABLE LABELS ( ;
  PARTNUM              C(10) , ;
  PONUM                C( 5) , ;
  CUSTID               C(10) , ;
  QUANTITY             N( 4)   )
USE LABELS EXCLUSIVE
ZAP


* Because they may want to put three parts in one box and two in another,
* permit adding lines so they can create extra labels manually.

ON KEY LABEL F2 DO INSERTER
@ 24, 0 SAY PADC ( "F2 - insert a duplicate of the current line",80)

SELECT EDITOR
BROWSE               ;
  FIELDS             ;
    HOWMANY  :4           , ;
    QUANTITY :4           , ;
    PARTNUM     :W=.F.    , ;
    PONUM       :W=.F.    , ;
    CUSTID      :W=.F.
@ 24, 0 CLEAR
* Any adjustments to number of labels was done above:
* Now, create a table consisting of one record for each label to print.

SCAN
   SELECT LABELS
   FOR I = 1 TO EDITOR.HOWMANY
      APPEND BLANK
      REPLACE NEXT 1 ;
         PONUM    WITH EDITOR.PONUM     , ;
         CUSTID   WITH EDITOR.CUSTID    , ;
         QUANTITY WITH EDITOR.QUANTITY  , ;
         PARTNUM  WITH EDITOR.PARTNUM
   ENDFOR
   SELECT EDITOR
ENDSCAN
```

10-6 Continued.

```
* FILE "LABELS" now has one record for each part number in each P/O.

SELECT LABELS
BROWSE TITLE " These are the labels that will be printed "

* The label printing command would be next:
* LABEL FORM LABELS TO PRINT

RETURN

FUNCTION INSERTERUnlike DELETE, INSERT is reflected immediately on the BROWSE
screen. Interested, Microsoft/Fox developers?
* Purpose....: Permits user to duplicate label records, F2 is the hot key.
SCATTER MEMVAR
INSERT BLANK BEFORE
GATHER MEMVAR
```

A program like this can bridge the gap between your file structures and the file structures required by LABEL FORM. This sort of feature adds value to a program, because it works the way the customer works.

Using a single validation table

If you have a number of character fields to be validated from lists, you can save yourself a few file handles and some repetitive coding by using a single table and a single VALID routine. TABLEVAL, presented in this section, is such a routine.

A friend of mine mentioned that he'd given up on such routines because the table displayed the data for the fields to be validated as if they were of the same width. Of course, the data in the table is indeed all the same width, but it doesn't have to display like that. You can use the width of the input field to determine the display size.

This example uses the file structure used in my January, 1990 newsletter article on the subject. While that article provided a table editor, it didn't have a generic validation routine. I was using FoxBASE at the time, and the required tools weren't present.

The test bed is shown in Listing 10-7, and function TABLEVAL follows in Listing 10-8. Each memvar must have been assigned a value of the correct length at the time of the GET. The size clause, which FoxPro always supplies correctly, doesn't help, and the default clause, which is always a single CHR(32), causes the table display to misinterpret the width of the field. Play with various combinations of the size and default clauses in the example, and you'll see what I mean. Each memvar's width must be initialized correctly in SETUP.

Listing 10-7 A test program for the Table Validation function.

```
FUNCTION TABTEST
SET TALK OFF
DEFINE WINDOW VALTEST FROM 5,5 TO 12,75 DOUBLE SHADOW
ACTIVA WINDOW VALTEST
@1, 1 SAY '     State:'
@3, 1 SAY ' Warehouse:'
@1,12 GET m.State PICT '!!' VALID TABLEVAL('STATE') SIZE 1, 2 DEFA SPACE(2)
@3,12 GET m.Whse  FUNC '!'  VALID TABLEVAL('WHSE' ) SIZE 1,10 DEFA SPACE(10)
READ COLOR ,W+/R
WAIT WINDOW
RELEASE WINDOW VALTEST
```

Listing 10-8 Using a single validation table for all fields.

```
FUNCTION TABLEVAL
PARAMETER FNAME
IF NOT USED ( 'CODES' )
   SELECT 0
   USE CODES
   ELSE
   SELECT CODES
ENDIF
SET ORDER TO CODES
* Structure of CODES.DBF:   Key FIELD + CODE
*    FIELD   Character 10
*    CODE    Character 10
*    DESCRIP Character 40
FLD  = LEFT ( FNAME + SPACE(10) , 10 )   && ensure proper length
FVAL = &FNAME
WIDE = LEN(&FNAME)
IF SEEK ( FLD + FVAL, [CODES] )
   RETURN
ENDIF

SaveAlias = ALIAS()
SELECT CODES
SEEK ALLTRIM ( FLD )

DEFINE POPUP CODEVALS FROM 1,25 SHADOW IN SCREEN ;
   COLOR N/W, N/W, N/W, N/W, N/W, W+/R, W+/W
I = 1
SCAN WHILE FIELD = FLD
   DEFINE BAR I OF CODEVALS PROMPT LEFT(CODE,Wide) + [ | ] + DESCRIP
```

```
   I = I + 1
ENDSCAN

ON SELECTION POPUP CODEVALS DEACTIVATE POPUP CODEVALS
ACTIVATE POPUP CODEVALS
mPrompt = PROMPT()
RELEASE POPUP CODEVALS

IF NOT EMPTY    ( mPrompt    )
   &FNAME = LEFT( mPrompt,Wide)
 ELSE
   RETURN .F.              && Comment this out if blank is permitted.
ENDIF
IF NOT EMPTY ( SaveAlias )
   SELECT    ( SaveAlias )
ENDIF
```

Provided you do that, you'll find this routine easy to use. The name of the GET variable is the name the routine looks for in the CODE table. If you have a case where several fields can use the same table (e.g., DEPT1, DEPT2), I recommend you do the name tweaking in TABLEVAL for such special cases. Figure 10-6 shows the validation for STATE, and Fig. 10-7 shows the one for Warehouse code.

I hope this works for you. It has saved me a considerable amount of coding, especially in prototypes.

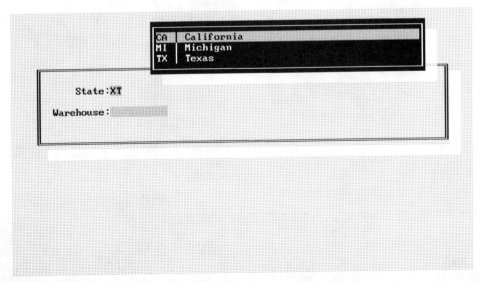

Figure 10-6 Validation of the STATE code.

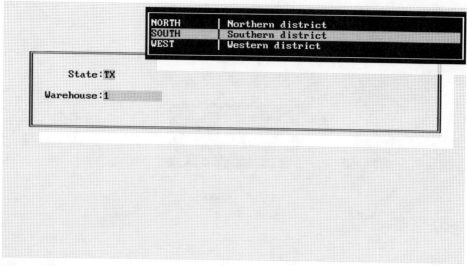

Figure 10-7   Validation of the WAREHOUSE code.

Code/name lookups

Customer files often have both a customer-code field and a customer-name field. Presumably, if the user knows the code, it's easier to type than the name. On the other hand, some customer files are so large that you're just guessing. Wouldn't it be great to have a lookup function that used whichever field made the most sense?

I use the function shown below with my customer database. In some cases, I know the code, which is derived from the customer's last name. The name field, on the other hand, contains the name that I print out on envelopes, in first-name order. It's great for printing, but not so great for searching. Still, each is just right some of the time.

This routine was written for a screen where the customer code or name is typed in at the top center of the screen—that's the @ 2, 22 location. If the function returns a record, the name is displayed at that same location. If no name is picked, the top center location is left blank. Figures 10-8 and 10-9 show the function in action.

This lookup is used in a point-of-sale application where the customer objects to having his name collected, so it isn't required. I almost wasn't allowed to buy something at a Radio Shack store when an overzealous employee insisted that I had to give them my name for a cash sale. Radio Shack makes a lot of money selling your name and address to list brokers, so I'm sure this kid's manager had drummed it into his head. The function is shown in Listing 10-9.

Sales graphs

If you have sales history going back a year or so, you'd probably like to know how things are going. Well, a picture is worth a thousand words, and

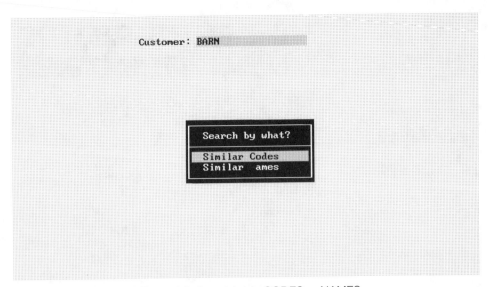

Figure 10-8 If no CODE match is found, table CODES or NAMES.

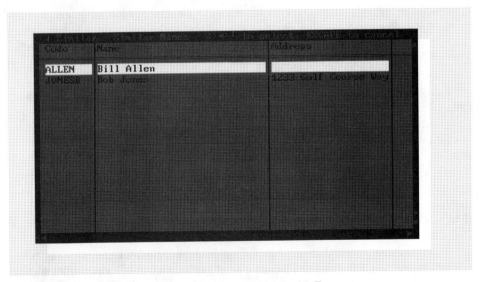

Figure 10-9 The user can either pick from the table or hit Escape.

a sales graph in the form of a histogram, from most recent to oldest, can be particularly informative.

The sales-history file in this example has an index tag consisting of the item description (a surrogate for item code in this example) concatenated with the date of the sale, like this:

```
INDEX ON DESCRIP + DTOC(DATE) TAG SALEHIST
```

Listing 10-9 Finding a customer using either code or name.

```
FUNCTION GETACUST
CLEAR TYPEAHEAD
m.CustName = SPACE(29)
@ 2, 22 SAY 'Customer:' ;
       GET mCustCode ;
       DEFAULT SPACE(19) ;
       FUNCTION "!"

READ COLOR R+/W

IF EMPTY ( mCustCode )
   mCustCode  = SPACE( 8)
   m.CustName = SPACE(29)
   @ 2, 22 SAY m.CustName
   RETURN
ENDIF

SaveAlias = ALIAS()

IF USED ( "CUSTOMER" )
   SELECT  CUSTOMER
  ELSE
   fil = [CUSTOMER]
   SELECT 0
   USE &fil
ENDIF

SET ORDER TO CODE
SEEK LEFT ( TRIM ( mCustCode ) + SPACE ( 8 ) , 8 )

IF FOUND()
   =ShowCust()
   IF NOT EMPTY ( SaveAlias )
      SELECT    ( SaveAlias )
   ENDIF
   RETURN
ENDIF

DEFINE WINDOW BROWSER FROM 2,5 TO 21, 70 DOUBLE SHADOW COLOR SCHEME 10

DEFINE POPUP HOWSEARCH FROM 10,30 ;
 COLOR N/W, N/W, N/W, N/W, N/W, W+/R, W+/W
DEFINE BAR 1 OF HOWSEARCH PROMPT [\] + PADC('Search by what?',20)
DEFINE BAR 2 OF HOWSEARCH PROMPT [\-]
DEFINE BAR 3 OF HOWSEARCH PROMPT PADC([Similar \<Codes],20)
```

```
DEFINE BAR 4 OF HOWSEARCH PROMPT PADC([Similar \<Names],20)
ON SELE POPU HOWSEARCH DEAC POPU HOWSEARCH
ACTIVATE POPU HOWSEARCH
mPrompt = PROMPT()
RELEASE   POPU HOWSEARCH


DO CASE
   CASE [Codes] $ mPrompt          SET ORDER TO CODE
   CASE [Names] $ mPrompt
       SET ORDER TO NAME
ENDCASE


Key = UPPER ( TRIM ( mCustCode ) )
SEEK Key


DO WHILE NOT FOUND() AND LEN ( Key ) > 0
   Key = LEFT ( Key, LEN ( Key ) - 1 )
   SEEK Key
ENDDO


IF EMPTY ( Key )                && Nothing matched....

   ON KEY LABEL ENTER KEYBOARD CHR(23)
   BROWSE                                 ;
     NOMODIFY                             ;
     WINDOW BROWSER                       ;
     COLOR SCHEME 10                      ;
      FIELDS                              ;
       CUSTOMER.Code :H=[Code]   , ;
       CUSTOMER.Name :H=[Name]   , ;
       CUSTOMER.Add1 :H=[Address] ;
     TITLE [ Nothing similar: Use ⏎ to select, ESCAPE to cancel]
   ON KEY LABEL ENTER

   IF LASTKEY() <> 27
      m.CustName = CUSTOMER.NAME
      mCustCode  = CUSTOMER.CODE
      ELSE
      m.CustName = SPACE(29)
      @ 2, 22 SAY mCustCode + SPACE(10)
      IF CONFIRM ( "Add this customer?" )
         =AddCust()
         ELSE
         mCustCode  = SPACE( 8)
         m.CustName = SPACE(29)
```

```
      ENDIF
    ENDIF

    @ 2, 22 SAY m.CustName
    IF NOT EMPTY ( SaveAlias )
       SELECT    ( SaveAlias )
    ENDIF
    RETURN
    ELSE  && Something matched; browse a subset of the customer file
    SET ORDER TO 0

    DO CASE
       CASE [Codes] $ mPrompt
                SELECT                                        ;
                   CUSTOMER.NAME,                             ;
                   CUSTOMER.CODE,                             ;
                   CUSTOMER.ADD1                              ;
                     FROM CUSTOMER                            ;
                     ORDER BY CUSTOMER.NAME                   ;
                     HAVING UPPER(CUSTOMER.CODE) =Key         ;
                     INTO CURSOR VIEWER
          CASE [Names] $ mPrompt
                SELECT                                        ;
                   CUSTOMER.NAME,                             ;
                   CUSTOMER.CODE,                             ;
                   CUSTOMER.ADD1                              ;
                     FROM CUSTOMER                            ;
                     ORDER BY CUSTOMER.NAME                   ;
                     HAVING UPPER(CUSTOMER.NAME) =Key         ;
                     INTO CURSOR VIEWER
    ENDCASE

    SELECT VIEWER
    ON KEY LABEL ENTER KEYBOARD CHR(23)
    BROWSE                         ;
      WINDOW BROWSER               ;
      FIELDS                       ;
        Code :H=[Code ]   ,        ;
        Name :H=[Name ]   ,        ;
        Add1 :H=[Address ]         ;
      COLOR SCHEME 10              ;
      TITLE  [ Similar ] + mPrompt + [: ↵ to select, ESCAPE to cancel]
    ON KEY LABEL ENTER

    IF LASTKEY() = 27
```

```
        m.CustName = SPACE(29)
        @ 2, 22 SAY mCustCode + SPACE(10)
        IF  CONFIRM ( "Add this customer?" )
           =AddCust()
        ENDIF
        @ 2, 22 SAY m.CustName
        ELSE
        m.CustName = NAME
        SELECT CUSTOMER
        SET ORDER TO NAME
        SEEK UPPER ( m.CustName )
        mCustCode  = CODE
        m.CustName = NAME
        =ShowCust()
      ENDIF
      @ 2, 22 SAY m.CustName
      IF NOT EMPTY ( SaveAlias )
         SELECT    ( SaveAlias )
      ENDIF
      RETURN
   ENDIF

   IF NOT EMPTY ( SaveAlias )
      SELECT    ( SaveAlias )
   ENDIF
   RETURN


   FUNCTION AddCust

   DEFINE WINDOW CUSTWIND FROM 2,10 TO 12, 70 DOUBLE SHADOW ;
    FOOTER 'Press ESCAPE to cancel customer entry'
   ACTIVA WINDOW CUSTWIND
   SCATTER MEMVAR BLANK
   @ 0,0   SAY PADC('Add new customer',WCOLS())
   @ 1,1   SAY '   Code: ' + mCustCode
   @ 2,1   SAY '   Name:' GET m.NAME
   @ 3,1   SAY 'Address:' GET m.Add1
   @ 4,1   SAY '   City:' GET m.City
   @ 4,$+1            GET m.State FUNCTION '!'
   @ 4,$+1            GET m.Zip   FUNCTION '!'
   @ 5,1   SAY '  Phone:' GET m.PHONE
   @ 6,1   SAY 'Comment:' GET m.COMMENT1
   @ 7,1   SAY '        ' GET m.COMMENT2


   READ COLOR ,W+/R
```

```
m.CustName = NAME

IF LASTKEY() <> 27
    APPEND BLANK
    GATHER MEMVAR
    ELSE
    mCustCode = SPACE( 8)
    m.CustName = SPACE(29)
ENDIF

RELEASE WINDOW CUSTWIND

FUNCTION ShowCust

DEFINE WINDOW CUSTWIND FROM 2,10 TO 12, 70 DOUBLE SHADOW
ACTIVA WINDOW CUSTWIND
SCATTER MEMVAR
@ 0,0   SAY PADC('Customer Information',WCOLS())
@ 1,1   SAY '   Name: '  + m.NAME
@ 2,1   SAY 'Address: '  + m.Add1
@ 3,1   SAY '   City: '  + m.City
@ 3,$+1              SAY m.State FUNCTION '!'
@ 3,$+1              SAY m.Zip   FUNCTION '!'
@ 4,1   SAY '  Phone: '  + m.PHONE
@ 5,1   SAY 'Comment: '  + m.COMMENT1
@ 6,1   SAY '         '  + m.COMMENT2

IF NOT CONFIRM ( ' Is this the correct customer? ' )
    m.CustName = SPACE ( 29 )
    mCustCode  = SPACE (  9 )
    ELSE
    m.CustName = CUSTOMER.NAME
    mCustCode  = CUSTOMER.CODEENDIF

RELEASE WINDOW CUSTWIND

@ 2, 22 SAY m.CustName
```

First I SEEK the description in question. If no records are found, I haven't had any sales for that item. If data is found, I can start to build the array of sales per month. Because the index is being used in descending order, I have to read back only one year. If I change description, pass the date corresponding to one year ago, or hit EOF( ), I'm done.

Figure 10-10 shows the histogram displayed by this program. The display requires you to normalize the monthly counts. This is a standard operation in graphing. The largest month's sales becomes 100%, and everything else is resized accordingly. The REPLICATE command finishes the job. See Listing 10-10 for the code.

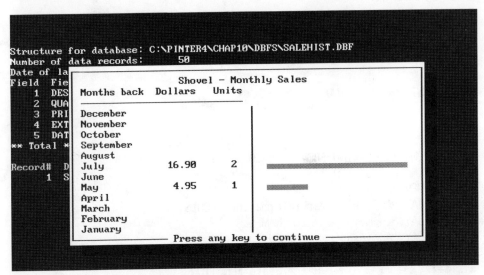

Figure 10-10 The monthly sales histogram.

Listing 10-10 Monthly-sales histogram from a history file.

```
* Program-ID....: MonthSal
* Purpose.......: Displays 1 year of monthly sales for one item

PARAMETERS cDescrip

SET TALK   OFF
SET BLINK  OFF4388 LIDSTSET CURSOR OFF

DIMENSION MONTHNAME(12)
MONTHNAME( 1) = [January  ]
MONTHNAME( 2) = [February ]
MONTHNAME( 3) = [March    ]
MONTHNAME( 4) = [April    ]
MONTHNAME( 5) = [May      ]
MONTHNAME( 6) = [June     ]
MONTHNAME( 7) = [July     ]
MONTHNAME( 8) = [August   ]
MONTHNAME( 9) = [September]
MONTHNAME(10) = [October  ]
```

```
MONTHNAME(11) = [November ]
MONTHNAME(12) = [December ]

SaveAlias = ALIAS()

IF USED ( 'SALEHIST' )
   SELECT  SALEHIST
  ELSE
   fil = mfile_dir + [SALEHIST]
   SELECT 0
   USE &fil
ENDIF


* Structure for database: SALEHIST.DBF
* Field   Field Name   Type        Width    Dec
*     1   DESCRIP      Character     28
*     2   QUANTITY     Numeric        4
*     3   PRICE        Numeric        7      2
*     4   EXTENDED     Numeric        7      2
*     5   DATE         Date           8
* ** Total **                        55


SET ORDER TO SALEHIST DESCENDING

* DESCRIP + CTOD ( DATE, 1 )

DIMENSION  MonthSales ( 12 )
DIMENSION  MonthUnits ( 12 )
STORE 0 TO MonthSales, MonthUnits

SEEK cDescrip

IF NOT FOUND()
   WAIT WINDOW [ No sales for this item in last 12 months] TIMEOUT 1
   IF NOT EMPTY ( SaveAlias )
     SELECT     ( SaveAlias )
   ENDIF
   RETURN
ENDIF

SCAN WHILE DATE > ( DATE() - 365 ) AND DESCRIP = cDescrip
    MonthNum =  MONTH ( DATE )
    MonthNum =  12 - MonthNum + 1
    MonthSales (MonthNum) = MonthSales (MonthNum) + Extended
    MonthUnits (MonthNum) = MonthUnits (MonthNum) + Quantity
```

```
ENDSCAN

DEFINE    WINDOW SHOWMonth FROM 5,10 TO 21, 70 SHADOW FLOAT ;
          COLOR N+/W*,N+/W*,N+/W*,N+/W*,N+/W*,N+/W*,N+/W*,N+/W* ;
          FOOTER [ Press any key to continue ]
ACTIVATE WINDOW SHOWMonth

SET COLOR OF SCHEME 13 TO SCHEME 1
SET COLOR OF SCHEME 1 TO N+/W*,N+/W*,N+/W*,N+/W*,N+/W*,N+/W*,N+/W*,N+/W*

@ 0, 0 SAY PADC([Monthly Sales],WCOLS() -1)
@ 1, 0 SAY [ Months back  Dollars    Units]
@ 2, 0 SAY [ ───────────────────────────────]

FOR I = 1 TO 12
    @ 2+I, 1 SAY MonthName(12 -I+1) +  [  ] ;
            + TRANSFORM ( MonthSales(I), [@Z ##,###.##] ) ;
            + TRANSFORM ( MonthUnits(I), [@Z #######] ) + [  |]
ENDFOR

SET COLOR TO BR/W+*

Max = 0
HighMonth = 0

FOR I = 1 TO 12
    IF MonthSales(I) > Max
        HighMonth = I
        Max = MonthSales(I)
    ENDIF
ENDFOR

FOR I = 1 TO 12
    IF MonthSales(I) > 0
        MonthSales(I) = MonthSales(I)/Max * 24
        @ 2+I,33 SAY REPL([■],MonthSales(I))
    ENDIF
ENDFOR

SET COLOR OF SCHEME 1 TO SCHEME 13

CLEAR TYPEAHEAD
a=INKEY(0)

SET CURSOR ON
```

```
RELEASE WINDOW SHOWMonth

IF NOT EMPTY ( SaveAlias )
   SELECT   ( SaveAlias )
ENDIF
```

Scroll control

The most frequent need among database software designers is parent-child screen management. Try as I might, I can't use the BROWSE model to make life easier. I can't delete lines and make them instantly disappear, I can't change a record's key and redisplay it in its new location, I can't get the speed I need, and the list is very, very long. Figure 10-11 shows the model we're going to use here.

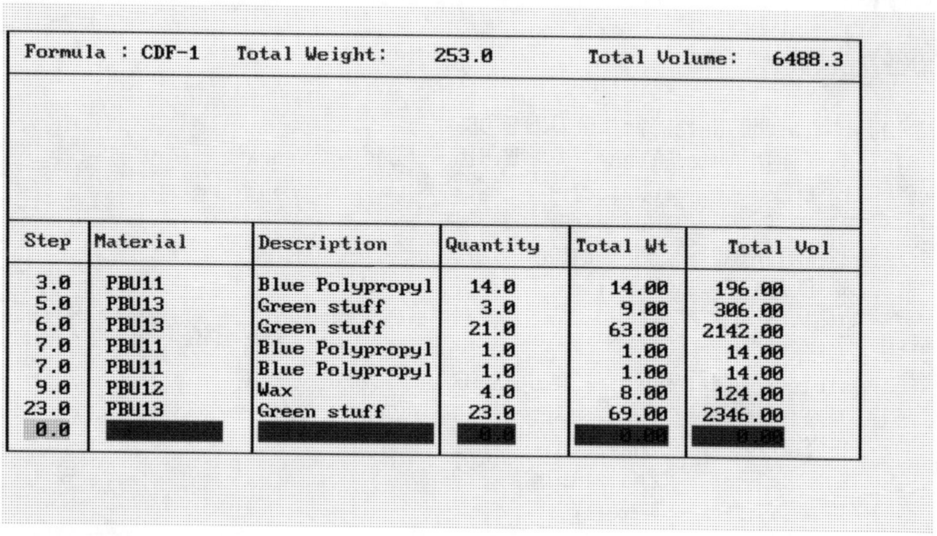

```
Formula : CDF-1    Total Weight:     253.0           Total Volume:    6488.3




  Step  Material       Description      Quantity    Total Wt      Total Vol

   3.0   PBU11          Blue Polypropyl    14.0       14.00         196.00
   5.0   PBU13          Green stuff         3.0        9.00         306.00
   6.0   PBU13          Green stuff        21.0       63.00        2142.00
   7.0   PBU11          Blue Polypropyl     1.0        1.00          14.00
   7.0   PBU11          Blue Polypropyl     1.0        1.00          14.00
   9.0   PBU12          Wax                 4.0        8.00         124.00
  23.0   PBU13          Green stuff        23.0       69.00        2346.00
   0.0
```

Figure 10-11   The Invoice Model screen.

This model is another variation on the one shown in chapter 6. To build this program, I took the program in chapter 6 and spent about two hours modifying the routines that construct the lookup keys to match the key fields in my new files. The code is shown in Listing 10-11.

This example contains a few additional wrinkles. The quantity entered on a line is multiplied by the weight and volume of the current material, but the material's weight and volume are located in yet another coordinated file. Continuous totaling is handled via a VALID clause that sums the products of quantity times weight and volume from the MATERIALS file over all the child records in the current order. Thanks to Rushmore, the speed of this is very acceptable even with a large number of child records.

Listing 10-11 Parent-child screen with several validations.

```
* Program-ID.....: FORMULAS.PRG
* Purpose........: Demonstrate file-following scrolling detail GETS

SET TALK OFF
SET SAFETY OFF

SET COLOR OF SCHEME 2 TO ;
  [BG/W,BG+/B,N/W,B/W,BG+/B,W+/R,W+/RB,N+/N,B/W,W/N,+]


**********************************************************
* Structure for database: MATERIAL.DBF
* Field  Field Name  Type        Width    Dec    Index
*   1    MATERIAL    Character     10             Asc
*   2    DESCRIP     Character     15
*   3    WEIGHT      Numeric        7      1
*   4    VOLUME      Numeric        7      1
* ** Total **                     40
*
* Structure for database: DETAILS.DBF
* Field  Field Name  Type        Width    Dec    Index
*   1    CODE        Character     12             Asc
*   2    STEP        Numeric        4      1
*   3    MATERIAL    Character     10
*   4    QUANTITY    Numeric        7      2
* ** Total **                     34
*
* Structure for database: FORMULAS.DBF
* Field  Field Name  Type        Width    Dec    Index
*   1    CODE        Character     12             Asc
*   2    DESCRIP     Character     30
*   3    WEIGHT      Numeric        7      1
*   4    VOLUME      Numeric        7      1
* ** Total **                     57
**********************************************************


IF NOT USED ( 'FORMULAS' )
   USE FORMULAS IN A ORDER CODE
ENDIF
IF NOT USED ( 'DETAILS' )
   USE DETAILS  IN B ORDER CODE
ENDIF
IF NOT USED ( 'MATERIAL' )
   USE MATERIAL IN C ORDER MATERIAL
ENDIF
```

10-11 Continued.

```
SELECT FORMULAS
GO TOP

SET TALK     OFF
SET ESCAPE   OFF
SET BLINK    OFF
SET RESOURCE OFF
SET MESSAGE  TO 24 CENTER
PUSH MENU _MSYSMENU
DEFINE MENU _MSYSMENU


ON KEY LABEL F1  DO HelpWindow
ON KEY LABEL F10 WAIT WINDOW [No menu active] TIMEOUT 1

Line       = 1
UpArrow    = 18                  && INKEY() value
PgUp       = 6
PgDn       = 7
ENTER      = 15
Done       = 14                  && Ctrl+W
Escape     = 12
CtrlPgUp   = 34
CtrlPgDn   = 35
Alarm      = .F.
Descrip    = []

CalcWt     = 0
CalcVol    = 0
TotWeight  = 0
TotVolume  = 0

WireFrame  = .T.
WireColor  = [BG+/B]
TextColor  = [GR+/B]
DataColor  = [W+/B]

TopLine    = 12
BottomLine = 21
MaxLines   = BottomLine - TopLine -1

RMargin    = 73
GrandTotal = 0
PageTop    = 0
```

```
NewRec      = .F.
KeyChanged = .F.

SELECT DETAILS
SEEK FORMULAS.CODE

* Data columns
c1 = 2                     && Code
c2 = c1+     7             && Material
c3 = c2+LEN(MATERIAL)+3 && Description
c4 = c3+    17             && Quantity
c5 = c4+    10             && Price
c6 = c5+    10             && Extended

* Vertical bar columns
v1 = c1-1
v2 = c2-2v3 = c3-1
v4 = c4-2
v5 = c5-1
v6 = c6-1

DO WHILE .T.

   SELECT DETAILS
   SEEK   FORMULAS.CODE
   SELECT FORMULAS

   =ShowPage()
   =ShowGets()


ACTIVATE SCREEN
@ 23, 0   PROMPT [ \<Add ] MESSAGE [ Add a formula ]
@ $, $+1 PROMPT [ \<Edit ] MESSAGE [ Edit this formula ]
@ $, $+1 PROMPT [ \<Delete ] MESSAGE [ Edit this formula ]
@ $, $+1 PROMPT [ \<Next ] MESSAGE [ Next formula ]
@ $, $+1 PROMPT [ \<Prev ] MESSAGE [ Previous formula ]
@ $, $+1 PROMPT [ \<Find ] MESSAGE [ Browse formula file ]
@ $, $+1 PROMPT [ \<Utilities ] MESSAGE [ Utilities ]
@ $, $+1 PROMPT [ E\<xit ]   MESSAGE [ Previous menu ]
Action = 1
MENU TO Action
Action = IIF(Action=0,'X',SUBSTR('AEDNPFUX',Action,1))
@ 23, 0 CLEAR

DO CASE
```

```
CASE Action = [X]
     EXIT
CASE Action = [U]
     @ 23, 0 PROMPT [ \<Renumber ] ;
         MESSAGE [ Renumber steps ]
     @ $, $+1 PROMPT [ E\<xit ]     ;
         MESSAGE [ Previous menu ]
     Action = 1
     MENU TO Action
     Action = IIF(Action=0,'X',SUBSTR('RX',Action,1))
     @ 23, 0 CLEAR

     DO CASE
        CASE Action = [R]
             SELECT DETAILS
             SEEK FORMULAS.CODE
             COUNT TO NUMRECS WHILE CODE = FORMULAS.CODE
             SEEK FORMULAS.CODE
             DIMENSION STEPS ( NUMRECS )
             I = 1
             SCAN WHILE CODE = FORMULAS.CODE
                STEPS(I) = RECNO()
                I = I + 1
             ENDSCAN
             FOR I = 1 TO ALEN(STEPS)
                GO ( STEPS (I) )
                REPLACE NEXT 1 STEP WITH I
             ENDFOR
             SEEK FORMULAS.CODE
        ENDCASE
CASE Action = [N]
     SELECT FORMULAS
     IF NOT EOF()
        SKIP
        IF EOF()
           GO BOTTOM
        ENDIF
     ENDIF
     LOOP
CASE Action = [P]
     SELECT FORMULAS
     IF NOT BOF()
        SKIP -1
        IF BOF()
           GO TOP
```

```
            ENDIF
         ENDIF
         LOOP
    CASE Action = [E]
         SELECT FORMULAS
         =EditForm()
         NewRec = .F.
    CASE Action = 'D'
         SELECT FORMULAS
         IF CONFIRM ( ' Delete this formula? ' )
            SELECT DETAILS
            DELETE FOR CODE = FORMULAS.CODE
            SELECT FORMULAS
            DELETE NEXT 1
            GO TOP
         ENDIF
    CASE Action = 'F'
         SELECT FORMULAS
         DEFINE WINDOW BROWSER  ;
          FROM 2,10 TO 22, 70    ;
          COLOR SCHEME 10          ;
          TITLE [ Press ← to select, ESCAPE to cancel ]
         ON KEY LABEL ENTER KEYBOARD CHR(23)
         RECORD = RECNO()
         BROWSE NOMODIFY WINDOW BROWSER
         ON KEY LABEL ENTER
         IF LASTKEY() = 27
            GO ( RECORD )
         ENDIF
         RELEASE WINDOW BROWSER
   ENDCASE
ENDDO

CLOSE DATABASESCLEAR
POP MENU _MSYSMENU
RETURN

FUNCTION EDITFORM

SELECT FORMULAS
Key = FORMULAS.CODE
SELECT DETAILS
SEEK   Key
SCATTER MEMVAR
```

10-11 Continued.

```
SET COLOR OF SCHEME 1 TO ,,,,,,,,,W+/BG

ON KEY LABEL DnArrow     KEYBOARD [{PgDn}]
ON KEY LABEL UpArrow     KEYBOARD [{PgUp}]
ON KEY LABEL CTRL+A      KEYBOARD [{PgDn}] + [A]
ON KEY LABEL CTRL+DEL    KEYBOARD [{PgDn}] + [D]
ON KEY LABEL CTRL+W      KEYBOARD [{PgDn}] + [X]
ON KEY LABEL Ctrl+F10    KEYBOARD [{PgDn}] + [X]


DO WHILE .T.
    =Gets(Line)
    IF KeyChanged
        KeyChanged = .F.
        =ShowPage()
        =ShowGets()
        LOOP
    ENDIF
    LastKey = MOD(READKEY(),256)
    DO CASE
        CASE LastKey = ESCAPE
            EXIT
        CASE LastKey = Done AND EMPTY ( m.Step )
            EXIT
        CASE LastKey = PgUp
            IF NewRec
                Line = Line -1
                SCATTER MEMVAR
                NewRec = .F.
                CLEAR TYPEAHEAD
                LOOP
            ENDIF
            SaveRec = RECNO()
            SKIP -1
            IF BOF() OR Code <> FORMULAS.Code
                =Alarm()
                IF SaveRec > 0 AND SaveRec <= RECCOUNT()
                    GO ( SaveRec )
                ENDIF
                LOOP
            ENDIF
            Line = Line-1
            IF Line = 0
            SCROLL TopLine+1, 1, BottomLine-1, RMargin-1, -1
                Line = 1
                =VertLines(Line)
```

```
      ENDIF
CASE LastKey = PgDn
      IF CHRSAW()
         SET CONSOLE OFF
         LastKey = INKEY()
         SET CONSOLE ON
         DO CASE
            CASE LastKey = ASC([A])
               DO AddLine
               LOOP
            CASE LastKey = ASC([D])
               DO DeleteLine
               LOOP
            CASE LastKey = ASC([X])
               EXIT
         ENDCASE
      ENDIF
      IF EMPTY ( m.Step )
         EXIT
      ENDIF
      SaveRec = RECNO()
      SKIP
      IF EOF() OR Code <> FORMULAS.Code
         SKIP -1
         NewRec = .T.
      ENDIF
      Line = Line+1
      IF Line > MaxLines
         SCROLL TopLine+1, 1, BottomLine-1, RMargin-1, 1
         Line = MaxLines
         =VertLines(Line)
      ENDIF
CASE LastKey = CtrlPgDn
      SaveRec = RECNO()
      IF Line > 1
         SKIP -Line
      ENDIF
      SKIP MaxLines
      IF EOF() OR Code <> FORMULAS.Code
         =Alarm()
         IF SaveRec > 0 AND SaveRec <= RECCOUNT()
            GO ( SaveRec )
         ENDIF
      ENDIF
      =ShowPage()
```

```
            =ShowGets()
        CASE LastKey = CtrlPgUp
            GO ( PageTop )
            SKIP -MaxLines
            IF BOF() OR Code <> FORMULAS.Code
                SEEK FORMULAS.Code              ENDIF
            NewRec = .F.
            =ShowPage()
            =ShowGets()
            CLEAR TYPEAHEAD
    ENDCASE
    IF NewRec
        SCATTER MEMVAR BLANK
        m.Code = FORMULAS.CODE
      ELSE
        SCATTER MEMVAR
    ENDIF
ENDDO

CLEAR TYPEAHEAD
POP KEY ALL


RETURN


FUNCTION ShowPage

CLEAR


@  1,0 TO BottomLine, RMargin        COLOR ( WireColor )
@  2, 2 SAY [Formula : ]             COLOR ( TextColor )
@  2,12 SAY FORMULAS.CODE            COLOR ( DataColor )
@  2,20 SAY [Total Weight: ]         COLOR ( TextColor )
@  2,50 SAY [Total Volume: ]         COLOR ( TextColor )

=ShowTotal()

=HorizLine(3)

=HorizLine(TopLine-2)
@ TopLine-1,v1+1 SAY [Step]          COLOR ( TextColor )
@ TopLine-1,v2+1 SAY [Material]      COLOR ( TextColor )
@ TopLine-1,v3+1 SAY [Description]   COLOR ( TextColor )
@ TopLine-1,v4+1 SAY [Quantity]      COLOR ( TextColor )
@ TopLine-1,v5+1 SAY [Total Wt]      COLOR ( TextColor )
@ TopLine-1,v6+4 SAY [Total Vol]     COLOR ( TextColor )
```

10-11 Continued.

```
=HorizLine(TopLine)

=DetLines()

FUNCTION DetLines

IF WireFrame
    @ TopLine-2   , v2 SAY [┬]              COLOR ( WireColor )
    @ TopLine-1   , v2 SAY [│]              COLOR ( WireColor )
    @ TopLine     , v2 SAY [┼]              COLOR ( WireColor )
    @ BottomLine  , v2 SAY [┴]              COLOR ( WireColor )

    @ TopLine-2   , v3 SAY [┬]              COLOR ( WireColor )
    @ TopLine-1   , v3 SAY [│]              COLOR ( WireColor )
    @ TopLine     , v3 SAY [┼]              COLOR ( WireColor )
    @ BottomLine  , v3 SAY [┴]              COLOR ( WireColor )

    @ TopLine-2   , v4 SAY [┬]              COLOR ( WireColor )
    @ TopLine-1   , v4 SAY [│]              COLOR ( WireColor )
    @ TopLine     , v4 SAY [┼]              COLOR ( WireColor )
    @ BottomLine  , v4 SAY [┴]              COLOR ( WireColor )

    @ TopLine-2   , v5 SAY [┬]              COLOR ( WireColor )
    @ TopLine-1   , v5 SAY [│]              COLOR ( WireColor )
    @ TopLine     , v5 SAY [┼]              COLOR ( WireColor )
    @ BottomLine  , v5 SAY [┴]              COLOR ( WireColor )

    @ TopLine-2   , v6 SAY [┬]              COLOR ( WireColor )
    @ TopLine-1   , v6 SAY [│]              COLOR ( WireColor )
    @ TopLine     , v6 SAY [┼]              COLOR ( WireColor )
    @ BottomLine  , v6 SAY [┴]              COLOR ( WireColor )

    @ TopLine+1   , v2 TO BottomLine-1,v2 COLOR ( WireColor )
    @ TopLine+1   , v3 TO BottomLine-1,v3 COLOR ( WireColor )
    @ TopLine+1   , v4 TO BottomLine-1,v4 COLOR ( WireColor )
    @ TopLine+1   , v5 TO BottomLine-1,v5 COLOR ( WireColor )
    @ TopLine+1   , v6 TO BottomLine-1,v6 COLOR ( WireColor )

ENDIF

FUNCTION ShowGets
PRIVATE I
I = 1
SELECT DETAILS
SaveRec = RECNO()
```

```
PageTop = SaveRec
SCAN WHILE I <= MaxLines AND DETAILS.CODE = FORMULAS.CODE
   =Says(I)
   I = I + 1
ENDSCAN
IF SaveRec > 0 AND SaveRec <= RECCOUNT()
   GO ( SaveRec )
ENDIF
Line = 1
=TotalCalc()

FUNCTION Gets
PARAMETERS CurLine

IF NewRec
   SCATTER MEMVAR BLANK
   m.Code = FORMULAS.CODE
   ELSE
   SCATTER MEMVAR
ENDIF

SELECT MATERIALSEEK m.Material
m.Descrip = DESCRIP
SELECT DETAILS

=TotCalc()                && show calculated variables

@ TopLine+CurLine, c1 GET m.Step       ;
       PICTURE [##.#] VALID Finished()
@ TopLine+CurLine, c2 GET m.Material   ;
       PICTURE [!!!!!!!!!!!] VALID FindMat()
@ TopLine+CurLine, c3 GET m.Descrip    DISABLE
@ TopLine+CurLine, c4 GET m.Quantity   ;
       PICTURE [###.#]        VALID TotCalc()
@ TopLine+CurLine, c5 GET m.CalcWt     ;
       PICTURE [#####.##] DISABLE
@ TopLine+CurLine, c6 GET m.CalcVol    ;
       PICTURE [#####.##] DISABLE

READ COLOR ,W+/R

IF LASTKEY() <> 27
   IF EMPTY ( m.Step )
   ENDIF
   =Replaces()
```

10-11 Continued.

```
ENDIF
=Says(Line)
=TotalCalc()

IF MOD(READKEY(),256) = ENTER
   KEYBOARD [{DnArrow}]
ENDIF

FUNCTION Finished
LastKey = LASTKEY()
IF EMPTY ( m.Step ) AND LastKey <> UpArrow
   KEYBOARD [{Ctrl+W}]
   RETURN
ENDIF

FUNCTION TotCalc
m.CalcWt  = m.Quantity * MATERIAL.WEIGHT
m.CalcVol = m.Quantity * MATERIAL.VOLUME
SHOW GET m.CalcWt  DISABLE
SHOW GET m.CalcVol DISABLE

=TotalCalc()

FUNCTION Replaces

RePaint = .F.
IF NOT EMPTY ( m.Step )
   m.Code = FORMULAS.Code
   IF NewRec
      APPEND BLANK    ENDIF
   RePaint = IIF ( m.Step = DETAILS.Step , .F. , .T. )
   GATHER MEMVAR
   NewRec = .F.
ENDIF
IF RePaint
   =ShowPage()
   =ShowGets()
ENDIF

FUNCTION Says
PARAMETERS CurLine

IF NOT NewRec

   SELECT MATERIAL
```

10-11 Continued.

```
    SEEK DETAILS.Material
    SELECT DETAILS

    m.CalcWt  = DETAILS.Quantity * MATERIAL.Weight
    m.CalcVol = DETAILS.Quantity * MATERIAL.Volume
    @ TopLine+CurLine, c1 SAY DETAILS.Step PICTURE [##.#]
    @ TopLine+CurLine, c2 SAY DETAILS.Material
    @ TopLine+CurLine, c3 SAY MATERIAL.Descrip
    @ TopLine+CurLine, c4 SAY STR(DETAILS.Quantity,5,1)
    @ TopLine+CurLine, c5 SAY STR(CalcWt, 8,2)
    @ TopLine+CurLine, c6 SAY STR(CalcVol,8,2)
  ELSE
    @ TopLine+CurLine,  1 CLEAR TO TopLine+CurLine, 78
ENDIF
=VertLines(CurLine)

FUNCTION VertLines
PARAMETERS HLine
IF WireFrame
    @ TopLine+HLine, v2 SAY [|] COLOR ( WireColor )
    @ TopLine+HLine, v3 SAY [|] COLOR ( WireColor )
    @ TopLine+HLine, v4 SAY [|] COLOR ( WireColor )
    @ TopLine+HLine, v5 SAY [|] COLOR ( WireColor )
    @ TopLine+HLine, v6 SAY [|] COLOR ( WireColor )
ENDIF

FUNCTION HorizLine
PARAMETERS CurLine
@ CurLine,0  TO CurLine,RMargin-1 COLOR ( WireColor )
@ CurLine,0              SAY '├'        COLOR ( WireColor )
@ CurLine,RMargin        SAY '┤'        COLOR ( WireColor )

FUNCTION Alarm
IF Alarm
 FOR I = 1 TO 3
   SET BELL TO 1000,1
   ?? CHR(7)
   SET BELL TO 1600,1    ?? CHR(7)
 ENDFOR
ENDIF

FUNCTION Finder

PUSH KEY CLEAR

DEFINE WINDOW FINDER FROM 3,10 TO 20, 70 DOUBLE SHADOW
```

```
SET LIBRARY TO JKEY
ON KEY LABEL ENTER KEYBOARD CHR(23)
=JkeyInit([U],FORMULAS.Code,[Formula Code: ])
BROWSE WINDOW FINDER ;
  FIELDS ;
    Code, Step :H=[Description] ;
  COLOR GR+/B,W+/R,B/W+*,GR+/B,GR+/B,GR+/B,W+/R ;
  KEY FORMULAS.Code, FORMULAS.Code
ON KEY  LABEL ENTER
RELEASE WINDOW FINDER
=JkeyCanc()
=ShowPage()
=ShowGets()
SCATTER MEMVAR
POP KEY


FUNCTION TotalCalc

SELECT DETAILS
SaveRec = RECNO()

SEEK FORMULAS.CODE
SET RELATION TO DETAILS.MATERIAL INTO MATERIAL

SUM quantity * MATERIAL.Weight, ;
    quantity * MATERIAL.Volume  ;
 TO TotWeight, ;
    TotVolume  ;
  WHILE Code = FORMULAS.Code

SET RELATION OFF INTO MATERIAL

IF SaveRec > 0 AND SaveRec <= RECCOUNT()
   GO ( SaveRec )
ENDIF

REPLACE NEXT 1 ;
  FORMULAS.WEIGHT WITH TotWeight, ;
  FORMULAS.VOLUME WITH TotVolume

=ShowTotal()

FUNCTION ShowTotal

@ 2,35 SAY FORMULAS.Weight    COLOR ( DataColor )
```

```
@ 2,65 SAY FORMULAS.Volume        COLOR ( DataColor )

FUNCTION AddLine
Key = FORMULAS.Code + [99.9]
SET NEAR ON
SEEK Key
SET NEAR OFF
IF EOF()
   GO BOTTOM
  ELSE
   SKIP -1
ENDIF
LastRec = RECNO()
HowMuch = MaxLines -2
SKIP -HowMuch
IF DETAILS.Code <> FORMULAS.Code OR BOF()
   SEEK FORMULAS.Code
   Line = 1
   SCAN REST
      SKIP
      IF DETAILS.Code <> FORMULAS.Code OR EOF()
         EXIT
      ENDIF
      Line = Line + 1
   ENDSCAN
 ELSE
   Line = MaxLines - 1
ENDIF
SaveLine = Line
=ShowPage()
=ShowGets()
IF LastRec > 0 AND LastRec <= RECCOUNT()
   GO ( LastRec )
ENDIF
Line = SaveLine +1
NewRec = .T.
SCATTER MEMVAR BLANK
m.Code = FORMULAS.CODE

FUNCTION DeleteLine
IF CONFIRM ( [ Delete this line? ] )
   SaveLine = Line
   DelRec   = RECNO()
   TopLineOffset = Line -1
   SKIP -TopLineOffset
```

```
   SaveRec  = RECNO()
   GO ( DelRec )
   SCATTER MEMVAR BLANK
   GATHER  MEMVAR
   DELETE NEXT 1
   IF SaveRec > 0 AND SaveRec <= RECCOUNT()
      GO ( SaveRec )
   ENDIF
   =ShowPage()    =ShowGets()
   GO ( SaveRec )
   Line = SaveLine
   SKIP ( Line-1 )
   IF Code <> FORMULAS.Code
      SEEK FORMULAS.Code
      =ShowPage()
      =ShowGets()
   ENDIF
   SCATTER MEMVAR
   KEYBOARD [{ENTER}]
ENDIF


FUNCTION HelpWindow

PUSH KEY CLEAR

DEFINE   WINDOW HELPWINDOW FROM 9,23 TO 19, 57 SHADOW DOUBLE
ACTIVATE WINDOW HELPWINDOW
@ 0, 0 SAY PADC('Hot Key Commands',WCOLS()-1)
@ 1, 0 TO 1, WCOLS()-1
@ 3,5 SAY 'Ctrl-A   - Add a line'
@ 4,5 SAY 'Ctrl-Del - Delete a line'
@ 5,5 SAY 'Ctrl-PgUp- Prev screen'
@ 6,5 SAY 'Ctrl-PgDn- Next screen'
@ 7,5 SAY 'F10      - Exit screen'

WAIT WINDOW
RELEASE WINDOW HELPWINDOW

POP KEY

FUNCTION FINDMAT

SaveAlias = ALIAS()
SELECT MATERIAL
SEEK m.Material
```

```
IF FOUND( )
   m.Descrip = LEFT(MATERIAL.DESCRIP,15)
   SHOW GET m.Descrip DISABLE
ENDIF
IF NOT EMPTY ( SaveAlias )
   SELECT    ( SaveAlias )
ENDIF
```

Note that features like removing the vertical bars separating columns—which is accomplished with the NOBORDER option in BROWSE—can also be done in a model like this; you can even let the user toggle them on and off if you add a hot key. That might make an interesting exercise.

This screen is typical of parent-child screens called *invoice model* screens. I published a model very similar to this one last year, and if you compare carefully you'll find a few "enhancements." The original bugs were brought to my attention by several readers—thanks for your support—and are corrected here.

I've had occasion to modify this model a number of times. The modifications required to adapt it to a new parent-child file take about two to three hours. The result frees you from a number of constraints imposed by BROWSE.

If you use BROWSE to add records, you'll use Ctrl–N to add a record. It adds a blank record immediately, forcing you to take remedial action if the add is canceled. Because these two files are related with a common key, the key has to be inserted into the child record; if you look carefully at the examples that come with FoxPro, they all require that the user type in the relating key. Not cool. FoxPro's logic does that automatically.

Repositioning added records is another problem. Child files often have a secondary key, in addition to the key that relates them to their parent. When you edit the value of the secondary key, BROWSE wants to redisplay the screen so as to correctly reflect the new position of the current record relative to the secondary keys of the rest of the records in the BROWSE. Sometimes that's okay, and sometimes it isn't. This code lets you decide how to handle it. In fact, you can turn off the secondary key ordering during adding, then let the user toggle secondary key ordering on and off. This often provides the best overall approach.

Summary

I'd like to be able to say that FoxPro straight out of the box is really all you need—no add-ons, no workarounds, no compromises involved in using only the built-in tools. Unfortunately, the view that you don't need to program to write applications in FoxPro sells well, but the after-sale is murder. I'm involved in the after-market. Clients call me when they've tried to follow the rules.

Index

Other Bestsellers of Related Interest

EASY PC MAINTENANCE AND REPAIR
—Phil LaPlante

Keep your PC running flawlessly—and save hundreds of dollars in professional service fees! This money-saving guide will show you how. It provides all the step-by-step instructions and troubleshooting guidance you need to maintain your IBM PC-XT, 286, 386, or 486 compatible computer. If you have a screwdriver. a pair of pliers, and a basic understanding of how PCs function, you're ready to go to work. 152 pages, 68 illustrations. Book No. 4143, $14.95 paperback, $22.95 hardcover

BUILD YOUR OWN COMPUTER ACCESSORIES AND SAVE A BUNDLE
—Bonnie J. Hargrave and Ted Dunning

Here are step-by-step, easy-to-understand instructions for 27 useful network management and computer diagnostic devices. Page after page of practical guidance for building accessories make complex, time-consuming computer network operations easier and faster. Plus, you'll find a special section on the tools necessary for basic soldering and cabling operations . . . information on how to read circuit diagrams and schematics . . . a list of component suppliers . . . and estimated total costs for each project. 376 pages, 222 illustrations. Book No. 4134, $19.95 paperback, $29.95 hardcover

ENHANCED BATCH FILE PROGRAMMING
2nd Edition—Dan Gookin

Create powerful batch files that automate your system, boost productivity, and improve efficiency with this guide—now updated for DOS 5 and Windows. It's packed with programming tricks, over 100 special utilities, and a working copy of the bestselling batch file compiler Builder—on two FREE 5.25" disks. 368 pages, 92 illustrations, two 5.25" disks. Book No. 4099, $34.95 paperback only

MEMORY MANAGEMENT AND MULTITASKING BEYOND 640K
—Lenny Bailes and John Mueller, Foreword by John C. Dvorak

Extend or expand your memory options for your IBM PC or compatible with this in-depth guide to breaking the 640K barrier. Even if you can't afford expensive memory expansions, the authors will show you a variety of ways to get the most bang for your buck out of applications and operating systems software. 456 pages, 140 illustrations, 5.25" disk. Book No. 4069, $29.95 paperback, $39.95 hardcover

GLOSSBRENNER'S GUIDE TO SHAREWARE FOR SMALL BUSINESSES
—Alfred Glossbrenner

Now, in as little as one hour, you can use a personal computer to keep track of your customers, ride herd on your inventory, and run your business with a degree of control you may have only dreamed about. This valuable book/disk package clears away the misconceptions surrounding today's computer jargon and products, offers solid advice on how to select IBM-compatible hardware, and reviews and recommends dozens of today's hottest shareware programs—all at the lowest possible prices! 432 pages, 64 illustrations, 5.25" disk. Book No. 4059, $27.95 paperback, $37.95 hardcover

FOXPRO®: The Master Reference
2nd Edition—Robin Stark and Shelley Satonin

Design and run powerful, customized databases in no time using all the exciting new features of FoxPro. this alphabetical guide to every FoxPro command and function covers all versions through 2.0—more than 350 entries in all. Its innovative three-part indexing system leads you quickly to all commands, functions, and examples found in the book. 512 pages, 135 illustrations. Book No. 4056, $24.95 paperback only

USING ONLINE SCIENTIFIC & ENGINEERING DATABASES
—Harley Bjelland

With this authoritative guide, you'll discover how to conduct successful online searches that take advantage of databases dedicated to computers, physics, electronics, mathematics, and other disciplines. Emphasizing efficiency, jargon-free language and simple procedures, Bjelland shows you how to use modem online services to locate information with minimal time, effort, and expense. 232 pages, 31 illustrations. Book No. 3967, $26.95 paperback only

ONLINE INFORMATION HUNTING
—Nahum Goldmann

Cut down dramatically on your time and money spent online, and increase your online productivity with this helpful book. It will give you systematic instruction on developing cost-effective research techniques for large-scale information networks. You'll also get detailed coverage of the latest online services, new hardware and software, and recent advances that have affected online research. 256 pages, 125 illustrations. Book No. 3943, $19.95 paperback, $29.95 hardcover

Order the source code on disk

This book probably contains more source code than most programming books. Although you can type them in, many readers will prefer to get the programs in ready-to-run form. The source code on disk is available from the author, using the order form at the bottom of this page. The disk includes all program code, screen, menu and project files, and all test data.

Source Code On Disk

Send me the source code, screen, menu and project files for the programs in your book, *FoxPro 2.5 Programming*. I enclose a check for US $29.95.

Name: _____

Address: _____

_____

_____

Phone: _____

❑ *Send information about the Pinter FoxPro Letter*
❑ *Send information about other training materials and products*

The Pinter FoxPro Letter
PO Box 10349
Truckee, CA 96162
(800) 995-2797